Asian Christianity in the Diaspora

Series Editors
Grace Ji-Sun Kim
Earlham School of Religion
Richmond, IN, USA

Joseph Cheah
University of Saint Joseph
West Hartford, CT, USA

Asian American theology is still at its nascent stage. It began in the 1980's with just a handful of scholars who were recent immigrants to the United States. Now with the rise in Asian American population and the rise of Asian American theologians, this new community is an ever-important voice within theological discourse and Asian American cultural studies. This new series seeks to bring to the forefront some of the important, provocative new voices within Asian American Theology. The series aims to provide Asian American theological responses to the complex process of migration and resettlement process of Asian immigrants and refugees. We will address theoretical works on the meaning of diaspora, exile, and social memory, and the foundational works concerning the ways in which displaced communities remember and narrate their experiences. Such an interdisciplinary approach entails intersectional analysis between Asian American contextual theology and one other factor; be it sexuality, gender, race/ethnicity, and/or cultural studies. This series also addresses Christianity from Asian perspectives. We welcome manuscripts that examine the identity and internal coherence of the Christian faith in its encounters with different Asian cultures, with Asian people, the majority of whom are poor, and with non-Christian religions that predominate the landscape of the Asian continent. Palgrave is embarking on a transformation of discourse within Asian and Asian American theological scholarship as this will be the first of its kind. As we live in a global world in which Christianity has re-centered itself in the Global South and among the racialized minorities in the United States, it behooves us to listen to the rich, diverse and engaging voices of Asian and Asian American theologians.

More information about this series at
http://www.palgrave.com/gp/series/14781

Marco Lazzarotti

Place, Alterity, and Narration in a Taiwanese Catholic Village

palgrave
macmillan

Marco Lazzarotti
Anthropology
Heidelberg University
Heppenheim, Germany

Asian Christianity in the Diaspora
ISBN 978-3-030-43460-1   ISBN 978-3-030-43461-8 (eBook)
https://doi.org/10.1007/978-3-030-43461-8

© The Editor(s) (if applicable) and The Author(s), under exclusive licence to Springer Nature Switzerland AG 2020
This work is subject to copyright. All rights are solely and exclusively licensed by the Publisher, whether the whole or part of the material is concerned, specifically the rights of translation, reprinting, reuse of illustrations, recitation, broadcasting, reproduction on microfilms or in any other physical way, and transmission or information storage and retrieval, electronic adaptation, computer software, or by similar or dissimilar methodology now known or hereafter developed.
The use of general descriptive names, registered names, trademarks, service marks, etc. in this publication does not imply, even in the absence of a specific statement, that such names are exempt from the relevant protective laws and regulations and therefore free for general use.
The publisher, the authors, and the editors are safe to assume that the advice and information in this book are believed to be true and accurate at the date of publication. Neither the publisher nor the authors or the editors give a warranty, expressed or implied, with respect to the material contained herein or for any errors or omissions that may have been made. The publisher remains neutral with regard to jurisdictional claims in published maps and institutional affiliations.

Cover illustration: LatitudeStock / Alamy Stock Photo

This Palgrave Macmillan imprint is published by the registered company Springer Nature Switzerland AG
The registered company address is: Gewerbestrasse 11, 6330 Cham, Switzerland

*To my wife and my son,
without whom I would have finished this book many years before.
But without whom my life would have been
much more empty and meaningless.*

Foreword

It is a particular pleasure for me to write these lines to accompany the publication of a book that began as Marco Lazzarotti's PhD thesis.

Since the inception of ethnography as part of the anthropological discipline, villages seemed to be the natural places to study. They were the sites where people conducted face-to-face sociality, they spoke to romanticist ideas about cultural authenticity in the countryside, and they were the places where most people lived in the colonial universe of early anthropology. With the rise of the postmodern critique of anthropological epistemology, with multisited ethnography reacting to globalized socialities, and with urban anthropology, the age of village studies seems long gone. Quite a number of authors have thus questioned the validity of the village as a unit of study.

However, this very situation allows for a reconsideration of the village as a theoretical and cultural construct. The insight that the village is not a self-explanatory category of human life raises the question: What is a village? How do people there turn the places they live in into villages? What kind of differences, what kind of practices does this involve?

Here is where Marco Lazzarotti's work provides a fresh approach. He explores the village as a spatial, social, and ontological entity that emerges through the practice of storytelling. The village he is concerned with is a peculiar one: Shuiwei in Taiwan is home to a majority of Christians who started converting in the early twentieth century. Thus, it sticks out from its environment that is dominated by the mix of Daoism, Buddhism,

Confucianism, and folk practices that is characteristic of Chinese religion. In particular, Lazzarotti highlights the difference from Chinese folk religion: The elaborate rules of geomancy and astrology that come with it are ignored by Shuiwei Christians, and the festive processions by which the gods visit neighboring temples steer clear of the village. As Lazzarotti describes for numerous events, told in and around Shuiwei, the village receives its identity through the absence of folk religious rules. This applies to both the space it occupies and the people it is home to. This also comes with other digressions from Chinese standards, like the accounts of genealogy, the layout of homes, or the relations with the ancestors. The internal order of village society and its external representation intersect, and both together produce a sense of a boundary that is both spatial and social. It is through little anecdotes and events that people tell to each other that this specific world is narrated into being. Remarkably, this does not appear to come with ostracization, which may be due to the important relationships Taiwan has with Christian countries, predominantly the USA. Still, it is important to point out that this profound difference is managed in a peaceful way. There are even signs of the kind of cosmological complementation found in other parts of Asia, like Laos or Indonesia. Due to their ontological disparities, neighbors can solve each other's problems. Like Laotian Buddhists who ask their animist neighbors to perform animal sacrifices that would affect their karma, adherents of Chinese folk religion give pigs with inauspicious birth defects to their Christian neighbors. Here, the diversity of ontologies does not create incompatibility but maps out digressing options for practice.

It is in this respect that Shuiwei is not the village of classic anthropology that represents a larger ethnicity. Shuiwei's specificity is a result of globalization, the spread of world religion, the alliance of Taiwan with the West (their East), the interlinkage of faraway places. It does not necessarily represent Taiwan or Chinese Christianity. But it is an exemplar of the way people create their specific communities through a sense of difference that permeates the nitty-gritty of the everyday and the place of human beings in the cosmos. Marco Lazzarotti skillfully introduces us into this local world, with a lively eye for detail and an empathic sense for the cosmological diplomacy that his interlocutors manage, their wit and their humor.

With his unique theoretical approach, he explores the analytic richness of the stories he has heard and experienced, and there are no signs that he is going to run out of stories anytime soon. In any case, I hope you will enjoy his book as much as I did.

Heidelberg, Germany
February 2020

Professor Dr. Guido Sprenger

Acknowledgments

This book has been made thanks to the constant and joyful inspiration from my beautiful wife Joo Young and my son Antonio. They followed all the steps of this project, and now we arrived together to see the conclusion of it. This project, which began many years ago, took somehow the form of a journey that led my family and me to travel across three continents and I no longer know across how many countries.

The longer the journey, the longer the list of people we met along the way. I would like to thank all the people who helped me when I started this project in Taiwan. First of all I want to thank my former Master and PhD adviser, Prof. Yeh, Chuen-Rong. He introduced me to the Catholic community of Shuiwei village. It is because of him that I started this project. I will always be grateful to him. Apart from Prof. Yeh, there are few persons who concretely helped me by finding materials and giving me any kind of support. Hao-Yu Cho and Chun Yu Chen helped me to collect extra materials and information during the writing process. But there is a person who supported me in a very concrete way, my big friend Martin Chouinard. Without him and without his purple sofa, my PhD studies would have been almost impossible. I want to thank also all the professors and the staff of the Department of Anthropology at the National Taiwan University, where I first discussed and started to be interested in the topic of this book.

Other big thanks must be addressed to the Xaverian fathers in Taipei and Makeni, who helped, encouraged, and gave me support during the time of my research. Another special thanks is for the professors and the staff of the University of Makeni, among them my brother Guliver, who followed my family and me and the development of my work. I am especially in debt to the students who attempted my courses at Unimak. It is because of them that I started to feel again the passion of the anthropological research.

Following the route of my life, it is time now to thank some important people in South Korea. Especially my parents-in-law who always encouraged me and helped my family and me to reach this important goal. I dedicate a special thought to Chang Ik Hoang. Knowing how much he loved my family, I believe he will be very happy to know about this book.

At the end of the journey (but just for the moment), I would like to thank my adviser at the University of Heidelberg, Prof. Dr. Guido Sprenger. He has been—and he still is—not only an adviser but a constant opportunity to learn and better understand what I was doing.

Apart from Guido, I want to take this opportunity to thank Prof. Philip Clart. He helped me by reading my thesis and giving me precious suggestions and advices. During my studies in Germany, I feel so lucky to have the opportunity to mention Eva Sevenig, Carmen Grimm, Frauke Mörike, and Elizabeth Rauchholz. Their kindness and generosity have been really remarkable. I am not afraid to say that they are the best PhD group I could even dream to find.

I want to reserve a special mention to Dr. Yves Menheere. He is the one who accompanied me—sometimes concretely, sometimes virtually—along all of my long journey. His help, his ideas, his support meant a lot to me. If the saying "who finds a friend finds a treasure" is true, it is because there are people like Yves.

Last but not least, I want to thank all my friends in Lunbei and in Shuiwei. When Fr. Chao introduced my wife and me to this community, I could not imagine that I would spend three beautiful years there. Three years in which the people of this wonderful Catholic community—and non-Catholic people as well—welcomed us into their families. My wife and I arrived there by chance few months after our wedding, and, when we left, we had an almost two-year-old small boy with us. Those wonderful people have opened their homes and their hearts to us. I hope this book can be a tribute to them.

Thanks to all these people and also to those who, because of my ingratitude, I forgot to mention in these pages. May my gratitude arrive to them, wherever they are.

A Note to the Reader

Before reading this book, the reader should know some important notes on language, romanization, and the use of Chinese characters.

This book is based on fieldwork carried out in Taiwan, more specifically in 水尾 Shuǐwěi, a small village located in 雲林縣 Yúnlín Xiàn, in western Taiwan. I conducted almost all the interviews in Chinese Mandarin and a few in Taiwanese with the help of some translators.

Apart from the names of the places (counties, cities, townships, and villages),[1] throughout this dissertation, I have chosen to give priority to the Chinese characters and to their transcriptions in pinyin with tones. Further exceptions have been made for the names of authors who already have a transcripted name.

I hope this choice will help both those who approach the Chinese writing for the first time and the Chinese native speakers.

I decided to change the name of the persons I met during my fieldwork, apart from those who explicitly—and even with a certain insistence—asked me to be named in my work.

---

[1] The names of the places follow the romanization made by the Taiwanese government. <http://www.moi.gov.tw>.

Contents

1 **Introduction**   1
   1.1 *The Narrative Construction of Reality*   1
   1.2 *Ethnography and the Field*   5
       1.2.1 *Defining the Field: Taiwan*   6
       1.2.2 *Defining the Field: Lunbei Township*   8
       1.2.3 *Shuiwei*   9
   1.3 *The Five Elements of Narration*   10
   1.4 *The World Is All That Is the Case*   14
   References   15

2 **Locus**   17
   2.1 *Stories from Shuiwei*   17
   2.2 *Telling Stories Makes the World*   20
       2.2.1 *Narration and Its Context: The Circuit of Narration*   20
       2.2.2 *Narration and Time: Need of Coherence*   24
       2.2.3 *Narration and Cultural Context*   25
   2.3 *Locus*   27
       2.3.1 *Space and Place*   30
       2.3.2 *Space and Place in the Anthropological Discussion: A Literature Review*   31
       2.3.3 *Locus and Alterity*   34

	2.4	Defining Locus: Operative Mode	36
		2.4.1 Five Elements	38
	References		40

3 Topos — 43
- 3.1 Narrating Topoi — 43
- 3.2 Topos — 45
  - 3.2.1 The Sense of Place — 46
  - 3.2.2 Creating a Context — 52
- 3.3 Shuiwei as Locus: Historical, Geographical, and Social Context — 56
  - 3.3.1 Yunlin County — 57
  - 3.3.2 Lunbei Township — 59
  - 3.3.3 Shuiwei Village — 64
- 3.4 Shuiwei in Context: Locus and Narration — 68
- References — 72

4 Epos — 75
- 4.1 Stories of Shuiwei — 75
- 4.2 Epos — 76
- 4.3 Shuiwei Christian Community, Between Myth and History — 79
  - 4.3.1 Shuiwei Catholic Community: At the Roots of the Myth — 82
  - 4.3.2 A Brief History of the Taiwanese Catholic church — 85
  - 4.3.3 How Catholicism Arrived in Shuiwei — 87
  - 4.3.4 Modern Times: Shuiwei and Lunbei Catholic Communities — 91
- 4.4 The Chinese Rites Controversy and the Dominican in Taiwan: History or Epos? — 94
- 4.5 Epos, Stories, History, and Everyday Life — 97
- References — 100

5 Genos — 101
- 5.1 Narrating Genos — 101
- 5.2 Genos — 103
  - 5.2.1 Genos, Kinship, and the Chinese Family — 104

	5.2.2 Chinese Kinship and the Importance of Ancestors' Rites	107
5.3	Christianity in Taiwan and the Reconstruction of Genos	109
	5.3.1 The Catholic Community of Lunbei	110
	5.3.2 The Catholic Community of Shuiwei	113
5.4	The Genealogy of the Zhong Family	115
	5.4.1 Mr. Zhong Qin Kinship Scheme	119
	5.4.2 First Branch	121
	5.4.3 Second Branch	122
	5.4.4 Third Branch	124
5.5	Reconstructing Genos	124
	5.5.1 From Ancestors to Ancestor	125
	5.5.2 Family Ceremonies	130
	5.5.3 We Are All Brothers and Sisters: The Holy Mary Pilgrimage	131
	5.5.4 Ancestors, Jesus, and the Zhong Clan	134
References		137

6 Ethos 139

6.1	Stories from Shuiwei	139
6.2	Ethos, Ritual, and the Taiwanese Daily Life	141
	6.2.1 Ethos and "As if" World	142
6.3	Different Ethos, Different Worlds?	145
	6.3.1 Open Rituals	150
	6.3.2 Open Rituals in Open Life	152
	6.3.3 Different Ethos and Shared Knowledge	157
References		159

7 Logos 161

7.1	Narrating Logos	161
7.2	Logos	165
	7.2.1 Logos, Common Sense, and Daily Life	166
7.3	Shuiwei Logos: Between Hegemony and Daily Life	168
	7.3.1 Logos, Politics, and Hegemony	169
	7.3.2 Logos and Common Sense	171
	7.3.3 Logos and the Ever-Changing Context	179
References		182

8 Conclusions — 183
   8.1 Other Stories, Other Worlds — 183
   8.2 The Discovery of the Other — 185
   8.3 Locus, Narration, and the Other Us — 187
   8.4 Alterity, Narration, and Our Life — 189
   References — 190

Index — 191

List of Figures

Fig. 2.1	The Circuit of Narration	22
Fig. 3.1	Schematic representation of a traditional Taiwanese home	47
Fig. 3.2	The characters in the lintel mean "Jesus is the Lord of my house"	48
Fig. 3.3	The true origin of all things	49
Fig. 3.4	煞 Shā.	55
Fig. 3.5	Yunlin County	57
Fig. 3.6	Yunlin County and Lunbei Township	58
Fig. 3.7	Lunbei Township with Shuiwei village. *Source*: Modified from Google Maps	60
Fig. 3.8	Shuiwei Village Christian community. *Source*: Modified from Google maps	65
Fig. 3.9	Shuiwei Presbyterian (yellow) and Catholic (red) communities. *Source*: Modified from Google Maps	66
Fig. 3.10	Temples' location in Shuiwei village. *Source*: Modified from Google Maps	67
Fig. 3.11	Theme park in Shuiwei village	70
Fig. 4.1	Mr. Zhong Qin, who began the Catholic community of Shuiwei village in 1905	83
Fig. 4.2	The images of Mr. Zhong Qin and his second wife	84
Fig. 5.1	The kinship structure of the Li family of Lunbei	111
Fig. 5.2	The kinship structure of the Han family of Lunbei	112
Fig. 5.3	Position of the Catholic households in Shuiwei. *Source*: Modified from Google Maps	114
Fig. 5.4	Catholic kinship situation. *Source*: Modified from Google Maps	119
Fig. 5.5	Schema of the traditional home altar	126

Fig. 5.6	Old version of the Catholic home altar	128
Fig. 5.7	Modern version of the Catholic home altar	129
Fig. 5.8	The poster of the 150th anniversary	134
Fig. 6.1	Offering for the ghosts	147
Fig. 6.2	Taiwanese measuring tape	149
Fig. 6.3	Table from David Jordan (2006)	155
Fig. 7.1	Traditional Chinese Calendar. *Source*: 農民曆系列. ACME Cultural Enterprise Co., Ltd.	164
Fig. 7.2	Logos Schema 1	172
Fig. 7.3	The Agape clinic	173
Fig. 7.4	In between myself (right) and my wife (left) is the text of The First Letter to the Corinthians	174
Fig. 7.5	May God bless you	175
Fig. 7.6	The First Letter to the Corinthians	176
Fig. 7.7	Logos Schema 2	177
Fig. 7.8	Logos Schema 3	178

CHAPTER 1

Introduction

1.1 THE NARRATIVE CONSTRUCTION OF REALITY

"When a 演戲 *Yǎnxì* traditional performance takes place in 水尾 Shuiwei, I will give you back your money." This is one of the first sentences I heard about Shuiwei village. The meaning of this joke is that you will never get your money back, because in Shuiwei village no *yǎnxì* is ever performed. As Taiwanese people know, a *yǎnxì* performance is offered to thank the deities for a gain, or because one has been released from a vow, or because of a happy event within the family. Usually a "stage-truck," a truck that carries a stage for performances, is parked in front of the temple or in front of the house where the *yǎnxì* is to be offered. Since the stage is positioned just in front of the main door of the temple, and since these shows are followed by few if any spectators, it is clear that the recipients, the real audience for these performances, are the deities and not the people.

The meaning of this joke derives from the fact that Shuiwei village is, for the most part, inhabited by Presbyterians and Catholics.[1] Consequently, no such performances are offered to any deity. Shuiwei is located in the

---

[1] I will refer to the Christian communities of Shuiwei by using the specific terms Catholic 天主教 (*Tiānzhǔjiào*) and Presbyterian 長老會 (*Zhǎnglǎohuì*). When I use the term Christian 基督徒 (*Jīdūtú*), I will refer to both Churches.

© The Author(s) 2020
M. Lazzarotti, *Place, Alterity, and Narration in a Taiwanese Catholic Village*, Asian Christianity in the Diaspora,
https://doi.org/10.1007/978-3-030-43461-8_1

northern part of 崙背鄉 Lunbei Township, just south of the 濁水溪 *Zhuóshuǐ* Stream that marks the border between the counties of 彰化縣 Changhua and 雲林縣 Yunlin.

This small village was the first village in Lunbei Township to accept the Christian religion. A majority of the villagers are still either Presbyterian or Catholic (廖救玲 2005). This large Christian community has had more than 100 years of interaction with the population of Lunbei. The evidence of these interactions can be found in the expressions, the words, and the stories that non-Christian people use in order to describe and contextualize the Christian community of Shuiwei. In the same way, this long interaction is also perceived in the words and stories told by the people of Shuiwei to describe both themselves and the non-Christian members of their community.

I had the opportunity to live in Shuiwei for three years, from August 2008 to October 2011; or more accurately, I spent one year in Lunbei and two years in Shuiwei, during a ten-year period living in Taiwan. Early in June 2008, my wife and I, hopeful and curious, arrived in this village almost by chance. At the time I was doing research into the effect of Catholicism on the tradition of ancestors' rites in Taiwan, while my wife was looking for a suitable place to carry out her fieldwork on Hakka people.[2] We spent the spring of that year visiting all the Hakka communities in both the north and south of Taiwan. Finally, my MA supervisor introduced us to his former classmate who was living in Shuiwei and to the parish priest of that little community. He presented Shuiwei village to us as a place where most of the population were Christian and where the inhabitants introduced themselves as Taiwanese people, but with Hakka ancestors. After a couple of visits, we decided to settle in Lunbei and, as my wife started her fieldwork, I started to think about what kind of project I could undertake for my PhD.

My project, and therefore this book, was born in the field. I had arrived in Shuiwei without a study plan and without a research project. The fundamental reason I had come was to follow my wife during her fieldwork. I did not create an abstract model that had to be verified (or disproved)

---

[2] Hakka people, whose Chinese name 客家人 *Kèjiā rén* literally means "guest people," are a subgroup of the 漢 *Hàn* Chinese that originated in Northern China. In a series of migrations, the Hakkas moved and settled in their present areas in Southern China, and from there, substantial numbers migrated overseas to various countries throughout the world.

through research in the field. The topic somehow made its own way to me during the time I spent in Shuiwei. It prompted me every time Lunbei people told me: "Shuiwei is a different place," or every time they told me: "Are you doing research on religion? You should go to Shuiwei, they are all Christians there." Many, if not all, of the narrations about Shuiwei made by the people of Lunbei spoke about difference. It is because I wanted to understand why and how this sense of diversity was manifested in these stories that I realized that this place was constructed as "a different place" and that it was constructed, above all, by narration.

The aim of my thesis was to show how the narration of stories about this particular place, Shuiwei, attaches to it a special agency. With this book I would like to share with a wider audience the results of this research: that the narration of stories is not only a consequence of the encounter of different cultures, faiths, and traditions but is perhaps the basic way in order to create cultures, faiths, and traditions. By narrating, telling, and naming the world, we substantially create it. We create a Narrative World.

The stories that I have chosen from those collected during my fieldwork include both stories and anecdotes that I have either been told or witnessed directly myself. I want to present both stories and anecdotes because it is through them that, when I was in Shuiwei, I tried to understand how people act or react in and to certain situations. In other words, they will help the reader understand the symbolic context of where people live. I have chosen this way because I consider both stories and anecdotes as narrations, since they have been narrated at least by myself. This choice mirrors the essence of anthropology, which I have always considered a comparative discipline. There is always a comparison going on between the anthropologist and the local culture, between the anthropologist and academia, and also between the outcome of the anthropological work, the text, and the reader. Stories, as well as anecdotes, are always linked to the present and with the practical and contingent situations which both the storyteller and the audience meet in everyday life.

Among the narrations about Shuiwei, the narratives that I heard from people who live outside this village occupy a privileged position. I decided to give greater importance to these stories for several reasons. First of all because in the context formed by the storyteller and the audience, great importance must be assigned to the cultural background of the interlocutors. Within this context, which I call the Circuit of Narration (Locus, Sect. 2.2.1), the cultural background of the interlocutors plays an important role: it selects the facts that create stories and provides the storyteller with the symbols which help him to select the facts that will become a story. At the same time, the cultural background provides the audience with the symbols which help her/him to interpret the story. In the case of Shuiwei, very often the frames of meanings through which both the storyteller and the audience are able to read the reality and interpret it are not the same. During my fieldwork, I noticed how the stories about Shuiwei were emerging both from the contrast between the storyteller and the frame of meanings that led the actions of the main actors of his stories and from the contrast between the storyteller's and the audience's cultural schemes. Through this contrast present inside the Circuit of Narration, symbols, concepts of the world and of the other, and consequentially stories are revisited and created.

There is another reason that convinced me of the importance of stories coming from people living outside Shuiwei. The reason lies in the fact that generally, scholars who analyze and work with the concept of "agency of place" use this idea in order to demonstrate how a specific place, linked with particular memories and facts, is able to produce a feeling of "belonging to a particular place." In other words, they stress the importance of the agency of place in order to explain how a place influences and shapes the sense of identity of a certain group of people. While basing myself on these studies, I would like to take the discussion a little further. In fact, the particular character of my fieldwork place allows me to affirm that we must put these above-mentioned research frames in a wider context. We cannot limit the potentiality of an agency of place to a discussion about identity and a sense of belonging. The theoretical implications of considering a place as an element full of agency power could lead us to do some very interesting theoretical experiments. But, as a first step, we have to put within this context elements such as narration and storytelling.

I will argue that it is through the narrations that Shuiwei is created as locus, where locus is a place where different historical roots, cultural traditions, personal experiences, and above all narrations meet and confront each other. In other words, locus refers to a place where alterity, or otherness, is discovered and reconceived according to narrative criteria.[3]

---

[3] Alterity is considered as the quality or state of being radically alien to the conscious self or a particular cultural orientation. Merrian-Webster.com 2017, Alterity.

1.2 Ethnography and the Field

The Catholic community of Shuiwei has been the focus of my ethnographic fieldwork, although I also had very deep and fruitful exchanges with the Presbyterian community and with villagers who had not joined the Christian faith. Within the Catholic community of Shuiwei, I especially focused my attention and my analysis on one specific lineage—the 鍾 *Zhōng* family. I chose this approach because the Zhong family was the first family to convert to Catholicism more than 100 years ago. The influence of this family on the conversions that followed, both in the village of Shuiwei and in the township of Lunbei, was and still is very big. It was with these first conversions that the missionaries started to have contacts and interact with the Lunbei area. Moreover, the anthropological analysis of this family will be helpful to understand the situation of the whole Catholic community in Lunbei.

During the perusal of this work, the reader will note how every entity (the Zhong Catholic lineage, the Catholic and the Presbyterian communities in Shuiwei, the Christian community of Lunbei, the non-Christian inhabitants of both Shuiwei and Lunbei) is never independent, but part of a system of relations that contribute to assign to each entity a specific value. These entities are interconnected and interdependent in many moments of daily life and above all within the Circuit of Narration. Their interactions and their narrations create the locus, the concept I would like to introduce in the field of anthropology of space and place (Locus, Sect. 2.3.3).

Among this relational system is located the anthropologist, who cannot but observe how complex the relationships between the different entities are. These different entities continuously intersect one another and contribute to form the "field" where the anthropologist should discover and select the data. In the process of writing this book, I reached a point where I had to decide whether to try to reduce the complexity of these relations to a more focused (and manageable) ethnographic description or to choose the interactions of these mentioned entities as the target of my research as suggested by Standaert (2011, p. 214) (please refer to Locus, Sect. 2.3.3).

The first choice concretely entailed focusing my ethnographic writing toward the description of the Catholic branch of the Zhong family in Shuiwei. This option, a quite traditional one, has the advantage of having a clear focus, but at the same time it covers up (eliminates, reduces, you name it) the presence and the importance of the other elements that I met in the field and with whom I (and more important the Zhong Catholics) constantly interacted.

The second option led me toward the discovery of locus as a place for interactions and made by the interactions of different agents and by their narrations (Sect. 2.3.3). The analysis of the specific situation of the Catholic part of the Shuiwei's Zhong family cannot be fully understood without the knowledge of the interactions of this community with the whole Lunbei's Catholic community, the Presbyterian community, and the non-Christian inhabitants of this township.

Because of this I decided to write down what I concretely met on the field. Even if the Catholic community of Shuiwei had been the focus of my ethnographic fieldwork, my interaction with all these entities helped me to better understand the Catholic branch of the Zhong family. At the same time, these entities were always present in the narrations made by the Catholic branch of the Zhong family.

My goal in the next page will be to describe together the Catholic Zhong of Shuiwei and the ethnographic context that consists of the relationships of the entities I previously mentioned.

1.2.1 Defining the Field: Taiwan

The ethnological particularities linked to the Christianity of Shuiwei are emphasized when considered within the Taiwanese religious context. Prior to the seventeenth century, Taiwan was inhabited by the Taiwanese aborigines of Austronesian stock, and there were small settlements of Chinese and Japanese maritime traders and pirates (Clart and Jones 2003, p. 11). The religious traditions of these people consisted of a combination of animism and ancestors worship (Yearbook 2006, p. 267).

Buddhism, Taoism, and Christianity made their appearance in Taiwan in the mid-seventeenth century when Han migrants from southeastern China arrived (Clart and Jones 2003, p. 15). Almost during the same time, Protestant missionaries and Roman Catholic missionaries arrived on the island. Other religions were introduced over the next three and half centuries as Chinese, Japanese, and Westerners came to the island, with a large religious influx following the Second World War, when a new wave of Mainland immigrants arrived in Taiwan along with the relocated Republic of China (ROC) government (Yearbook 2016, p. 267).

Nowadays the Taiwanese religious background presents a strong diversification of religious beliefs and practices. Among these practices, those pertaining to Chinese culture and Chinese traditional religions are indubitably predominant. In fact, Taiwan has one of the world's highest densities of religious structures, especially Taoist and Buddhist temples and shrines (Yearbook 2016, p. 268). The census of 2005 made by the Taiwan Ministry of the Interior shows that Taoism and Buddhism have the largest numbers of adherents. 35% of the population is composed of Buddhists, and 33% are Taoists (including local religion). Among the rest of the population, 3.9% are Christian, 18.7% identify themselves as not religious, and approximately 10% are adherents to religious movements of Taoist or Confucian origin (among whom 3.5% adhere to Yiguandao) (Yearbook 2006). It is possible to note how in Taiwan only a sizable minority of people adheres to Christianity. Specifically, Taiwan's 400,000 Catholics represent only 1.7% of Taiwan's total population (Brown and Cheng 2012, p. 60).

Researchers and academics estimate that as much as 80% of the population believes in some form of traditional folk religion. Such folk religions may overlap with an individual's belief in Buddhism, Taoism, Confucianism, or other traditional Chinese religions (Department of State 2007).

Within the context delineated by the Taiwanese religious background, the village of Shuiwei, whose population is composed of a Christian majority, shows itself as a special place. A place where the minority become majority, subverting in this way many of the cultural cornerstones (e.g. kinship, cultural and ethnic identity) defined by the many anthropologists who worked on the 漢 Han population of this island.

Moreover it is worth mentioning that many of the researches about Christianity in Taiwan are pointed toward the Taiwanese aborigines who converted to Christianity in a bigger number. According to some of these researches, many of the aborigines converted to Christianity because of the missionaries' help, especially because many of them were medical doctors (洪秀柱 1973). The importance of missionaries as bearers of medical aid played an important role also in the conversion of the Han people. The parish of 鹿寮 Luliao in Yunlin (not far away from Shuiwei) started because of the intervention of a Dominican missioner who "healed" a non-Christian who was ill.[4]

---

[4] Please refer to Lazzarotti (2008).

From another point of view, Shepherd (1996) suggests that the aboriginal people, whom the Han people considered as a sort of marginal ethnic group (Shepherd 1996, p. 135), converted in order to get closer relationships with the Western missionaries. In other words, their conversion should be considered as a way to balance the power relations between them and the Han people. In these researches, the relevant position of the missionaries and the discriminating attitude of the Han people against the Taiwanese aborigines are evident.

The importance of the missionaries as one of the centers of power was important also in the context of the Han people. Those who converted to Catholicism were always a minority of the local population, and especially in small villages the conversion—and as we will see all the interdictions and new rules that this conversion involved—was considered a non-filial act, especially because the newly converted were forbidden to pay honor to their ancestors. The missionaries concretely implemented strategies apt to defend the newly converted.

Not too far from Shuiwei, in the county of Changhua, is the parish of 田中 Tianzhong. In this parish the Dominican missionaries bought the lands surrounding the church to let the newly converted Han peoples build there their homes. Living together, the newly converted were helping and defending themselves from the Han people who did not convert to the Catholic faith (Genos, Sect. 5.3).

In Shuiwei the situation is a bit different for several reasons. First of all, in the village of Shuiwei, the converted families were the majority; second (at least in the Catholic part), missionaries did not take part at the beginning of the Catholics' conversion. The first Catholic to arrive in Shuiwei was a layman, and only after that did some of the village's inhabitants convert to Catholicism (Epos, Sect. 4.3.3). The very first time I asked the Catholic believers of Shuiwei if they felt somehow discriminated against by the non-Christian population because their faith is in the minority, they answered: "here they [non-Christian people] are the minority, and we don't discriminate against anyone."

1.2.2 Defining the Field: Lunbei Township

Lunbei Township offers a great concentration of different religious, ethnic, and political groups in one little township. Different religious groups (Taiwanese Popular Religion, Christian Presbyterian, Catholic, Buddhist,

Yiguandao),[5] different ethnic groups (Minnan, Hakka, Mainland Chinese, Southeast Asia people), and people of different political orientations inhabit the same place. However, these religious and ethnic differences tend to disappear if we look at the situation from an economic point of view. Intensive agriculture is the most important economic activity. Sharing agricultural machinery and physical labor is a common practice among farmers in Lunbei (as it is in other parts of the Taiwanese countryside). This mutual help promotes contact between persons and families, helping to enhance mutual knowledge and respect.

Apart from Shuiwei, Christianity is also well represented in other villages of Lunbei Township. The Catholic and Presbyterian churches are both located in the village of 南陽 Nanyang. Catholic believers run pharmacies, medical and dental clinics, and stores carrying agricultural products. In all these places, people can find images of Holy Mary, verses from the Holy Bible, crucifixes, and so on. In contrast with many other places in Taiwan, it seems to me that the Christian faith is not only well accepted but also well known in Lunbei. It is very common for people in Lunbei to have a Christian workmate or classmate. Living in this kind of environment has, in my view, caused people in Lunbei to start to relate to the Christian religion as a local religion rather than as a foreign element.

1.2.3 Shuiwei

From many points of view, Shuiwei is not so different from the other villages of Lunbei. The younger generations tend to leave the village and to move around Taipei or Kaohsiung, the two biggest cities of the island, which offer more job opportunities and are more lively (as they say, 比較熱鬧 *bǐjiào rènào*). This situation reflects the fact that nowadays fewer people take up agricultural work on the land. However, the presence of a strong Christian community is a particular characteristic of this small village. Being two-thirds of the entire village, the influence that the Christian community has on the whole community of Shuiwei is very strong and concrete. Apart from the fact that, unlike the rest of the township, there is not a main temple, the influence of the Christian community is also felt in the political

---

[5] In this book, following the indication of Professor Philip Clart (2007), I will use the term "Popular Religion" instead of the term "Chinese folk religion."

field. For example, without the support of the Christian community, or at least part of it, it is difficult for anyone to become the head of the village.

For the most part, the villagers are farmers or have jobs linked to agricultural activities. In fact, the village economy is not too different from the rest of the villages in Lunbei Township. Among the male part of the Catholic community of Shuiwei, almost 70% are farmers, but different professions are also represented: plumbers, deer farmers, agents of commerce. The women especially are involved in different kinds of businesses or other community activities. The Presbyterians and the Catholics are located in a specific part of the village (Topos, Sect. 3.3.3, Fig. 3.9), which is also the most densely populated.

The part of the village occupied by the Christian community is the oldest part of the village and the place originally called Shuiwei. Other residential areas are located in the southern part of the village, in a place called 下街 *xiàjiē*, and in the northern part of the village. This last group of households is called 新生 *xīnshēng*, and it is inhabited by Hakka people from the northern county of 新竹 Hsinchu, who moved into the village around 30 years ago.

As I will explain in detail, the Catholic community is mainly composed of two big lineages, the Li and the Zhong.

1.3 THE FIVE ELEMENTS OF NARRATION

As mentioned above, the evidence of the interactions between the Christian community of Shuiwei village and the non-Christian population of Lunbei can be found in their expression, in their words, and in the stories that the people of Shuiwei, both Christian and non-Christian, tell themselves and one other. It is easy to understand that the people involved in what I call the Circuit of Narration very often belong to different religious and cultural backgrounds. In order to reduce this complexity to a more simple and effective analytical approach, I decided to use an operative mode that allows me to organize this complexity within a precise analytical schema.

Following some indications I found in the work of the Italian anthropologist Carlo Tullio Altan (1995), I have selected five aspects that I named *Topos*, *Epos*, *Genos*, *Ethos*, and *Logos*, by which reality and daily events are identified, selected, and (re)organized in stories. Through these points, everyday events take on a specific value and thus form the foundation of the stories about Shuiwei and its inhabitants.

Altan originally uses these categories to analyze the formation and the development of ethnic groups. The goal of his analysis is the understanding of the phenomena linked to the creation of national identities (Altan 1995, p. 7). In my work I will use the five elements selected by Altan in a somewhat different way. I will consider these five elements as the main points around which the sense of otherness coalesces and shows itself. This sense of alterity, discovered by the analysis of these five elements, is the creator of the stories about Shuiwei. Alterity is, thus, the main source of the stories that create Shuiwei as locus—as a place where different concepts and ideas meet and interact together.

There is actually another reason that led me toward the choice to use the five points from Altan to describe the situation of Shuiwei. During the process of writing this book, these five elements helped me also in reconstructing my personal experience in the field. I would like, with this division into chapters, to introduce gradually to the reader this village and the people who inhabit it. The progressive reconstruction in the text of the knowledge that I have acquired during my fieldwork is none other than the mirror of my experience in the field. As I said, I arrived in Shuiwei without a previous knowledge of this place and, above all, without having built a hypothetical picture of it in a research plan. My knowledge of Shuiwei has increased gradually through the contact with the people who lived in the village, and thanks to the narratives about it that other people made.

I consider this division into chapters very important in order to preserve this sense of progressive "disclosing" of Shuiwei, both to me and to the reader. The reader will achieve a bigger knowledge through the reading of the chapters, and the reading of each single chapter will cast a new light upon the chapters she/he has previously read. In this way the reader will be able to take part in my process of discovering Shuiwei, how I get more and deeper knowledge every time a new story enlightens the elements I had gathered till that time.

I am aware that this choice entails the risk that all the stories I will introduce in the chapters will appear covered by my voice-over. I think that this is a real risk, and I am the first to say that my presence within each chapter is sometimes even cumbersome, but indeed it is my voice, the voice of the anthropologist who with his questions and his presence raises memories and thus stimulated the creation of stories.

This approach has deep roots in the reading of the book of Alessandro (Dell'Orto 2003), one of the anthropologists who most influenced the choice of topic for my research and especially the style of my writing.

I particularly got inspiration from his idea that the process of writing—and consequentially the process of reading—should, obviously within certain limits, reflect the experience in the field, which is never the solitary experience of the anthropologist, but it is the result of the meetings and the exchanges that the anthropologist has on the field.

> As in the field so in the text, in fact, the construction of anthropological knowledge is an ongoing process in which different 'poles' of experience and interpretation, those of the anthropologist and those of the people 'on the ground', are created and recreated in the same ethnographic process. (Dell'Orto 2003, p. 134)

Another approach to the process of writing that Dell'Orto stressed in his book is that the reader should have an active role in the process of discovering the stories that the anthropologist selected in order to create a text.

> What I wish to ask of the reader is to become an 'author' himself or herself by telling his or her own story in the same process of reading other people's stories.(Dell'Orto 2003, p. 12)

This is what I tried to do by choosing to present my ethnographic material through the analysis of the five elements I am going to introduce in the next pages.

It has been previously introduced that the five elements selected by Altan are topos, epos, genos, ethos, and logos.

Topos represents both the image of the positive value of the territory and a source of aesthetic and emotional charm. In the Taiwanese context, traditionally, the concept of territory is linked to the idea of 風水 *fēngshuǐ*, to the concept of ancestors, and with many other concepts that characterize the rich Chinese cosmology. In the specific case of Shuiwei, the conversion to a new faith produced small but important changes in the architecture of the domestic homes (Lazzarotti 2013, p. 303 et seq.). These visible changes indicate some significant structural modifications of the cosmology and of the social relations within and between households. On the one hand, these sensorial changes expressed by topos are constitutive of the Christian people of Shuiwei. On the other hand, they are one of the main signs of alterity for the non-Christian people who interact with this village.

Epos has been considered as the symbolic transfiguration of historical memory as a celebration of the common past (Altan 1995, p. 21). In more specific terms, the epos of Shuiwei is strongly related to the village's history with the Catholic church in Taiwan. The Dominicans required the new believers to have a clear break with all the traditions related to the cult of ancestors and of Confucius. These practices were considered heresies or treated as pagan cults. The consequence of this has been the separation and estrangement of the converted from the rest of their lineages.[6] On the other hand, this separation helped to create the starting point of the history, and thus of the epos, of the Catholics of Shuiwei.

Genos is the element that Altan relates to kinship, lineage, and dynasty. Kinship has a fundamental importance in Chinese culture. Chinese kinship is based on the idea of patrilinearity. The consequence is that the blood relationship between father and son is the most important element of society. These blood links continue even after death and have their visible implementation in the rites for the ancestors. In other words, for many Taiwanese people, the concept of family also encompasses those members who have already passed away. One of the consequences of the conversion to Christianity was that the believers were forbidden to perform any ceremonies in honor of the ancestors. Through a long historical process, this prohibition created a new sense of identity among the converted families—a sense of belonging to a new family, with new ancestors and with a new sense of brotherhood.

Ethos was conceived by Altan as the sacralization of the norms and institutions, by religion or social origin, on which the sociability of a group of people is based (1995, p. 21). Almost everybody among the non-Christian inhabitants of Lunbei knows that the ethos of the people in Shuiwei is linked to a different cosmology which leads them to act in different ways and be subjected to different taboos. Everybody also knows that the ethos of the Shuiwei people is somehow based on Christian

---

[6] In the Chinese tradition, a lineage is an organized group of descendants of a single, specific ancestor. The ancestor is referred to as an "apical" ancestor because he is at the "apex" of the genealogy by which the lineage membership is determined, and the descent links to this person are known (or written in a genealogy where they can be looked up). A clan is a property holding group made up of descendants of an apical ancestor, but the details of the descent lines from that ancestor are unknown. In some cases the ancestor is clearly mythical, and in some societies, the apical ancestor may even be non-human. Please refer to David K. Jordan (2006).

concepts, concepts that are felt to be unknown or at least felt as 不一樣 *bù yīyàng* (different) or 奇怪 *Qíguài* (strange) by the neighboring inhabitants. The acknowledgment of this diversity became a sense that the surrounding non-Christian people share and on which they build their narrations on Shuiwei.

Logos is the element which represents the language. The analysis of logos underpins the analysis of the linguistic situation in Shuiwei. Language is considered as a sense of things held in common and, thus, to the idea of local culture (Gramsci et al. 1971; Forgacs and Nowell-Smith 1985). From this point of view, it is possible to recognize the contrast between certain idioms, anecdotes, and common sayings used by non-Christians and the ones used by both Presbyterians and Catholics. Christians and non-Christians use different terms to refer to specific concepts or events linked to a particular system of beliefs. The use of specific words such as Amitofo (a Buddhist mantra) or 天主保佑 *Tiānzhǔ bǎoyòu* (may God bless you) immediately situates the speaker within a precise social group. Certain words, then, have the power to identify those who pronounce them. In a certain sense, it is possible to say that non-Christian people—when they heard words or expressions linked to the Christian community—directly linked the speakers to Shuiwei village.

1.4 The World Is All That Is the Case

These elements of topos, epos, genos, ethos, and logos will represent both a modus operandi and the structure of this thesis. They could be conceived of as a filter, through which the stories are created and inserted in a shared horizon of beliefs and values held in common. At the same time, these basic elements are how a people, through narration, maintains its own identity.

This division will help to explain how through the narration of concrete experiences and abstract thought, the people of Shuiwei keep and reinforce—but also adapt and change—their own identity and therefore the identity of the locus they inhabit. At the same time, within the Circuit of Narration, the sharing of stories about Shuiwei and the Christian community lets the people of Lunbei recognize, along with the differences, their own cultural categories.

The narrations that come out from the sense of alterity shaped by the five elements construct Shuiwei village and its identity. From an analytical point of view, the choice of these elements is helpful for understanding the historical processes which are underlined in the social and cultural structure of Shuiwei village and its surrounding areas. In order to understand how a place is created, it is thus necessary to underline what these elements mean, how they are created and considered by Shuiwei inhabitants, and the different meanings that these elements—because they are involved in different historical processes—have for the people who live outside the village.

It is through the sharing of narrations about concrete experiences and abstract thought that the people of Shuiwei keep and reinforce, but at the same time adapt and change their own identity and consequently the identity of the place they inhabit. This process also works in the opposite way: the sharing of stories about Shuiwei and the Christian community—which is historically and socially linked to this village—lets the people who are living outside the village recognize, along with the differences, their own cultural categories. In this never-ending dialogic process of narration, Shuiwei is created as a locus, a place where differences are reconceived through the narration of stories about them.

In conclusion, we can say with Ludwig Wittgenstein (1922, 25) that the world is all that is the case. Everything that happens, and also things that never happened, can become part of a narration. Both things that happen and things that never happened are symbols that are recognized and interpreted. All the symbols are able to create a contrast with a standard common sense—a public symbolic system made by shared meanings. Therefore everything that happens has the power to affect our symbolic systems, build a world, and create a narration that will give us the certainty of being alive in a more or less friendly and known world.

References

Altan, C.T. 1995. *Ethnos e Civiltà. Identità Etniche e Valori Democratici*. Milano: Feltrinelli.
Brown, D.A., and T.-J. Cheng. 2012. Religious Relations Across the Taiwan Strait: Patterns, Alignments, and Political Effects. *Orbis* 56 (1): 60–81.
Clart, P. 2007. The Concept of 'Popular Religion' in the Study of Chinese Religions: Retrospect and Prospects. In *The Forth Fu Jen University International Sinological Symposium: Research on Religions in China: Status quo and Perspectives; Symposium Papers*, 166–203.
Clart, P., and C.B. Jones. 2003. *Religion in Modern Taiwan: Tradition and Innovation in a Changing Society*. Honolulu: University of Hawaii Press.

Dell'Orto, A. 2003. *Place and Spirit in Taiwan: Tudi Gong in the Stories, Strategies and Memories of Everyday Life.* New York: Routledge.
Department of State, U. 2007. *International Religious Freedom Report 2007.* https://www.state.gov/j/drl/rls/irf/2007/90134.html. Accessed March 19, 2017.
Forgacs, D., and G. Nowell-Smith. 1985. *Selections from Cultural Writings.* Cambridge: Harvard University Press.
Gramsci, A., Q. Hoare, et al. 1971. *Selections from the Prison Notebooks.* London: Lawrence and Wishart.
Jordan, D.K. 2006. *Traditional Chinese Family and Lineage.* http://pages.ucsd.edu/~dkjordan/chin/familism.html. Accessed Aug 08, 2017.
Lazzarotti, M. 2008 How Histories make History. Two Taiwanese Cases: Shuiwei Village and Luliao Village Catholic Communities. In *The Annual Conference of the Taiwan Society for Anthropology and Ethnology.*
——. 2013. How the Universal Becomes Domestic: An Anthropological Case Study of the Shuiwei Village, Taiwan. In *The Household of God and Local Households: Revisiting the Domestic Church,* ed. T.K.-P. le Roi, M. Gerard, and D.M. Paul, 301–314. Leuven: Peeters Publishers.
Merrian-Webster.com, T. 2017. *Alterity.* https://www.merriam-webster.com/dictionary/alterity. Accessed Mar 09, 2017.
Shepherd, J.R. 1996. From Barbarians to Sinners: Collective Conversion among Plains Aborigines in Qing Taiwan, 1859–1895. In *Christianity in China: From the Eighteenth Century to the Present,* ed. D.H. Bais, 120–179. Palo Alto: Stanford University Press.
Standaert, N. 2011. *The Interweaving of Rituals: Funerals in the Cultural Exchange between China and Europe.* Seattle: University of Washington Press.
Taiwan Yearbook, T. 2006. Taipei: Government Information Office, 2007.
Taiwan Yearbook, T. 2016. Taipei: Government Information Office, 2016.
Wittgenstein, L. 1922. *Tractatus Logico-Philosophicus with an Introduction by Bertrand Russell.* Paperback.
洪秀柱. 1973. 南投宰人的宗教信仰.
廖救玲. 2005. 掌中崙背. Yunlin County Government.

CHAPTER 2

Locus

2.1 Stories from Shuiwei

Mister Yang is the president of a cultural association in Lunbei. He is very involved in preserving local customs and in particular the local Hakka culture and language. My wife and I, especially during the first phase of our fieldwork, were often invited to take part in the activities of his association. One night, after one of these activities, we started to drink tea and talk about our life and our studies.

There are not many things that can help an anthropologist in the Taiwan countryside more than a relaxing conversation in front of a cup of good tea on a summer night. The weather, usually very hot and humid, makes people sit down together outside the house, searching for a pleasant breeze. At this moment it seems that there are no fences between persons, and everybody enjoys the conversation.

That night the topic of the conversation was the Christian village of Shuiwei and its interesting peculiarity. As Mister Zhong (a non-Christian inhabitant of Lunbei) told me, "That village is very different from our places. They have no main temple and when the procession of the 太平媽祖 *Tàipíng Māzǔ* arrives in Shuiwei, they started to run in order to leave that place as quickly as possible. He told us that this decision is taken because nobody goes on the road to welcome the goddess. Therefore, the persons who have the charge of carrying the statue of Mazu, 覺得很不好意思 *Juédé hěn bù hǎo yìsī*, felt this situation very embarrassing for her.[1] "

During my fieldwork, I have been a witness to this event. I can testify that only two people were on the road when Mazu came across the main road of Shuiwei: my son and I. Arriving in Shuiwei, the people who were carrying the traditional flags and the statues of the deities jumped on a small truck and left that place in a hurry.

Mister Yang also told me a very interesting history about Shuiwei village. He has been a pig farmer for a certain time. As everyone knows, the hoof of the pig is formed of four parts, but occasionally it may happen that a fifth "finger" shows up in the pig's paw. Mr. Yang told me that this situation is difficult to resolve. Due to the belief in the cycle of reincarnation, the fact that the pig has five fingers instead of four places the pig in an intermediate state between man and pig. The pig is not a man, but certainly it can no longer be regarded as a pig. In other words, the animal is not yet completely purified to be reborn as a man, but because it has five fingers, it is reborn at a higher level than that of the pig. The difficulty is how to solve this problem. Mister Yang told me, most of the farmers who encounter this problem tend to set the pig free, which will have to find a way to survive on its own. But for the people of Lunbei, there may be another solution. Mister Yang sought advice from another pig farmer in the area, and he told him to give the pig to the people of Shuiwei. "They don't believe in these things! When I meet these problems, I always give them the pig." And so did Mr. Yang, bringing the pig to a Christian pig farmer. When he brought the pig, he asked this Christian farmer how he will solve the problem. The answer of the Christian farmer was "I will cut off the fifth finger and then I will sell it."

In addition to these two stories told by Mr. Zhong and Mr. Yang, there are also many anecdotes that, as introduced above, help to interpret the meaning of the narrated stories and of the world created by them. One of the people who most helped me during my fieldwork, by telling these stories and helping me to interpret them, was Zhong Fengrong. Fengrong

---

[1] 媽祖 *Māzǔ*, whose real name was 林默娘 *Línmòniáng*, is one of the most popular deities in Taiwan. Mazu was originally worshiped as the goddess of the sea, but now she is worshiped as an all-powerful protective deity (Katz 2003, p. 395). The 太平媽祖 *Tàipíng Māzǔ* is the Mazu of the 福興宮 *Fúxìng* temple in 西螺 Siluo. Every year this temple organizes a big pilgrimage that passes through Lunbei, after touching the neighboring county of Changhua.

is a Catholic believer from Shuiwei village who works around Lunbei as a plumber. Because of his job and his sunny personality, he is very well known in all Lunbei Township. He worked on the construction of many temples of Lunbei; therefore he knows some aspects of the Taiwanese Popular Religion. I am going to report one of the many anecdotes that he shared with me. Fengrong told me that during the construction of a temple, it is necessary to continuously burn sticks of incense inside the big incense burner located inside the temple and usually dedicated to 天公 *Tiāngōng*, the lord of heaven. During the construction of a temple where he had worked, Fengrong told me that people of the temple met a very serious problem. As we will see in the next pages, very often the lives of many Taiwanese people are linked to various taboos and elaborate geomantic calculations that affect the choice of the proper name, the choice of house orientation, and many other concrete aspects of their lives. Therefore, it is very important to calculate who, in a determinate moment, in a determinate place, can or cannot do certain things. For example, on certain days people cannot marry, buy or sell things, go out, and so on. It is very important to continually change the incense sticks, but that day, as a result of geomantic calculations and after asking the deities, at that precise time, no one present was allowed to go into the temple. The reason for this unusual situation lies in the fact that these geomantic calculations were made to sort out which sign of the 12 terrestrial branches (the Chinese zodiac), in that particular moment, was forbidden to enter the temple. The knowledge of this is important in order to avoid misfortune to the person and to the temple.

Looking at this situation, even if he is a Catholic believer, Fengrong decided to help these people. He said: "no problem, just give me the incense sticks. I will go inside and I will put them in the incense burner." The first thing that people asked him was: "to what birth sign do you belong?" and Fengrong: "Monkey." At this point, since monkey was one of the interdicted signs, people agree to not let him go inside the temple, but Fengrong replied: "No problem, I am a Catholic believer, therefore I absolutely don't care about these things. If you want, I can help you." Finally, Fengrong entered the temple and changed the incense sticks inside the incense burner, thus allowing the ritual to continue.

2.2 Telling Stories Makes the World

The stories I mentioned above help me to introduce a basic assumption of this thesis, which is linked to the importance of narration: when we tell a story, we tell the story and also the world in which this story takes place. Each narrative (a short story, a novel, a movie, a TV show, a comic book, etc.) is always composed of two essential elements: a story and the world in which the story takes place.

We learned in school and we read in many manuals of creative writing that to narrate means to tell a story. If we have a closer look, however, a narrative is always composed of two basic elements: a story and a world. Each story, in fact, is linked and inserted in—and takes form and originality from—a specific world (physical, social, cultural, political, religious, professional, relational, etc.). On this basis, then, it is possible to say that to narrate is to tell the world through the telling of a story. Inside the narrative process, *to tell* means *to build*. Especially if we consider this process as a dialogue between stories, their symbolic background, the concrete experiences of their narrators, and the interpretations made by the audience.

From an extreme point of view, this statement could lead us to another assumption: that "the world" does not exist. There are "worlds," worlds continuously created and recreated by philosophy, religion, science, psychology, marketing, and so on. I am not arguing that "there are no facts, only interpretations": there are interpretations exactly because there must be something to be interpreted. Even if every interpretation is an interpretation of an earlier interpretation, it would assume the nature of a fact. In any case this *regressum ad infinitum* should stop from the point from which it started (Eco 1994, p. 35 et 38–39).

What I am arguing is that each interpretation can be made and can be better understood if framed within a specific narrative context. Or, in Jerome Bruner's words, the narrated events need to be constituted in the light of the overall narrative (Bruner 1991, p. 8). This assumption directly leads us to another important point: the importance of the context.

2.2.1 Narration and Its Context: The Circuit of Narration

According to many scholars, the processes by which we are able to give a name to things are not separable from those by which we think about them (Eco 1997; Violi 1997). When we classify a thing, in one way or another, we select it from the other things, and therefore when we give it a name, we identify that particular thing (Eco 1997, p. 4–8). If we take into consideration the assumption I made at the beginning (see Sect. 2.2), this process is true also for narration. When we narrate, we identify the other (the characters), ourselves, and the world where the event happened and the world we live in. This becomes evident if we consider what Eco defined as the "contractual" dimension of meaning and reference. According to him, "contractual realism" means that we discuss a certain thing because that thing exists (realism) but also because we agree with a community about how to discuss that certain thing (contract). When we are talking about something that does not exist (or that we cannot see), there is always the certainty that we are not talking nonsense (Eco 1997, p. 234 et seq.). Therefore, the consensus becomes a complex operation of negotiation between the speakers. This complex operation of negotiation, which Eco calls consensus, is nothing other than the context.

In our case, the context is thus designed as a circuit composed by the narrator and his audience. As Alberto Melucci pointed out, "we cannot separate the narrative from the relationship in which it is situated. The narratives are always stories that individual or collective actors create *to* someone and *for* someone. Narratives are communicative activities that take place in a specific relational context" (Melucci 2000, p. 114. My translation, my emphasis).

To this context, however, it is necessary to add a third element: what Bruner called "overall narrative" or, in other words, the cultural context, which has a great importance in the study on narratives. This cultural context consists of socially established frames of meaning in terms of which people perform their actions. These frames of meaning are used both to interpret everyday facts and to create or interpret the stories raised by them.

I will refer to this complex set of relationships as the *Circuit of Narration*. In our peculiar case, the one represented by the Christian village of Shuiwei, the Circuit of Narration should take into consideration that sometimes the narrator and the audience (even if they speak the same language) belong to different cultural systems. Certainly the diversities linked to different cultural systems are very often neither absolute nor irreconcilable. Contrariwise, they are overlapping and have much in common.

Even so, it is undeniable that sometimes there are significant differences between the storyteller's and the audience's cultural backgrounds and also between the storyteller and the characters of the story he is telling. These differences can seriously affect the whole Circuit of Narration.

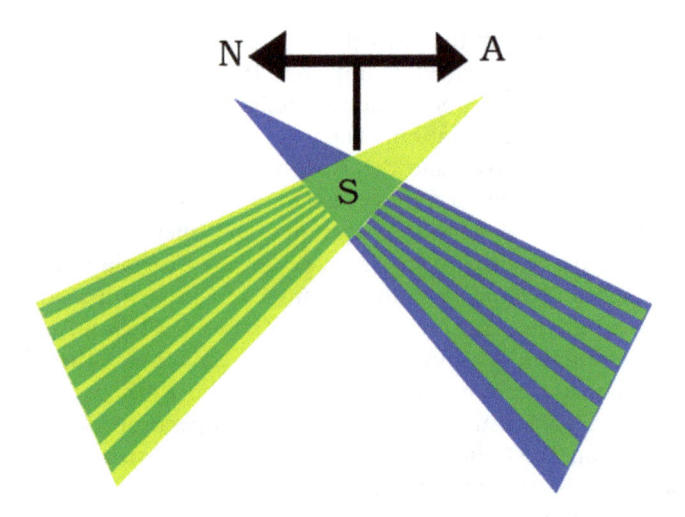

Fig. 2.1 The Circuit of Narration

Within the many Circuits of Narration that I am going to introduce in this thesis, both sides are aware of their reciprocal differences and, in some ways, incorporate these differences into their narrations. The narration of the other is thus built and acquires meaning through the differences that are immanent to the context made by them.

I tried to exemplify some of these differences in Fig. 2.1. In this image N represents the narrator, A is the audience, and S is the story which is created by the interactions of N and A.

At the same time, this interaction helps to create the imagined reality which we could define as the narrative world. The different colors represent the diversities among the different cultural systems.

Because of this complexity, I decided to choose a theoretical approach able to understand, absorb, and let operate together all these differences. A good theoretical approach seems to me the one elaborated by Alfred Gell in order to create a universal approach to the anthropology of art (Gell 1998). The key term to understand the work of Gell is *agency*. In fact, Gell believed that the art objects should be studied only for their agency and not for their aesthetic value.

According to Gell, art objects are not agents in themselves, they are *index*, a term that Gell borrows from the semiology of Peirce. Peirce points out that index is different from icon because icon has a relation of similarity with the referent, while index has with the referent a causal connection. "An 'index' in Peircian semiotics is a 'natural sign,' that is, an entity from which the observer can make a *causal inference* of some kind, or an inference about the intentions or capacity of another person" (Gell 1998, p. 13).

This logical operation is called *abduction* (again, a term which Gell borrows from Peirce), that is, the construction of an acceptable but not demonstrable explicative hypothesis, at least with the data we have in our hands. In other words, the members of a community, through the abduction process, infer from the art object a certain quality or intentionality (agency) of the creators.

Artists, recipients, art objects, and referents become a complex of social relations which Gell calls the Art Nexus. This Art Nexus leads to a big variety of combinations because every component of this Nexus is able to operate in two directions, as agent and as patient (Gell 1998, p. 21–22, 29).

It is possible to adapt the concept expressed by Gell, with appropriate modifications, to explain what happens inside the above-mentioned Circuit of Narration. Therefore I would say that the listeners of a story, through a process of abduction such as the one described by Gell, infer a certain quality or agency of the characters of a story and, of course, of the narrator.

I think that the concept of "interpretive cooperation" proposed by Eco (1980, 1984) could help me to clarify what I have just tried to expose. Eco exemplifies the two more extreme tendencies which could come out from the situation I named the Circuit of Narration. According to him, the interpretation of a text—but, in our case, we can take it as an interpretation of a narrated story—could be fully determined by the author (the narrator), or it could be fully given by the reader (the audience). In between these two extreme conclusions, Eco places the notion of "interpretive cooperation."

Through this interpretive cooperation, what the audience perceives about the environment and the characters of a story is directly linked to how the narrator described or, as we already mentioned at the beginning of this chapter, created it. In other words, the audience perception is linked to how the narrator creates and organizes the characters in a specific environment and in a time sequence. The story is, thus, a sort of negotiation between the will—the creativity—of the storyteller and the acceptance and the interpretation made by the audience. But this dialogue is not limited to this relationship (even though we must consider it as a primary one) between storyteller and audience. As we already highlighted, the cultural contexts—the frames of meanings by which facts are selected as stories and by which stories are created—play an important role within the Circuit of Narration.

In the structure of this book, the Circuit of Narration should be considered as an archetype through which all the stories I will introduce in my work should be read. The composition of all elements which form the Circuit of Narration (storyteller, audience, cultural backgrounds) will be not analyzed but introduced and made explicit by the description and analysis of the cultural environments that I realized in each chapter. The goal of this approach is to encourage the readers to put themself within the Circuit of Narration and reconstruct it, as I did during my fieldwork, through a progressive knowledge of the frames of meaning that give a sense to the lives of the people involved in the moment of the storytelling.

2.2.2 Narration and Time: Need of Coherence

At this point, it is necessary to take into account that a story is something that is born on the spot, by the meeting of a storyteller with an audience. And it is precisely at this moment, linked to a specific time belonging to the Circuit of Narration, that the participants in this Circuit start to influence, more or less heavily, the rhythm, the time of the story, and thus the story itself.

The narrated story is always linked with the present and with practical and contingent situations which both the storyteller and the audience meet in everyday life. People tell stories about Shuiwei village because they live in the same social context where these "extraordinary" facts happen.

Because the Circuit of Narration is always linked with the mentioned social context, it is possible to recognize in it an internal coherence, within the story itself, and an external coherence, which links the story with the public sphere. These two coherences should be considered as two faces of the same coin. As Chris Rideout pointed out:

> In cohering externally with shared social and cultural knowledge, that shared knowledge lends meaning to the narrative. The key to external coherence lies in understanding that its thematic framework derives not from the content of the narrative as an empirical description of social reality, but rather from the social and cultural presuppositions that it conjures and with which it coheres, structurally. Burns, in summarizing how narrative works in a trial, notes that

this thematic framework is unavoidable: "The story told...inevitably assigns a meaning to the human action..." (Burns 1999, p. 163). The thematic framework is a powerful part of the coherence—and hence the plausibility—of narrative because, as a given narrative links to our shared expectations, that narrative is also contextualized in a way that guides its meaning. (Rideout 2013, p. 72)

2.2.3 Narration and Cultural Context

The process of narration has been analyzed by many cognitive psychologists, who argue that an essential cognitive activity of human thought is to narrate, and to narrate means to re-weave the events of our life in a timeline and in a logical sequence—that is, telling stories. If we have a look at the work *Acts of Meaning* of Jerome Bruner (1990), we can see how the author proposes a fresh approach to psychology that retrieves and places at the center of analysis, "a science of mind based on the concept of meaning and processes by which meanings are created and traded within a community." The revolution lies in the proposal to shift the focus from the concept of "information processing," which became prevalent in those days (we are speaking about the early 1990s), to the "construction of meaning." In doing so, Bruner turns to the so-called folk psychology or common sense and leaves us some critical reflections on the narrative and the role of narrative in our daily lives.

> Folk psychology [is] narrative in nature rather than logical or categorical. Folk psychology is about human agents doing things on the basis of their beliefs and desires, striving for goals, meeting obstacles which they best or which best them, all of this extended over time. (Bruner 1990, p. 42–43)

Bruner observes how in everyday experience narrative is an omnipresent activity, which serves several functions: coding experience intra- and interpersonally, negotiating our explanations, supporting mutual rhetorical performance, and so on. The popular or daily narrative then serves the very important task of maintaining order, incorporating the dissimilar and the extraordinary on a shared background.

Many of the popular narratives are stories of transgressions. They do not tell how things are, but how they should be. They do it incorporating into a fabric of common references facts that otherwise would be exceptional. Bruner believes that it is thus through narrative, or storytelling, that individual actors are able to mediate transactions between the ordinary, the unexpected, and the possible (Mattingly et al. 2008, p. 14).

The first act that human thought does attempt in order to re-order and give meaning to reality, through the storytelling process, is to build and reconstruct the worlds in which those personal and/or fictitious stories will find their environment and will be structured. We simply, all the time, manipulate the world around us according to narrative criteria, in order to orient, adapt, and defend ourselves against it.

I found this vision very close to the one of Clifford Geertz, the anthropologist who mostly influenced my studies and the way of understanding and interpreting my work in the field. One of the most important statements made by Geertz is that culture is an acted document in a public arena (Geertz 1973, p. 10) and that "human thought is consummately social: social in its origins, social in its functions, social in its forms, social in its application... thinking is a public activity" (Geertz 1973, p. 360).

Basing himself on these fundamental premises, Geertz structures his idea of culture, which he considers as "a historically transmitted pattern of meanings embodied in symbols, a system of inherited conceptions expressed in symbolic forms by means of which men communicate, perpetuate, and develop their knowledge about and their attitudes toward life" (1973, p. 89). An important point in Geertz's theory is that "cultural acts, the construction, apprehension, and utilization of symbolic forms, are social events like any other; they are as public as marriage and as observable as agriculture" (1973, p. 90). It follows that culture can be considered as a public symbolic system, where symbols "are historically constructed, socially maintained, and individually applied" (Geertz 1973, p. 364). Here we can read the importance of symbols and of their function in building and keeping together cultural patterns because "it is through culture patterns, ordered clusters of significant symbols, that man makes sense of the events through which he lives" (1973, p. 363).

And it is precisely because man lives constantly surrounded by a horizon full of common sense, surrounded by a system of meanings, that the sharing of experiences, through narration, is one of the most powerful ways to know, recognize, and integrate/reject new symbols and experiences. It is this symbolic background which, in my view, constitutes the hard core of the storytelling process and that immerses us in a narrative world. It helps to build the world where the story takes place and provides the tools to interpret it. Being public, this system of meaning cannot be considered as a closed system. It changes and adapts itself to the new contributions—and consequentially new stories—that everyday life brings with it. The Circuit of Narration is, therefore, one of the most powerful ways to introduce, change, or reinforce symbols inside the system of meanings which we commonly call culture.

Considering it as an inter-worked system of construable signs (which Geertz calls symbols), culture is not a power, something to which social events, behaviors, institutions, or processes can be causally attributed; it is a context, something within which they can be intelligibly described. This is for me the basic point in order to understand the situation I found in Shuiwei village, in the stories about it, and the people who inhabit it. It is the public aspect of culture that builds the sense of immanent difference and thus allows the audience of these stories—and, among them, the anthropologist—to bring to light and define the cultural system of the participants to the Circuit of Narration.

2.3 Locus

With the three stories by which I started this chapter, I tried to introduce the reader to the village of Shuiwei. At the same time, I provided knowledge that would be useful in order to construct an image of that world.

From these stories, we can try to read out some basic point linked to the concept of narration. According to Pinardi and De Angelis, "each story comes from conflict, without conflict there are no events, and therefore no story" (Pinardi and De Angelis 2008). If we consider this affirmation inside the context represented by the stories about Shuiwei village, we can see how these narrations are clearly delineated by a "context of contrast" formed by the narrator's encounter with a kind of experiences and people who strongly differ from the ones they met in everyday life and especially in other places. These stories are talking about contrasts, about encounters with someone or something which is not easily understandable through the system of meaning by which people are used to orienting themselves in the world. And, above all, these stories are always linked with a particular place: Shuiwei village.

It is through the meeting and sometimes the contrast of people who belong to different universes of meanings (but we can even call them cultures, cosmologies, world-views, faiths, etc.) that stories arise and are shaped. What I would like to suggest here it is that, in the same way, people become "other" and cultures (cosmologies, world-views, faiths, etc.) are identified as different because the narrations of them are built following a schema of contrast. The dialogue between event, narration, and interpretation is, therefore, a continuous exchange which continuously reinforces and renovates itself.

Within the Circuit of Narration, the elements of a story—the characters, the selected events, and the world which embodied the story—evoke specific symbolic categories. These categories are necessary in order to build a narrative world. These categories come out from the contrast, from the sense of alterity that the event and the narration of it stress when compared with the one belonging to our own cultural system. These differences are not necessarily profound and irreconcilable. During many everyday practices, Christian and non-Christian ways of behaving overlapped. Very often, however, since people are living inside a symbolic world, and being man, an animal able to see and interpret reality only in symbolic terms, it happens that the differences of behavior are interpreted in a way that reinforces the immanent sense of diversity that is a constitutive part of the knowledge system of the people of Lunbei. I will introduce in later chapters how the inhabitants of Lunbei acknowledge that the people of Shuiwei act in a different way. These different actions are often linked to the fact that Shuiwei's inhabitants are subject to different taboos from those that govern and affect the lives of the most part of Taiwanese people.

These differences are linked to the interpretation of the history of the encounter between the Catholic church and the Chinese world. Specifically, the method of evangelization chosen by the missionaries who worked in Taiwan during the nineteenth century and in the first half of the twentieth influenced the interpretation that Taiwanese people practiced the Catholic religion. Christianity was regarded—and narrated—as something ontologically different. This sense of difference has been strengthened over the years, and it is the first parameter used by most Taiwanese people when they come into contact with Christianity. The differences are, in other words, immanent.

Because of this, within the narrations by the non-Christian people of Lunbei, Shuiwei very often becomes a place where "other" people live and where "other" things happen. People and things that are considered as "other" because they challenge the system of meaning through which the non-Christian people of Lunbei commonly construct and interpret the reality they meet every day. Since people share their experiences of Shuiwei, stories arise from this place through the above-mentioned contrast. At the same time, this place—its agency—is built up by these narrations.

I would like to define this particular place as locus, as a symbolic cluster constructed by the creation and the sharing of stories as well as the intentional actions of thinking agents. Mister Zhong and Mister Yang were not only telling something about Shuiwei. By narrating it, they were building Shuiwei as locus, as well as Fengrong, who—being a resident of Shuiwei village—was (and still is) one of the main protagonists of the many stories about Shuiwei village circulating in Lunbei.

Locus is certainly related to the definition of place given by many scholars that I will introduce in detail in the next pages, but above all a locus is made by the encounter—and very often by the contrast—with the "other." Meeting/contrasting with the other that does not seem to have received an analytical centrality in previous anthropological studies on space and place.

People who live outside Shuiwei acknowledge that this place is "different." Mister Zhong and Mister Yang know very well that Shuiwei is a particular place and that people who live there are not subjected to the many taboos and prescriptions that somehow model the behavior of their life. It seems to me that it is the awareness of these differences and above all their narrations that contribute to creating a special agency linked with this particular place.

Considering place as a locus will help to consider people who live outside a specific place, and especially their narrations, as active agents in the construction of a place. Traditionally a locus could be considered as the place where something is situated or occurs, as well as a center of activity, attention, or concentration. Giving some examples, we can say that in democracy the locus of power is in the people or that a certain area became a locus of resistance to the government (Merriam-Webster.com 2017, Locus).

Locus, thus, could be considered as a space, which can be a physical space, like a street, a house, a square, a room, as well as a symbolic space such as the above-mentioned locus of power, or the web, and so on. In my view this formal division between physical and symbolic spaces is in some ways misleading because as such made by man, also a physical space could be considered ultimately as a symbolic space. With the notion of locus, however, I would like to bring the discussion about place a little further.

2.3.1 Space and Place

In many of the works about anthropology of space and place and in many definitions and analysis, space and place are conceptually, phenomenologically, and analytically linked. If space is "having an address," place is "living in that address" (Agnew 2005, p. 82). It is the fact that places are spaces that are inhabited, which gives them a special history and meaning. These meanings are linked with all sensorial experiences that attach to them a peculiar identity (Tuan 1979). Place is thus a "practiced space" (Merrifield 1993, p. 524), and these two entities cannot be conceived as separate from each other. They are dialectically interrelated, for the one is conceived in relation to the other (cf. Lefebvre and Nicholson-Smith 1991; Merrifield 1993).

Space and place contribute to developing our concept of identity and our sense of positioning. The construction of spaces through different representational devices can serve as powerful forms of social categorization, which position localities and people in cultural codes and narratives (Le Grand 2010, p. 9). Many authors stressed how, in our contemporary world, the concept of space stems from the emergence of modernity (Giddens 2013), and it is connected to the rational control and regulation of people and locality through planning (cf. De Certeau 1984) or the capitalist market (cf. Harvey 1989; Lefebvre and Nicholson-Smith 1991). Thus, according to these authors, spaces are generally constructed by powerful actors with ample access to economic, cultural, and social resources (Le Grand 2010, p. 9). I consider this point of view highly suggestive, but as I will try to demonstrate through the narration of stories and through a different analytical approach, this is a limited and limiting point of view.

If it is true that "spaces receive their essential being from particular localities and not from 'space' itself" (Heidegger 1971, p. 154), it follows that the interest of the researcher should be directed in how people form meaningful relationships with the locales they occupy, how they occupy, how they attach meaning to space, and how they transform "space" into "place." In other words, the focus will be in understanding how experience is embedded in place and how space holds memories that implicate people and events (Low and Lawrence-Zúñiga 2003, p. 25). I will argue that if it is certainly true that places are attached with specific and particular meanings and memories, this is true not only for the people who inhabit these places but also for outsiders. The specificity of my fieldwork place allows me to affirm that in the specific Taiwanese context, the special agency linked with Shuiwei village is concretely felt also—and, in some ways, especially felt—by the people who are not directly linked—economically, religiously, socially—with that village.

2.3.2 Space and Place in the Anthropological Discussion: A Literature Review

Within the discourse of the social sciences, space occupies a very important position, especially since Durkheim's definition of it as one of the Aristotelian categories of understanding (together with the ideas of time, class, number, cause, substance, personality, etc.) (Durkheim 1915, p. 9). Recently many anthropologists started to consider space not as a mere container for social and cultural activity but in fact as something produced by such activities (Lefebvre and Nicholson-Smith 1991). According to Setha M. Low and Denise Lawrence-Zúñiga, the increasing interest in space and place "is not accidental; it is necessary for understanding the world we are producing" (2003, p. 2). This new methodological approach leads many anthropologists to rethink and reconceptualize their understanding of culture in spatialized ways. Therefore the researches should pay attention not only "to the material and spatial aspects of culture, but in the acknowledgment that space is an essential component of sociocultural theory" (Low and Lawrence-Zúñiga 2003, p. 1).

The same position is shared also by other anthropologists such as Marc Augé (1995) with his study on non-places. In Augé's analysis, "place" or rather "anthropological place" is socially and culturally organized around relations, perceptions, and images defining the nature of the group inhabiting it. Augé points out that the world of supermodernity does not correspond precisely to the world in which we think we live; we actually live in a world that we have not yet learned to observe. "We have to re-learn to think space" (Augé 1995, p. 35–36).

If it is true that this interest is linked with the fact that space is everywhere (Geertz 1996), it is also true that a certain kind of "sense of place" (Feld and Basso 1996) is always "influenced by knowledge, by knowing such basic facts as whether the place is natural or man-made and whether it is relatively large or small" (Tuan 1977, p. 32). Place is, in other words, a physical dimension directly linked with human body and senses. As Edward S. Casey pointed out, "it is by body that places become cultural in character" (Casey 1996, p. 34), "body is 'lived body' and space is humanly constructed space" (Tuan 1977, p. 35). Therefore, it follows that knowledge of a place comes from the experience that we have of it. The sense of place comes from the interrelations that our bodies establish with the space that surrounds us. But not only, there is always a symbolic mediation that lets humans feel that the "experience [of a place] can be direct and intimate, or it can indirect and conceptual, mediated by symbols. We know our home intimately; we can only know about our country if it is very large" (Tuan 1977, p. 6).

According to Chen, Orum, and Paulsen, who are talking about cities, places "are distinct and meaningful sites in which people live out their lives. These meanings derive from the histories of places, whether the formal history found in books or the informal history that is created by individuals as they go about their daily routines. In turn, these histories reflect the use to which these places are put. (...) Histories, uses, and experiences imbue places with memories and meanings that distinguish one place from another. Places are thus inherently social creations" (Chen et al. 2018, p. 7).

It is because places are "complex constructions of social histories, personal and interpersonal experiences, and selective memories" (Kahn 1996, p. 167) that they receive such attention from the community of the social scientists. Among their works, apart from some impressive treatises and essay collections about space and place (Low and Lawrence-Zúñiga 2003), the senses of place (Feld and Basso 1996), landscape (Hirsch and O'Hanlon 1995), memory, and history (Stewart and Strathern 2003), as well as conflicts, migrations, and exile (Bender et al. 2001), the anthropological research analyzed aspects linked to space and place, such as home (Munro et al. 1999), the sense of belonging (Cohen 1982), and even one of the foundations of the anthropological thought: the field (Coleman and Collins 2006).

In the Taiwanese context, a very interesting work is the one of Dell'Orto (2003), who wrote about the Taiwanese deity 土地公 *Tǔdì gōng*, the God of Earth, a protective deity linked with the local territory, a god whose deification and functions are usually determined by local residents. One of the most "localized" characteristics of Tudigong is the limitation of his jurisdiction to a single place, a bridge, a street, a temple, a public building, a private home, or a field. In his work Dell'Orto tried to delineate the intricate relationships between place, identity, memory, and the contribution that the anthropologist put in building these elements with his presence during the fieldwork. According to him, the stories linked to the Tudigong temples and their narrations help people to preserve and even increase their sense of belonging to a specific place and therefore their identity. Inside this process, the anthropologist—stimulating the circulation of these narrations by his questions or even through his presence—stands on an important and dialogical position.

Interesting is the concept of "multilocation"—images and statues of Tudigong could be found in homes, shops, tombs, restaurants, rural villages, urban neighborhoods, field, and so on—which Dell'Orto links with the concept of "multilocution"—each place he guards has its stories to tell—which according to him are in some ways linked with the various range of functions and connotations that are attributed to this deity by people's interpretations of his cult and by textual sources. According to Dell'Orto, the multilocation, multilocution, and the various roles that people ascribe to Tudigong:

> To a certain degree, [they] reflect the ambiguity of defining, in a theoretical manner, key terms such as place, locale, territory, locality, location, senses of place, community and identity, and the problems of sorting the complexity of the interrelationships among these key words. (…) On the other hand, they also replicate the differential, multiple and somewhat contrasting senses of place, community and identity that people experience and imagine in the practice of everyday life. (Dell'Orto 2003, p. 2)

Among the Taiwanese researches linked with the concepts of space and place, we should consider Boretz (2011) and his work on rituals and the links between martial arts and the Taiwanese underworld. The focus of his studies are people described as 江胡 *Jiānghú*, "rivers and lakes," a term that Boretz uses to refer to "the marginal world of drifters, outlaws, con artists, thieves, bodyguards, loan sharks and debt collectors" (Boretz 2011, p. 16). They form "a diverse class of people who live by their wits, skill, and, sometimes, brutality," in "a world that can exist only beyond the stability and security of village and family and conventional occupations" (Boretz 2011, p. 33). Boretz links the identification of these people to the concept of masculinity, to the martial arts, and to the Popular Religion rituals. The people identify themselves with some localized rituals (e.g. the "Blasting of Lord Handan," a yearly ritual that has been carried out in Taitung since the 1950s), where the performance of the ritual becomes a space of creative agency, in which agents are able to materialize their "fantasies of supernatural powers, of knight-errant heroics, as well as cruel violence" (Boretz 2011, p. 16).

2.3.3 Locus and Alterity

As I mentioned above, central to the definition of locus is the concept of alterity, which is considered as the quality or state of being radically alien to the conscious self or a particular cultural orientation. The peculiarity of the place where I did my fieldwork is given by the presence of different religions concentrated in a small village. Presbyterians, Catholics, and those practicing the Taiwanese Popular Religion share the same living place, the same living time, and basically the same economic situation. It is especially in the field of everyday religious practices that alterity comes out and gains strength. But since, as we will see in the next chapters, the religious elements shape many aspects of most Taiwanese people's daily life, alterity is experienced in many fields of the everyday practices. The localized presence of many Christians in this small village, and the sense of alterity that those who converted to Christianity brought with them, is thus involved in the construction of the concept of locus. As I mentioned above, it is from this sense of alterity that stories come out and help to build a locus. On this subject, Lozada (2001) pointed out the importance of the places where the evangelization process has been carried out:

> The missionaries who arrived in China to import a foreign cosmology and ritual system spent enormous time and money constructing buildings. Once a space becomes a place, it is animated by the experiences of the people who use it; like commodities, places develop a social life through both mundane and spectacular social exchanges. Buildings like the churches built by the French and American Catholic missionaries accrete stories grounded in local experiences and meaning. (Lozada 2001, p. 86)

And again:

> The stories are kept alive because they tell the people of Little Rome [the place where Lozada carried out his fieldwork] who they are – not primarily in relation to the state, but in relation to each other. It is their shared memory, especially of the Catholic faith held by their ancestors and themselves, that makes a community like Little Rome a coherent social unit. (2001, p. 87)

This helps us to see how the encounter between Chinese people and Catholic faith transformed this space in a place animated by the presence, the memories, and the stories of people who use it. It is through this kind of place that cultures, throughout people and their narrations, can meet each other. This is basically what the anthropological research about space and place tells us. Basing myself on these assumptions, I would like to take a further step, saying that this local context, made alive by the interaction of the people who inhabit it, affects and is created also by the narrations made by people who live outside it.

The choice to consider the narration of people who live outside a specific place as one of the most important place-makers, and considering also the theoretical issues linked to it, was the consequence of the situation I found in Shuiwei village. Through the reading of its history, Shuiwei village appeared as a triangular body, composed of missionaries, the local Christian community, and the people who did not accept the new faith. I took this idea from St. Augustine and his discussion on linguistic signs.[2]

According to him, a dialogue cannot only be a question between two persons. Therefore he inserts a third element into the circuit of dialogue. If the third element or person cannot understand what the two previous persons are talking about, we cannot consider it as a dialogue. The third vertex of the linguistic triangle is necessary for the construction of a dialogue. It is this triangular composition which created a game that was—and still is—played by these three players in a continuous and endless symbolic negotiation or, in other words, in a continuous and changing dialogue (Lazzarotti 2010, p. 28).

The decision to consider the context as a triangle is the consequence of what I have experienced during my fieldwork. These three appearances exist and concretely let the others feel their influence. The context where the missionaries worked, and where the current parish priest is living, is the same context where some of the people of Shuiwei converted to Christianity and where they are still practicing their Christian faith. This context is undoubtedly also formed by the people who did not convert and perhaps opposed themselves to the missionaries work. As we will

---

[2] "De Doctrina Christiana Libri Quatuor" and "De Magistro Liber Unus." Fully available on: <http://www.sant-agostino.it/latino/index.htm>; Simone (1992), see especially the Chapter "Semiologia Agostiniana" 63–92.

see, the presence of non-Christian people deeply influences the practical performance of certain rituals (Ethos, Sect. 6.3.1).

To consider this particular context in this way brought me toward a particular methodological approach, which helped me to construct the concept of locus. First of all, I needed to define my (the anthropologist) other (object of research). During my fieldwork, I soon realized that my goal was not to understand how the missionaries (subject) acculturate themselves to the Taiwanese culture (object) nor how the converted Taiwanese people (self) receive the Catholics' message (other). Nor how to relate myself in the context created by them. The choice to see this situation within a triangular context helped me to consider the whole context—the triangle, the dialogical encounter, and cohabitation in the field of Shuiwei village of these different entities—as the object of my research.

Methodologically I found the framework created by Standaert (2011) very useful to define the concept of locus. As Standaert points out:

> Missionaries [arriving in China] created a space of interaction that led to the reframing of that space wherein traditional actions and ideas are reconceived. Therefore focus is neither on the transmitter (*agent*) nor on the receiver (*structure*), but on what is "in between." (Standaert 2011, p. 214. My Italics)

The methodological shift consists in the search not for others but for the space of interaction. Of course this space can be physical, like a church; it can be a moving space, such as a funeral procession. But this space is often mediated by symbols: language, texts, images, songs, rituals (Standaert 2011, p. 214–215).

Therefore, we can define locus as a *space of interaction*, where the different entities which take part in its construction (place, alterity, identity, etc.) could be considered and analyzed.

The first step in the analysis of a locus should be done in order to understand how a place could be defined. And more concretely, in our case, we have to find the elements which will help us to define a village: which are the elements that form the boundaries—real or symbolic—which delineate and define a village?

2.4   Defining Locus: Operative Mode

Among the social sciences discourse, identity, narration, and history are the major contributors to the definition of a place. I already explained how these concepts, linked with the concept of alterity, created that space for interaction which I called locus.

The main goal, at this point, will be to reduce the complexity of the relationships between these concepts, and their different symbolic levels, to a more simple modus operandi which will allow us to analyze the relations which link, and make interdependent, locus and narration. This approach should take into consideration the importance of man in building the concept of place, as pointed out by Casey (1996) and Tuan (1977); the symbolic peculiarity of human beings, as pointed out by Geertz (1973); and the importance that the symbolic construction of identity has inside this process, as pointed out by anthropologists mentioned in the previous paragraphs.

In order to overpass this problem, it seems to me indispensable to make a further step to reduce this complexity to a more simple and analyzable model.

We already said, talking about Bruner and Eco, that the first thing we do when we reorganize the narrative material (existential or fictional), in order to create the world which surrounds us, is to select to create an order. But, one might ask, an order of what? I think that we can answer this question in this way: an order of existents.

According to Seymour Chatman (1990), these existents, within the narratology area,[3] are the characters and environments of a story. Therefore, we can try to give a first definition: a narrative world is an order of existents, a set of characters and environments related in order to create a coherent unity, a complex body with a recognizable structure but at the same time capable of evolving.

In other words, we have to make clear what are the tools, within the infinity of all possible representations, which allow us to reconstruct (even unconsciously) which order of existence is more useful, more plausible, and more believable.

I found the method offered by the Italian anthropologist Carlo Tullio Altan (1995a) very useful in order to carry out this task. In his work, Altan considers ethnicity—or, in his words, *ethnos*—not as a merely "physical" identity, but as a "symbolic complex lived by different people, as a constitutive element of their identity, and as a principle of social aggregation"

---

[3] Please refer to Todorov (1969).

(Altan 1995a, p. 21). According to him, considering ethnos in this way, "the key elements that characterize it will be easily recognized."

For this purpose, he selects five elements, or maybe it would be better to say dimensions, that according to him interact in order to form the ethnos of a people. These five elements, *topos*, *epos*, *genos*, *ethos*, and *logos*, are delineated by Altan in order to analyze the formations of a specific kind of nationalism. More specifically, Altan designed these elements in order to understand how the process for the creation of a national identity failed in the Italian case. Altan, in fact, considers Italy an incomplete democracy, a country without a civil religion (Altan 1995b).

I am not interested, at least not in this work, in understanding how nationalism is or is not created. My purpose is to expand the framework offered by Altan into a more general framework of ordering the world. Therefore, I will use these five elements in order to analyze the narrative world made by the Circuit of Narration I previously introduced. Furthermore, I will use them in order to demonstrate how locus is created inside this Circuit.

These five elements may be thought of as a sieve through which we continuously sift the reality in order to make one of the more important "alchemical" transformations for our survival: the reduction of the magmatic chaos in which we are immersed into the image of a world endowed with sense and stability. I would consider the generative elements proposed by Altan as factors by which the world takes on identity and coherence. Reality—or, better yet, the interpretation we make of it—framed by these elements, becomes the background of a believable story and, at the same time, the basic elements for the construction of a *verisimilar* world.[4]

2.4.1 Five Elements

According to Altan, the five elements are the structure of the ideal type to which he constantly refers to perform the historical analysis of ethnic identities. These ethnic identities are always subject to historical and geographical changes. But the changes will touch the single elements, not the whole structure of the ideal type.

---

[4] I borrow the word *verisimilar* (*verosimile* in its original Italian) from Vico, which means "that seems to be the truth, that may have happened the way it's been reported."

What will change in these two dimensions of time and space, is not the structure of the whole model ethnos, but the contents of the individual components, in relation to the changing of the historical equilibrium of which ethnos is one of the most significant cultural factors, but not the only one. (Altan 1995a, p. 21)

As I pointed out before, these five points proposed by Altan should be considered as a sieve, through which the stories are created and through which are sifted and inserted in a symbolic system, in a shared horizon of things held in common. At the same time, these basic elements are the ways through which a people maintains its own identity and how it narrates it. It follows that the way a people narrates itself and its world is the way how it identifies itself. At the same time, the way people narrate about a place is the way locus is created. In other words, the five elements are both analytical, because they help the researcher, and descriptive, because they are universally used by people.

These elements help us to establish a modus operandi and at the same time will help us to understand how the narrated stories are sifted and incorporated into a precise symbolic universe or, in Geertz's words, a system. This symbolic system is neither close nor limited, because it is always put in confrontation/contrast with other narrations belonging to people who don't belong to the same community. It is through the sharing of narrations about concrete experiences and abstract thought that the people of Shuiwei keep and reinforce, but at the same time adapt and change their own identity and consequentially the identity of the locus they inhabit. At the same time, this process also works in the opposite way: the sharing of stories about Shuiwei and the Christian community—which it is historically and socially linked with this village—let the people of Lunbei recognize, along with the differences, their own cultural categories. By confronting different taboos and different traditions, the people of Lunbei better understand their own taboos and their own traditions.

The importance of alterity and the relation with others in the construction of the identity of ethnic groups is an important point among the anthropological literature on identity, especially in regard to minorities. Most of the literature (starting with Barth (1969)) argues that it is the relations with others which form and shape identity. While I described alterity as the fundamental and characterizing point of locus, it seems that this point is not covered by Altan's framework. Altan seems to suggest that the people whose identity is constructed have sovereignty in that construction. I think that this is a limiting point in Altan's model for the construction of ethnos, especially because it lacks all the contributions that the concept of alterity could offer to the analysis of this topic.

Anyway, my main goal is not to understand how a group identity is created and maintained, but to understand how identity, alterity, place, and narration cooperate in order to form locus. In order to achieve this task, I consider the framework proposed by Altan as very useful, on condition that alterity becomes one of the main analytical perspectives. In fact, from an analytical point of view, the choice of these elements will help me analyze the historical processes which are underlined in the social and cultural structure of Shuiwei village and its surrounding areas. Therefore, I will be able to underline what these elements mean, how they are created and considered by Shuiwei inhabitants, and the different meanings that these elements—because they are involved in different historical processes—have for the people who live outside the village. I found this extremely important, especially if we refer to the assumption I made at the beginning of this chapter that "every story comes from conflict, without conflict there are no events, and therefore no story" (Pinardi and De Angelis 2008).

References

Agnew, J. 2005. Space: Place. In *Spaces of Geographical Thought: Deconstructing Human Geography's Binaries*, ed. P. Cloke and R. Johnston, 81–95. London: Sage.

Altan, C. T. 1995a. *Ethnos e Civiltà. Identità Etniche e Valori Democratici*. Milano: Feltrinelli.

———. 1995b. *Italia: Una Nazione Senza Religione Civile: Le Ragioni Di Una Democrazia Incompiuta*. Udine: Istituto Editoriale Veneto Friulano.

Augé, M. 1995. *Introduction to an Anthropology of Supermodernity*. London: Verso Books.

Barth, F. 1969. *Ethnic Groups and Boundaries: The Social Organization of Culture Difference*. Bergen–Oslo: Universitets Forlaget.

Bender, B., M. Winer, and S. A. Cape Town World Archaeological Congress 1999. 2001. *Contested Landscapes: Movement, Exile and Place*. Oxford: Berg.

Boretz, A. 2011. *Gods, Ghosts, and Gangsters: Ritual Violence, Martial Arts, and Masculinity on the Margins of Chinese Society*. Honolulu: University of Hawai'i Press.

Bruner, J. S. 1990. *Acts of Meaning*, vol. 3. Cambridge: Harvard University Press.

———. 1991. The Narrative Construction of Reality. *Critical Inquiry* 18 (1): 1–21.

Burns, R. 1999. *A Theory of the Trial*. Princeton: Princeton University Press.

Casey, E. S. 1996. How to Get from Space to Place in a Fairly Short Stretch of Time: Phenomenological Prolegomena. In *Senses of Place*, ed. S. Feld and K. Basso, 14–51. Santa Fe: School of American Research Press.

Chatman, S. B. 1990. *Coming to Terms: The Rhetoric of Narrative in Fiction and Film*. Ithaca: Cornell University Press.

Chen, X., A. M. Orum, and K. E. Paulsen. 2018. *Introduction to Cities: How Place and Space Shape Human Experience*. Chichester: Wiley.

Cohen, A. P. 1982. *Belonging: Identity and Social Organisation in British Rural Cultures*, vol. 11. Manchester: Manchester University Press.

Coleman, S., and P. Collins. 2006. *Locating the Field: Space, Place and Context in Anthropology*. Oxford: Berg.

De Certeau, M. 1984. *The Practice of Everyday Life*. Berkeley: University of California Press.

Dell'Orto, A. 2003. *Place and Spirit in Taiwan: Tudi Gong in the Stories, Strategies and Memories of Everyday Life*. London: Routledge.

Durkheim, E. 1915. *The Elementary Forms of the Religious Life*. London: George Allan and Unwin.

Eco, U. 1980. Two Problems in Textual Interpretation. *Poetics Today* 2 (1a): 145–161.

———. 1984. *The Role of the Reader: Explorations in the Semiotics of Texts*, vol. 318. Bloomington: Indiana University Press.

———. 1994. *The Limits of Interpretation*. Bloomington: Indiana University Press.

———. 1997. *Kant e l'Ornitorinco*. Milano: Bompiani.

Feld, S., and K. Basso. 1996. *Senses of Place*. Santa Fe: School of American Research Press.

Geertz, C. 1973. *Interpretation of Cultures*. New York: Basic Books.

———. 1996. Afterword. In *Senses of Place*, ed. S. Feld and K. Basso, 259–262. Santa Fe: School of American Research Press.

Gell, A. 1998. *Art and Agency: An Anthropological Theory*. Oxford: Clarendon Press.

Giddens, A. 2013. *The Consequences of Modernity*. London: Wiley.

Harvey, D. 1989. *The Condition of Postmodernity: An Enquiry into the Origins of Cultural Change*. Oxford: Blackwell.

Heidegger, M. 1971. *Poetry. Language, Thought*. New York: Harper and Row.

Hirsch, E., and M. O'Hanlon. 1995. *The Anthropology of Landscape: Perspectives on Place and Space*. Oxford: Clarendon Press.

Kahn, M. 1996. Your Place and Mine: Sharing Emotional Landscapes in Wamira, Papua New Guinea. In *Senses of Place*, 167–196. Santa Fe: School of American Research Press.

Katz, P. R. 2003. Religion and the State in Post-War Taiwan. *The China Quarterly* 154 (S.): 395–412.

Lazzarotti, M. 2010. The Internal Structure of Dialogue. Two Taiwanese Case Studies. *Fu Jen International Religious Studies* 4 (1): 19–36.
Le Grand, E. 2010. *Class, Place and Identity in a Satellite Town*. Ph. D. thesis, Acta Universitatis Stockholmiensis.
Lefebvre, H., and D. Nicholson-Smith. 1991. *The Production of Space*, vol. 142. Oxford: Blackwell.
Low, S. M., and D. Lawrence-Zúñiga. 2003. *The Anthropology of Space and Place: Locating Culture*, vol. 4. Oxford: Blackwell Pub.
Lozada, E. P. 2001. *God Aboveground: Catholic Church, Postsocialist State, and Transnational Processes in a Chinese Village*. Stanford: Stanford University Press.
Mattingly, C., N. C. Lutkehaus, and C. J. Throop. 2008. Bruner's Search for Meaning: A Conversation between Psychology and Anthropology. *Ethos* 36 (1), 1–28.
Melucci, A. 2000. Costruzione di Sé, Narrazione, Riconoscimento. In *Identitá, Riconoscimento, Scambio*, ed. M. Greco and D. Della Porta, 30–44. Bari, Roma: Laterza.
Merriam-Webster.com, T. 2017. Locus. https://www.merriam-webster.com/dictionary/locus. Accessed March 9, 2017.
Merrifield, A. 1993. Place and Space: A Lefebvrian Reconciliation. *Transactions of the Institute of British Geographers* 18 (4): 516–531.
Munro, M., R. Madigan, and I. Cieraad. 1999. *At Home: An Anthropology of Domestic Space*. Syracuse: Syracuse University Press.
Pinardi, D., and P. De Angelis. 2008. *Il Mondo Narrativo: Come Costruire e come Presentare L'Ambiente e i Personaggi di una Storia*. Torino: Lindau.
Rideout, C. J. 2013. A Twice-told Tale: Plausibility and Narrative Coherence in Judicial Storytelling. *Legal Communication & Rhetoric: JAWLD* 10: 67.
Simone, R. 1992. *Il Sogno di Saussure: Otto Studi di Storia delle Idee Linguistiche*. Bari, Roma: Laterza.
Standaert, N. 2011. *The Interweaving of Rituals: Funerals in the Cultural Exchange between China and Europe*. Seattle: University of Washington Press.
Stewart, J., and A. Strathern. 2003. *Landscape, Memory and History Anthropological Perspectives*. London: Pluto Press. Citeseer.
Todorov, T. 1969. *Grammaire du " Décaméron": par Tzvetan Todorov*, vol. 3. The Hague: Mouton.
Tuan, Y.-F. 1977. *Space and Place: The Perspective of Experience*. Minneapolis: University of Minnesota Press.
———. 1979. Space and Place: Humanistic Perspective. In *Philosophy in Geography*, ed. S. Gale and G. Olsson, 387–427. Berlin: Springer.
Violi, P. 1997. *Significato ed Esperienza*. Milano: Bompiani.

CHAPTER 3

Topos

3.1 Narrating Topoi

It is common in Taiwan to associate the presence of a church or a temple with some particular place. Sometimes people hears "sounds" or "voices" coming from an abandoned land or house. It is a very polite way to say that a place is haunted by ghosts. Because of these presences, the land cannot be sold and cannot be built upon. Usually the solution is to ask for the intervention of a Daoist priest or a shaman, who through the help of some deities will solve the problem. One of the most radical ways to eliminate the problem is to build a temple on that land. This drastic solution reflects the hierarchical and power relationships between ghosts and deities in the Chinese pantheon (Feuchtwang 1974, 2003).

Another, quite radical, way to solve this problem is to sell the land to some Christians, principally because, as many in Taiwan told me, they don't believe in this kind of taboo. A good friend of mine, a Catholic believer, told me that when he bought his house, some of the neighbors came to him to tell him that the *fēngshuǐ* of that house was not good. This is another polite way to say that there is something, some strange presence, living or visiting that house. My friend told me that as soon as they saw the big cross he had hung on the wall, they said: "Oh, you believe in Jesus, therefore no problems for you." Near Shuiwei village, there are at least one

© The Author(s) 2020
M. Lazzarotti, *Place, Alterity, and Narration in a Taiwanese Catholic Village*, Asian Christianity in the Diaspora,
https://doi.org/10.1007/978-3-030-43461-8_3

church and one hospital which have been built on this kind of land. The church is located in the nearby township of 虎尾Huwei, in a land nobody wanted, because voices were always coming out from there. The Catholic missionaries bought it for a very cheap price in 1955. Till now, both the Catholic community and the surrounding neighbors are convinced to have done a good deal. A little bit away from Shuiwei is the Catholic Hospital of Saint Martin, located in the city of 嘉義 Chiayi. The hospital was built on the land that was used by Kuomintang soldiers to execute Taiwanese people after the 2/28 massacre.[1] Nobody wanted that land, except from the missionaries who built on it a hospital and a convent.

In the village of Shuiwei, there is a church which had been built in 1968. The Catholic community started to use it on Christmas of that year. Before this church, a smaller church made of wood (and, even before, a smaller one made of canes) was present on the same compound. I started to inquire about this church because I was thinking that a sort of "ghost story" may have been linked with its presence. After some round of questions (and, as it is usual in the Taiwanese countryside, after some round of dinners), I figured out that the presence of a church was linked to another reason. As I have observed also in other Catholic villages, the presence of a church is somehow related to the fact that one of the sons of the family who owns the land became a priest. As I will explain in detail in Genos, in Taiwan the land is divided between the male line of the family. Even today when the Taiwanese law allows daughters to take part in the land division, many families ask their daughters to sign a document attesting their renunciation of the land in favor of their brothers. In many Catholic communities present in Taiwanese countryside, a church has been built on the land traditionally assigned to the son who became priest, even if he was not able to guarantee the continuity of the family surname.

One evening we were sitting in the garden of A-Liang's house, a two-floor and well-maintained villa. Just a few days before, my master's thesis adviser came to see how my fieldwork was proceeding. I took the

---

[1] The 2/28 symbolizes the February 28, 1947 massacre of an undefined number of Taiwanese people by the soldiers of the Republic of China who came with Chiang Kai-shek.

opportunity to introduce him to the Catholic villagers of Shuiwei. Talking about his visit, A-Liang told me:

"Maybe you did not understand because he was speaking in Taiwanese, but your professor asked me who had helped me to make the *fēngshuǐ* calculation when I built this house.[2] "

"And what did you say?"

"That I have done it by myself!"

Knowing how important the concept of *fēngshuǐ* was for the Taiwanese people, I asked again:

"Did you really calculate the *fēngshuǐ* by yourself?"

"I don't even know how to do it! I just made sure that the final result of the house was harmonious, and this was enough for me. You know, we don't believe these traditions."

"You know?" said A-Liang's wife, who came from a non-Christian family, "When my relatives ask me about it and I answer that my husband took care of *fēngshuǐ* by himself, everybody start to laugh. For them it is strange that we built the house without the help of a *fēngshuǐ* master. But we don't believe in these things, so my husband decided in this way. Actually, after we built this house, other people come to ask my husband tips on how to build their home."

My own field notes. Spring 2011

3.2 Topos

Topos, from Greek "place," is the territory. It refers to the external environment, to the place, and it may indicate the different sites where the events are set. According to Altan (1995, 21):

> Topos is the symbolic image of the motherland. The image of the territory lived as value because it is perceived as the origin of the genealogy and of the products of the land. It is also a source of aesthetic and emotional suggestion (…). [Topos] is one of the values closest to natural phenomena in their effects on social life, and also one of the most striking as an inspiration of poetic imagery and political ideologies.

---

[2] The term used by Taiwanese people is 看 *Kàn*, 看風水 *Kàn fēngshuǐ* (to see). This expression is used when it is necessary to calculate the geomantic position of an object.

Topos is, thus, a symbolic image, the symbolic transfiguration of the place where a people live. This view of topos seems to me well linked with the recent developments of the anthropological research about space and place I already introduced in the previous chapters (Logos, Sect. 2.3.2). The works of many anthropologists and social geographers are pointed at exploring the connections that space and place interweave with concept such as identity, culture, and so on. According to Dell'Orto (2003), this new research development "has started to acknowledge the primary role of experience and senses as privileged topoi in the construction of anthropological knowledge, as well as in attempting to reduce the dichotomy between mind and body and subjectivity and objectivity" (Dell'Orto 2003, p. 136). The sense, the feeling of place is indeed one of the new and more interesting categories which tries to connect the person, through his body, with the physical and sensorial worlds in which man is living. If we bring these concepts to the context of Shuiwei village, it appears that very often it is through the recognition of sensorial differences that Shuiwei is felt and understood as a different place, not only by its inhabitants but also by the people who are living in the surrounding areas.

3.2.1 The Sense of Place

A traditional countryside household in Taiwan is a large U-shaped compound (Fig. 3.1), constructed as closely as possible to conform to an ideal of perfect symmetry. A home of this type is usually built in stages, the growth of the building reflecting the growth of the family.

The original structure is a long, rectangular building partitioned internally into three, five, or seven rooms. It is expanded by the addition of wings, first to the left side (believed to be the dragon side, it is the part where the elder son will inhabit) and then to the right (Wang 1974, p. 183).[3] This particular form is full of meanings linked with Chinese cosmology (patriliny, *fengshui*'s concepts of dragon and tiger) and Confucian elements (predominance of the elder son and, in general, of the elders on youth).

Many of the houses of Shuiwei present some important and highly visible changes. Perhaps the most important is represented by the change of

---

[3] According to the Chinese usage, the right and left parts are considered according to the perspective of a man standing with his back to the front of the house.

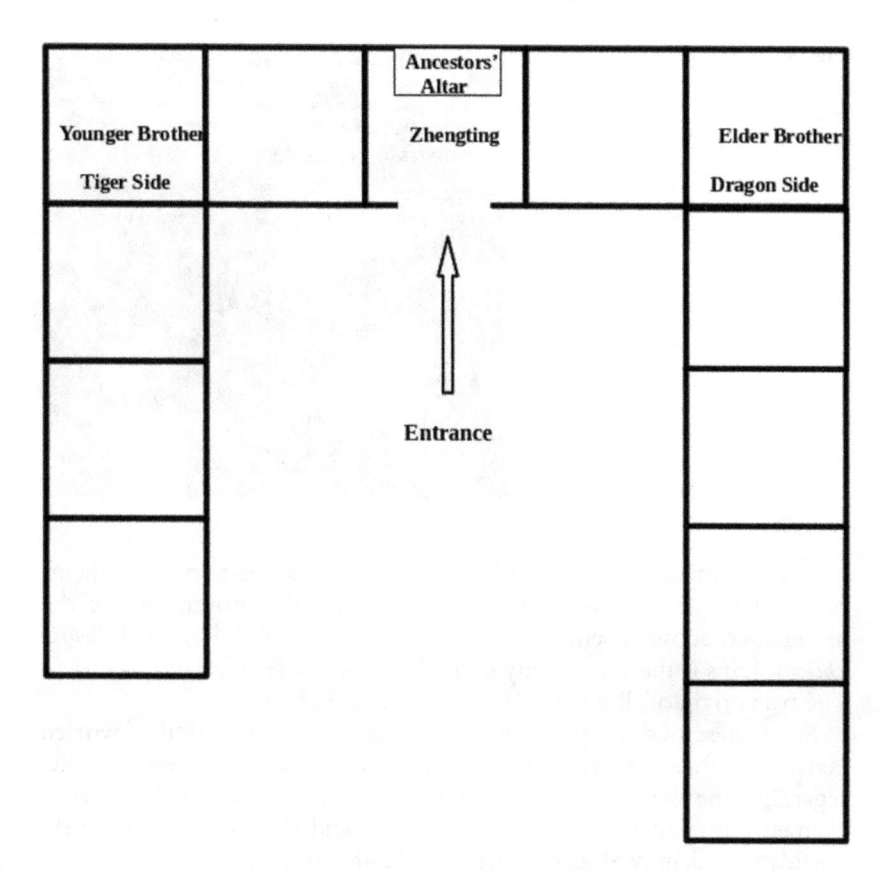

```
|Younger Brother|         | Ancestors' Altar |         | Elder Brother |
|  Tiger Side   |         |     Zhengting    |         |  Dragon Side  |
                                   ↑
                               Entrance
```

Fig. 3.1 Schematic representation of a traditional Taiwanese home

the inscription on the lintel of the main door of the home. Usually the lintel of the main door shows an inscription indicating the place of provenience of the inhabitants. Through the reading of the characters written in the lintel, an outsider could easily understand the surname of the people who inhabit that house. For example, a household belonging to people of the clan 李 Li will place these characters 龍西堂 *Lóngxī Táng* above their main gate. This shows that the people who live in the house are coming from Longxi, a place situated in north China (a county located under the 定西 Dingxi municipality in 甘肅 Gansu province) that is believed to be the ancestral homeland of the Li lineage.

Fig. 3.2 The characters in the lintel mean "Jesus is the Lord of my house"

The Christian inhabitants of Shuiwei village (at least some of them) removed the traditional inscription linked with the provenience of the lineage and adopted sentences such as "基督是我家之主 *Jīdū shì wǒjiā zhī zhǔ* Jesus is the Lord of my house" or "萬有真原 *Wàn yǒu zhēn yuán* The true origin of all things" (Figs. 3.2 and 3.3).[4]

Since these traditional inscriptions are considered as a kind of written genealogy, their change is full of meaning, especially, as we will see, regarding the concept of genos (see Genos, Sect. 5.5.2). These visual changes represent one of the most obvious and visible signals that help outsiders to identify Shuiwei village as a "different place."

Apart from the changes in the house, the sensorial differences between Shuiwei and the surrounding villages involve also visual, olfactory, and auditive sensations. In other villages of Lunbei, it is very common to find tables decked lavishly for the ghosts (at least twice a month), weddings or funerals celebrated in tents set up in the middle of the road, funeral ceremonies that seem to have no end, noisy and colorful ceremonies and

---

[4] This sentence comes from the very origin of Catholicism in China. It refers to the year 1775 in which the Beijing cathedral built by Jesuits was damaged by fire, and 乾隆帝 the Emperor Qianlong donated 10,000 teals of silver for the restoration work and also bestowed a board with calligraphy made from the Emperor's own hand, inscribed with the above-mentioned characters 萬有真原 on it, meaning "The true origin of all things."

Fig. 3.3 The true origin of all things

processions of deities who parade on their sedan chairs, and so on. During my stay in Taiwan, I had noticed many times how these activities, which look quite surprising to the visitors, are considered absolutely normal and common for Taiwanese people. In fact these activities are so common and frequent to be considered, without real risk of getting things wrong, a very important part of the common heritage of the people in Taiwan. This heritage includes all the "sensations" related to these activities: the noise, the smell of incense or smoke, the visual impressions of tables full of food, as well as the presence of little red stoves used to burn paper money, and so on. All the above-mentioned things and sensations could be grouped together under the everyday life events and, thus, symbols.

Paper money, for example, is one of the most common things that can be found on the roads of Taiwan. This money, called 金紙 *jīnzhǐ* or 陰司紙 *yīnsīzhǐ*, often translated as joss paper or ghost money, is nothing but sheets of yellow paper with a small rectangle in the center painted with a golden, silver, or bronze color (depending on the use and especially who will be the recipient of these offerings). This money, in fact, is offered to deities in the temples, to the dead, to the ghosts, and to other spirits more or less evil.[5] Anyone who walks the streets of Lunbei Township may notice the presence of these yellow sheets on the roadside. These are remainders of deity processions or funerals, where these moneys are used in a massive way. Even the smell of burnt paper that comes from the small red burners where this money is offered to gods or ghosts is a very common experience, especially on some specific days.[6]

Similarly, the sounds of Chinese clash cymbals (小鈸 *Xiǎobó*), of the Chinese trumpet (嗩吶 *Suǒnà*), and of the small-sized double-reeded pipe (管 *Guǎn*) are commonly heard at almost any time of the day. All these sensory experiences are somehow linked with the presence—although it would be more appropriate to say with the cohabitation—in the same territory of natural and supernatural entities. The spirits, as well as humans, live and give life to the place. Their presence is constantly indicated by these sensorial signs, which are able to link a place—and the people who inhabit it—with a specific cosmology or, in other words, with a specific conception of man and a specific way to position it in the universe. These sensorial signs, or better their absence, are the first—and very often striking— things that an outsider notices when he gets in contact with Shuiwei. Consequently these are the elements that contribute in a substantial way to create stories about this place.

Perhaps a short extract from my field note will help the reader to get more familiarity with these concepts:

> I was in the Township library with Chunlin, a Catholic believer who worked many years in the Township administration. We were talking with one of the librarians while my wife was looking for books. We came to talk about the fact that I was living in Shuiwei and that a new public park was opened in the village. The librarian told us, "I have been to visit that park. It is really beautiful and well maintained. I actually found Shuiwei clean and well maintained." After a short pause she added, "I think that this is linked with the fact that villagers share a different faith. Look here in Lunbei, even around our library. It is always dirty and everything seems a big mess. I think this is for sure linked with their faith."

---

[5] There is a vast literature on this subject. For more information, you may consult articles by Seaman (1982) or Gates (1987).

[6] Usually the 1st, 2nd, 15th, and 16th day of the lunar month, when food and money should be offered to the ghosts.

In the words of the librarian, it is possible to read how the absolute absence of the above-mentioned elements—little tables full of food, loud music and bursts of firecrackers, paper money and its smell—was a strong signal of opposition to the everyday reality which surrounds the people of Lunbei. It is this sense of difference, this way of perceiving the place as an entity somewhat stranger or different, which attaches a special agency to Shuiwei. This agency strongly contributes to create the stories that help to give life to Shuiwei as locus. As it has been previously discussed (locus, Sect. 2.3), locus is a space of interaction, and these above-mentioned sensations have an active part in its process of construction.

From this point of view, it is possible to detect this phenomenon in many of the stories I selected in the various chapters. The story told by Mr. Zhong (Locus, Sect. 2.1) about the passage of the Taiping Mazu in Shuiwei could help us to understand the concepts I introduced above. The people who were in charge of carrying the statue of Mazu encountered a place where all the sensorial experiences they were used in that particular context (a pilgrimage of Mazu) were absent. Their absence takes tangible meaning only in contrast with the narrative that creates the world for Taiwanese people. All these differences became key symbols in the narration Mr. Zhong created about Shuiwei village, contributing in this way to create the narrative about Shuiwei and, at the same time, to create Shuiwei as a place.

This happens because sensorial differences are interpreted and understood through narrative processes that consider the alterity of the other as immanent. The different sensorial experience is given by the interpretation of symbols—or in this specific case by the interpretation of their absence—which are difficult to insert (because they are new or they break with tradition) within the frames of meaning that help people to orient themselves in the world in which they live. If topos, as stated by Altan, is a "source of aesthetic and emotional suggestion," Shuiwei as topos is a source of aesthetic and emotional suggestion not only for the inhabitants of the village but also, in a more contrasting way, for the people who live outside it. Place is built also by the narrations made by the people who don't belong to it but contribute to its symbolic construction through the creation and the sharing of stories based on incomprehension and misunderstanding of the symbolic heritage embodied—and publicly exposed—in places.

The identification of Shuiwei as a place "other" to the standard places in Taiwan could be better understood if we consider this village within a wider context. This context will help us to consider Shuiwei as inserted within a specific conception of place. In fact, at least for most Taiwanese people, the concept of place is directly linked with a lot of taboos and with a myriad of cosmological concepts that concretely affect their lives. In the next pages, I will provide the reader with a context where she/he will be able to situate and interpret the stories about Shuiwei I narrated and also those I will narrate later in this work.

3.2.2 Creating a Context

Among the anthropological literature on Taiwan, the relationships between space and place, narration and religious concepts, have been discussed by many scholars such as 林瑋嬪 (2000, 2005), Lin (2009), and Allio (1998) or the already mentioned works of Dell'Orto (2003) and Boretz (2011). This topic has attracted the interest of many scholars who have been in China and have written about Chinese culture. Going back to the 1930s, the French sinologist Marcel Granet already stated that

> In China no philosophers have been interested in considering space as a simple extension coming from the juxtaposition of homogeneous elements [...]. While two portions of space, as well as two portions of time, could differ in radical ways, each period is connected to one specific region, each orient is linked to a season. To each part of time there is a corresponding, single, portion of the extension. A proper nature, indicated by a common set of attributes, belong to them. (Granet 1968, p. 55. My Translation)

The correspondence between spatial and temporal aspects was made explicit by the series of cosmological symbols by which the various doctrinal tendencies interpreted the world. The yin and yang, the 五行 *Wǔ xíng* (the five elements),[7] the 八卦 *Bāguà* (eight symbols), and other emblematic

---

[7] Sinologists cannot agree on the best translation of the word 行 *xíng*; the basic idea is one of "changing states of being." The elements themselves with their associated colors and directions are (1) East, green, wood, sour; (2) South, red, fire, bitter; (3) North, black, water, salty; (4) West, white, metal, hot; and (5) Center, yellow, earth, sweet. These five metamorphoses or states of being form a whole: in the "Hong fan" chapter of the "Book of Documents," we read: "water is said to soak and descend; fire is said to blaze and ascend; wood is said to curve or be straight; metal is said to obey and change; earth is said to take seeds and give crops" (tr. Karlgren). Dozens of parallel series are correlated with the five elements: for example, the four seasons of the year (here, "earth" is the odd man out, either receiving

groups, related to spatial and temporal properties, were used as a "model of the world."

This kind of "net of correspondences," which spread out during the period of Warring States to become orthodoxy with the birth of the empire, could give an interpretation of each natural and human phenomenon, which in China are concepts devoid of any epistemological barrier between "nature" and "culture." Every point in space, as well as every moment in time, was an expression of a qualitative reality that was possible to understand through the knowledge of analogical laws.

Perhaps this "theory of space" finds in *fēngshuǐ* (often translated as geomancy) its best explanation. This tradition is based on the assumption that there is a qualitative difference between different places. These differences are expressed by the 生氣 *Shēngqì* (translated as natural force, life force, energy flow, or even the word energy), a subtle energy present on the landscape. This energy is not fixed, but it focuses and disperses itself following the cycles associated with the system of space-temporal correspondences developed by the long Chinese tradition. The place where the 氣 *qì* coagulates is the site where the qualitative character of the space is at its height. This point is defined as the point where the equilibrium condition of yin and yang has been reached (Paolillo 2007, p. 440).

Within the Taiwanese context, these ideas have the power to concretely influence the construction of houses and public spaces such as roads, buildings, cemeteries, and so on. Usually the construction of a building or the choice of a proper land is an activity that requires the presence of a specialist, usually a 風水師 *fēngshuǐ shī* (master of *fēngshuǐ*). *Fēngshuǐ masters* are usually well respected, and their opinion is very often taken in high regard. I remember that one of the most renowned masters of *fēngshuǐ* in Taipei was able to convince the mayor to move one of the four doors of the train station in Taipei because, according to him, it was a cause of bad *fēngshuǐ* (朱詠薇 2005; CRNTT 2005).

---

no season specifically associated with it or, at most, a few days from each of the four seasons), animals (hairy, feathered, scaly, armored, naked), the five tastes (salty, bitter, sour, hot, sweet), and so on. As a whole, the system is bound up with Chinese astrology, geomancy, and also a branch of ancient Chinese astronomy, medicine. In ancient times, ceremonial garb varied according to the season of the year. Even the administration of justice was not unaffected by the doctrine of the five elements: thus we find that criminals could only be executed in autumn, the time of year when everything dies. All human actions had to be in harmony with nature (Eberhard 1986, p. 106).

What I would like to communicate to the reader is that these concepts, which lead to considering place as a living entity and in relation with a myriad of cosmological ties, are very much present in the life of many Taiwanese people and cut across social or politic hierarchies and classes.

Because of these beliefs, a place could be a spring of good luck or a cause of continued misfortune. The choice of the wrong place could bring people misfortunes, could let them become sick, could let a business lose lots of money, and so on. The choice of the right place for a grave, the right place where to put a tent that will be used as a parking lot, the right place in the apartment where to put the ancestors' shrine: all these activities are directly linked with the everyday life of the people who inhabit or have chosen a particular place. And this in the countryside as well as in Taipei, the capital city, the most modern and West-oriented city in Taiwan.

Because of these beliefs, people laugh when the wife of A-Liang tells them that her husband has decided by himself the orientation and the dimensions of their own house. The strangeness attributed to A-Liang's choice should be read in contrast to the narration on *fēngshuǐ* which I have summarized above. Apart from the concept of *fēngshuǐ*, space is shaped also by many other entities (which in Western tradition would be called "supernatural") that live among people and concretely give life to the concept of place.

Very often the conversion to Catholicism led to their elimination. Just to give another example, if a person stumbles and falls in front of a house, she/he must go to the temple to "get cleaned" off the spirits who inhabit that place and that might be clinging to her/him. If the house belongs to a Catholic or to a Christian, it is not necessary for the non-Christian person to go to the temple to be cleaned off these presences (Lazzarotti 2008, p. 114).

In Taiwan, place is always a living place, especially because it is inhabited or under the control of supernatural presences, such as ghosts, deities, or ancestors. In the stories by which I started this chapter, we can see how places, because of a particular event, could be inhabited by ghosts whose presence concretely will afflict and give identity to that specific place.

Following this vision of the world, it is easy to understand why there are places considered dangerous because of their position (Fig. 3.4) and, above all, why places are always considered as a living entity by the majority of Taiwanese people.

Not only ghosts inhabit and animate a place. Also, gods and ancestors have the power to concretely afflict a specific place. In Taiwan, ancestors

Road N. 1

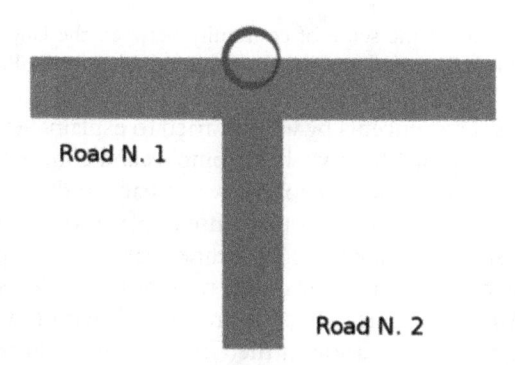

Road N. 2

Fig. 3.4 煞 *Shā*. This concept is commonly called *Shā*, and it is also linked with *fēngshuǐ* concepts. A road junction with T shape (路沖 *Lù chōng*) is considered a dangerous place because all the "dirty" (when people refer to dirty things, they usually refer to ghosts, bad spirits, and misfortunes) coming through the road N.2 will stop to the point marked with a circle. No one will build a house in this place that is usually left abandoned or where a temple could be built on it

are traditionally buried in their own land. It is traditionally believed that a person had to come back to his "ancestors' place" (故鄉 *Gùxiāng*) in order to die, or at least he has to be buried there.[8]

Very important scholars, at least in the field of Chinese religion, discussed and demonstrated—even if with different conclusions—how the choice of a good place for graves is linked with the concept of ancestors and how it will influence the lives of the descendants (Freedman 1967; Li 1976). As stated by Dell'Orto:

> The attachment that the Chinese have towards their place is felt in this life, but is also imagined and 'talked about' for the afterlife. I have often heard elderly people expressing an intense desire to be buried on the land of their place of origin. The land of their ancestors is a representation of stability and continuity and it is imagined as the right location for their own burial and location in the afterlife. Furthermore, the cult of the ancestors has played

---

[8] Regarding this last point, many people in Taiwan believe that their country has a so "unlucky" history and it cannot reach an independent status because the former dictator Chiang Kai-shek is buried in Taiwan and therefore unable to go back to his ancestors' place.

an important role in the sense of continuity between the land, family and community, thus creating a specific 'place-bound' identity. (2003, p. 161)

These are just few concepts by which I tried to explain—even if in a very elementary and incomplete way—how complex and concrete is the "sense of place" for many Taiwanese people. If we go back to the stories by which I started this chapter, I think that this sense of place will appear evident.

With these stories I wanted to underline that the concept of Shuiwei as a place, as a stage where these stories took place, could be understood only inside a wider discourse which is linked both with the presence and the experience of evangelization of the Catholic church in central Taiwan and with the cultural interpretation of it made possible by the Taiwanese Popular Religion cultural background.

3.3 Shuiwei as Locus: Historical, Geographical, and Social Context

In order to better understand its peculiarity, I would like to present Shuiwei village within the bigger context offered by both Lunbei Township and Yunlin County. The narration linked to these geographical entities is, in fact, strongly linked with the concepts of the Taiwanese Popular Religion. The aim of showing the context where Shuiwei is located will be to stress the peculiarity of this Christian village compared with the standard Taiwanese situation.

The contribution of the people who live outside the boundaries of a particular place, it is necessary in order to build a locus identity. The dialogic relationships between the people who inhabit the place—in our case the village of Shuiwei—and the people who live outside it, as the inhabitants of Lunbei, and especially the narrations which come from their exchanges, are perhaps the main constituents of the specificity of a place.

In order to give the most complete and clear description of this particular village, we have to put it inside its historical, geographical, and social context. Only in this way, it will be possible to deeply understand the peculiarity of Shuiwei as a place, especially highlighting the contrasts in order to create stories and consequently place identity.

3.3.1 Yunlin County

With its numerous and impressive temples, its purely agricultural landscape, the touching hospitality of its people, Yunlin is one of the most fascinating and traditional counties in Taiwan. Despite these attributes, Yunlin is often referred to as one of the country's least developed regions, at least on the west coast.

Yunlin (Fig. 3.5) is an agricultural county with 68% of farmland in its total area. Due to its fertile land and good weather, Yunlin produces many kinds of agricultural products in different seasons. During the past decade,

Fig. 3.5 Yunlin County

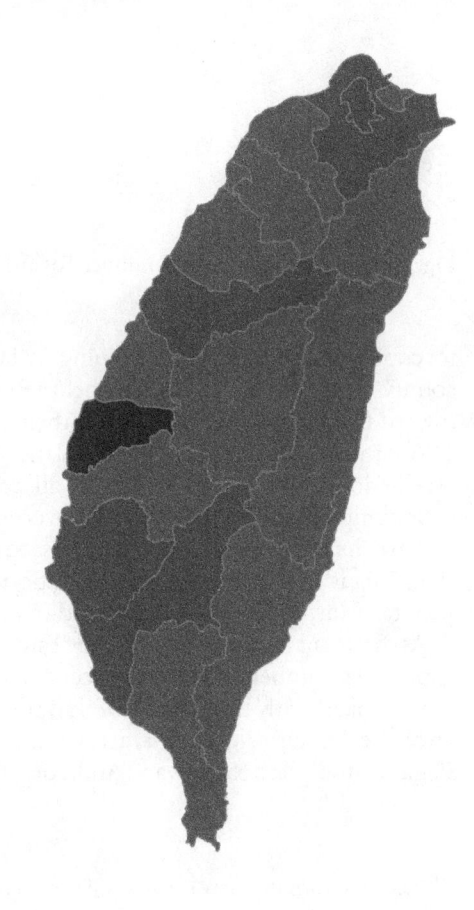

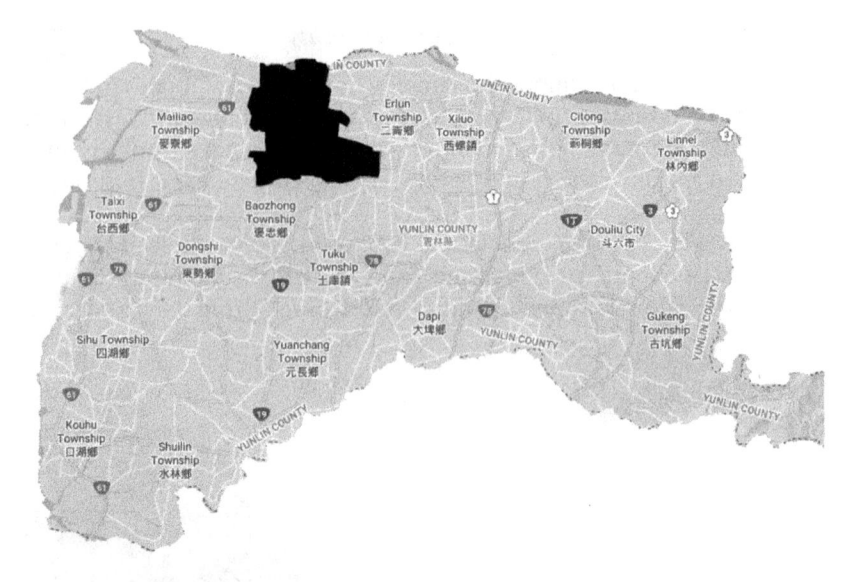

Fig. 3.6 Yunlin County and Lunbei Township

to cope with the impact of joining WTO on Taiwan agriculture,[9] the county government has tried to help farmers to improve their techniques toward fine farming, so to increase their competitiveness.

An integrated program of farmland has been used to improve the production environment and, above all, toward fine farming, so to increase their competitiveness. The county government pushed each rural township to have its own specific product. As consequence of this, now Lunbei (Fig. 3.6) is specialized on the cultivation of cantaloupe, Citong on garlic and star fruit, Gukeng on coffee and oranges, and so on.

As with many counties on the Taiwanese west coast, Yunlin has an impressive number of old and recent temples of all types and sizes. This fact is linked with the history of Taiwan and especially with the fact that since the Dutch ruled era, a great number of Chinese people started to illegally immigrate to Taiwan (Andrade 2008).

---

[9] Taiwan is a member of WTO, under the name of Chinese Taipei, since January 1, 2012. (WTO).

Journeys across the turbulent Taiwan Strait were always perilous. They became more so when opportunistic ship captains exploited the desperation and naivete of the illegal immigrants. Under such hardships, the migrants sought help from different deities, especially from the goddess Mazu, and established numerous temples in her honor (周明鋒 1994, p. 47–48).

Many of these boat people *ante litteram* arrived in Yunlin, where some of the older and most important Mazu temples of all Taiwan are present, such as 北港朝天 *Cháo Tiān Gōng* in Beigang Township or 麥寮鄉拱範宮 *Gǒng Fàn Gōng* in Mailiao Township, both of which have more than 300 years of history. The presence of these temples helped to establish a strong and deeply religious feeling among the people of Yunlin. Apart from these old and important temples, Popular Religion is present everywhere in this county: temples of all kinds and dimensions, family shrines, the smell of burning incense sticks, paper money almost everywhere on the roads. These and many another experiences—funerals, processions, sounds linked with temple or other religious activities—show themselves as a sensorial background where other daily activities are embedded.

3.3.2 Lunbei Township

Lunbei Township (Fig. 3.7) sits at the southern part of the 濁水溪 *Zhuóshuǐ* Stream, which slopes from east to west and marks the border between the counties of Changhua and Yunlin. The area is generally flat, the highest spot being 21 meters and the lowest spot 7 meters above sea level. Rainfall is usually concentrated in the flood season between April and September. The annual average temperature is about 20.4 °C (Lunbei Township 2009a).

This kind of situation favors farming, and some of the most characteristic agricultural products are watermelon and cantaloupe (Lunbei Township 2009b).

Thanks to the assistance of the Farmers' Association, cantaloupe has become a specialized produce in Lunbei. Every year a Cantaloupe Festival is organized by the Township government. The growing area of cantaloupe is mainly concentrated in three villages: 羅厝村 Luó cuò, 阿權村 Ā quán, and 豐榮村 Fēng róng. As we saw above for the Yunlin situation, the Township government started to improve economic construction in agricultural villages and effectively used the labor force in villages to set up a dairy area in Lunbei. In order to improve production costs, dairy farmers

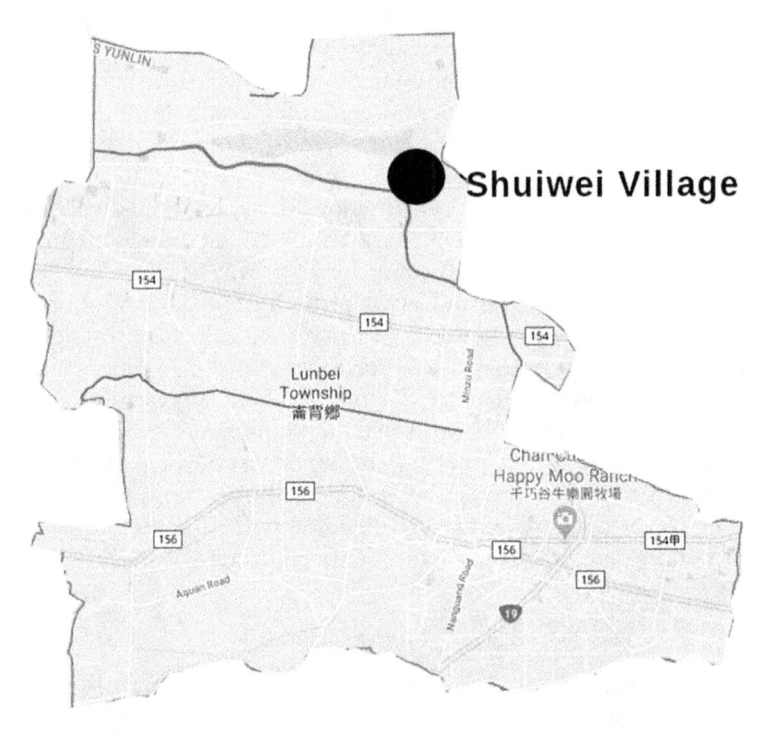

Fig. 3.7 Lunbei Township with Shuiwei village. *Source*: Modified from Google Maps

have cooperated. By 2002, the township had 58 dairy farms raising about 10,000 cows. With an annual production value of approximately NT$500 million to NT$600 million, dairy is an important industry in the township (Lunbei Township 2009a).

It is difficult to clearly define the origins of Lunbei Township. The area used to be 貓兒干(*Māo er gàn*) Vasikan, a settlement of the aboriginal 平埔族 *Píng pú* tribe (Lunbei Township 2009a). The Vasikan culture is a prehistoric archaeological culture from the Metal Age (or Iron Age) approximately 800–400 years ago. The culture was mainly distributed in Lunbei and the Mailiao alluvial plain along the river on the south bank of the *Zhuóshuǐ* Stream (Caltonhill 2013).

This makes sense if we consider that the zone around the township of Huwei was called by the Dutch people "Favorlang," a single aboriginal village which was located near Huwei Township, not far from Lunbei.[10] To date, the most certain archaeological remains related to the Favorlang were found at the Vasikan archaeological sites, demonstrating that the Favorlang were an important aborigine tribe in the Midwest region in early Taiwan history (施正鋒 et al. 2003). I mentioned all these historical and archaeological elements because they concretely play an active role in the construction of a "local" Lunbei identity.

Many factors, in fact, contribute to the formation of the narration of the nowadays Lunbei. One of these is linked with the fact that Yunlin is commonly considered as one of the most underdeveloped and poorest counties in all Taiwan. Till today Yunlin is the only Taiwanese province without an airport and the last one—among the west regions of Taiwan— to obtain a High Speed Railway Station (December 2015).

In addition, the emigration phenomena affected this area so much that in many townships—among which we can also put Lunbei—the presence of young people is dramatically low. In recent years, the Yunlin County government—which belongs to the Democratic Progressive Party (DPP)—tried to change this "bad" reputation by stressing the local "Taiwanese" identity of Yunlin, especially in opposition with big cities such as Taipei, Taichung, or Kaohsiung, which were more developed but ruled by the Kuomintang party. Therefore great importance was given to the Traditional Puppet Opera, which started in Yunlin—actually the founder was born in Lunbei—where a museum and an International Puppets Exhibition have been created in Huwei Town. Great importance also is given to all the cultural peculiarities present in the county: Hakka people, aboriginal people—Favorlang and Vasikan culture especially have been stressed both by the County government and by local scholars—local temple activities such as the annual pilgrimage of the goddess Mazu in Siluo Town or the one which ends in Beigang Town, and so on.

This effort to construct, or at least to empathize the authenticity of the Taiwanese culture in Yunlin, is linked with the general political orientation of the Democratic Progressive Party. The DPP tried to accentuate the local

---

[10] Translated in Chinese as 虎尾人 *Húwěi rén* (which in Taiwanese is pronounced Fuweilan), but which was also transliterated as 費落郎 *Fèi luò láng*; besides, Favorlang was also spelled as Favorang, Vavorlangh, and Vavorolangh.

Taiwanese identity in contrast with the "Chinese-ness" of the historically dominant Kuomintang party, mostly supported by Chinese who arrived in Taiwan after 1949 from Mainland China. In 1949–1950, following the victories of the Chinese Communists on the mainland, a stream of Nationalist troops, government officials, and other refugees under the lead of KMT poured onto the island. The KMT and ROC leader Chiang Kai-shek declared martial law. The KMT ruled Taiwan as a single-party state for 40 years, until 1985 when Chiang Ching-kuo, the son of Chiang Kai-shek, opened communications with the Chinese Communist mainland and with domestic political opposition. The opposition formed the DPP in 1986, stressing the local identity of the Taiwanese inhabitants. Under the pressure of the DPP political opposition, of the public and international opinion, in 1987 the KMT lifted martial law and started some democratic reforms, which led to the first-ever direct presidential election in 1996. The 2000 elections were the first presidential elections in which parties other than the KMT were allowed to participate. Chen Shui-bian, the DPP candidate, was elected as president of the Republic of China. This put an end to more than half a century of Kuomintang rule on Taiwan. Under his government, Chen Shui-bian gave a great impulse to policies pointed to stress the local aspects of Taiwan. This process could be summarized by the term 本土化 *Běntǔhuà* (indigenization). The DPP government put a big effort, even (and especially) with financial support, in order to let every place discover its local roots, where local means, of course, Taiwanese.[11]

In Lunbei the effects of the *Běntǔhuà* characterized (and still characterize) the direction of local politics. With the slogan "雲林好客" "*Yúnlín hàokè*" "Yunlin is welcoming you," the County government openly approved and encouraged the choice of Lunbei Township to choose their own Hakka roots as a sign of cultural distinction. The slogan plays with the meaning of the different pronunciations of 好客 which at the same time could mean *hàokè* "welcomes guests" as well as *hǎokè* "good Hakka people." Hakka culture has become one of the distinguishing traits, probably the most important, of the local culture in Lunbei. The choice of Hakka identity—詔安客家 *Zhàoān* Hakka people—that is a minority among the Hakka minority in Taiwan comported the introduction of Hakka Zhaoan language in the elementary school curriculum (at least in the elementary schools of the villages with Hakka presence), the cultural

---

[11] Please refer to Makeham and Hsiau (2005).

exchange with Hakka people from the Zhaoan County in Mainland China, and the building of a Hakka Traditional Palace style (called 土樓 *Túlóu*) as a cultural center with space for performances, studies, and conferences on Hakka culture.[12]

Actually, the choice of Hakka culture as the principal characteristic of Lunbei Township has been facilitated by the substantial economic contribution of the Hakka Affairs Council, a cabinet-level unit under Executive Yuan of the government of the Republic of China.

The Zhaoan Hakka group is the only Hakka group, among the ones recognized in Taiwan, which came from Fujian province. In historical times, the majority of the immigrants from Mainland China came from this province. In fact, most of the Taiwanese population has roots in this province, which is located just in front of the Taiwanese west coast. The main language spoken by these immigrants was Minnan (the language of the southern part of Fujian province). The other Hakka groups that arrived in Taiwan came from Guangdong province. The Zhàoān Hakka were thus already able to talk in Minnan language when they arrived in Taiwan. The other Hakka groups spoke only other Hakka dialects and were unable to speak the Minnan language. Because of this the Zhàoān Hakka were not considered as Hakka people, even by the Taiwanese Hakka community itself. Very often even Zhaoan people did not consider themselves as "truly" Hakka people. I heard several times people in Lunbei saying "我們不是真正的客家人 *Wǒmen bùshì zhēnzhèngde kèjiārén* we are not truly Hakka people."

The Hakka presence in Lunbei Township is concentrated in the villages of Lunqian, Gangwei, Fangnan, and Luocuo, and the families that still speak Hakka, and that according to the genealogical records are coming from the Zhaoan province, are the 李 Li, the 廖 Liao, and the 鍾 Zhong families. During my fieldwork, I noticed that in contrast to the effort made by the Township government, few families were concretely and enthusiastically involved in this Hakka ethnic revival. The Catholic families of Shuiwei (Zhong and Li), as we will see, are not interested and do not care about their identification as Hakka.

---

[12] The Hakka, who make up about one-fifth of the Han population in Taiwan, have a long history of periodic migration—hence the name Hakka, which literally means "guest people." Large Hakka communities can be found today in the Taoyuan, Hsinchu, Miaoli, Taichung, Kaohsiung, Yunlin, and Pingtung areas. (Yearbook 2014, p. 48).

Apart from this Hakka movement, which, as we saw, is mainly supported by the Township and the County governments, an important place inside the above-mentioned localization process—or better revaluation of the local customs and traditions—could be found in the private cultural association called 貓兒幹 *Māo ergàn* (Vasikan, as the old aboriginal culture present in these places linked to the Favorlang culture). This association actively cooperated with the Township government in order to discover the Hakka roots of Lunbei and in reevaluating agriculture and a traditional way of farming.

3.3.3   Shuiwei Village

The Christian community of Shuiwei lives mostly in the southern part of the village, which is also the most populated. Most of the area of the village is occupied by agricultural fields. The favorable climate allows for several harvests during the year. If the choice is growing rice, it is possible to have two harvests, one in June–July and another in October–November. If farmers choose to grow vegetables, they can have three or more harvests during the year depending on the kind of vegetables they want to cultivate.

Usually, rice is grown by older farmers, because both the sowing and the harvest are now completely mechanized. Furthermore, this kind of cultivation requires less physical work. I stress this aspect because, as I explained at the beginning of this chapter, there is a very strong link between land, inheritance, family structure, and the ancestors' cults. This link is still visible also among the Christian community even if, as we will see, with some important exceptions.

As I mentioned earlier, the Christian community of Shuiwei village is mostly composed of Presbyterian and Catholic believers. The only exception is a household which belongs to the Christian Church called 真耶穌教會 *Zhēn yēsū jiàohuì* "The True Jesus Church." This family, whose surname is Li, is a local family. They were previously belonging to the Presbyterian community of Shuiwei. A few years ago, however, they had some contrasts with the other Presbyterian families. As a consequence, they decided to join another Christian Protestant Church. The members of this family were the only Christians active in proselytizing within Shuiwei. While neither the Catholic nor the Presbyterian communities tried to convert the believers of the other Church, this family was always putting in each family's post-box brochures about the various activities of the True Jesus Church.

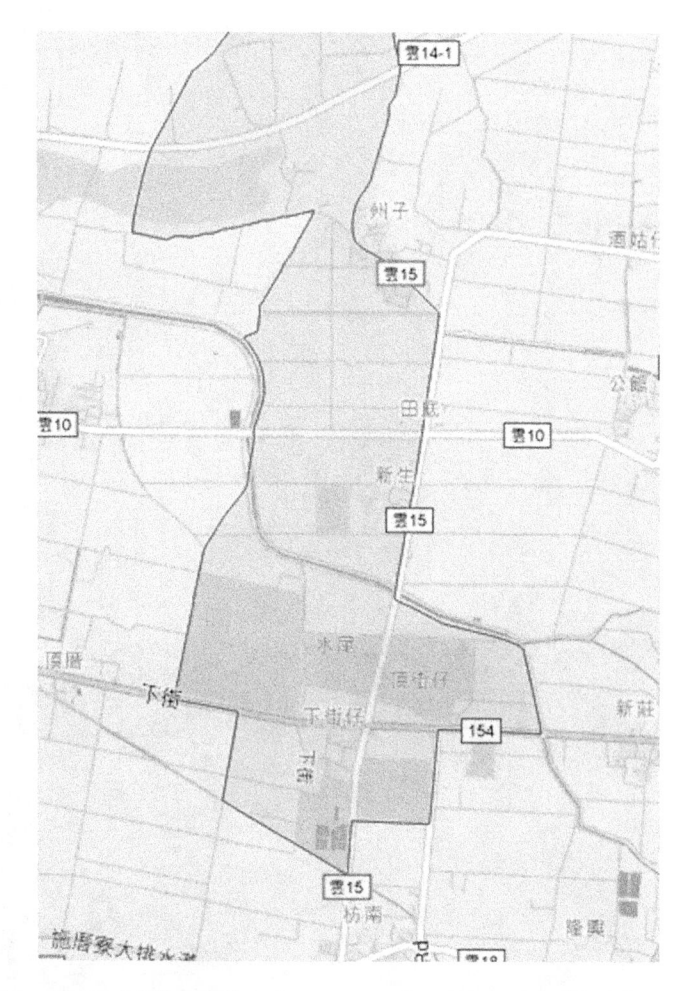

Fig. 3.8 Shuiwei Village Christian community. *Source*: Modified from Google maps

In Figs. 3.8 and 3.9, it is possible to see the distribution of the Christian community within the village of Shuiwei. In particular, Fig. 3.9 describes the different areas belonging to the Presbyterian community (the yellow one) and the Catholic community (in red).

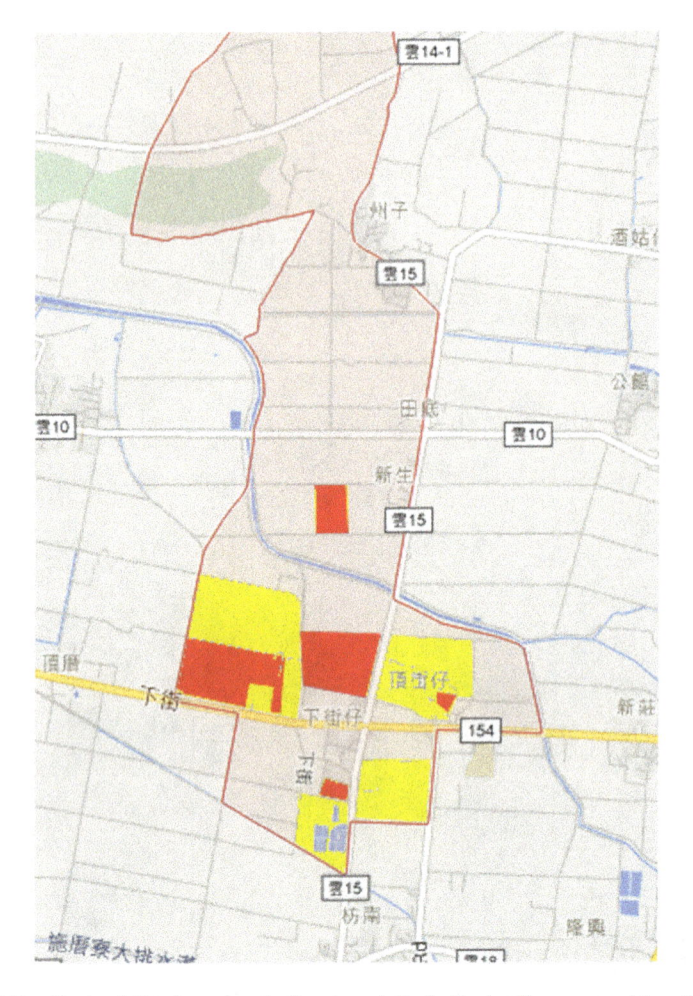

Fig. 3.9 Shuiwei Presbyterian (yellow) and Catholic (red) communities. *Source*: Modified from Google Maps

As we can see in Fig. 3.8, the Christian community occupies a definite area located in the southern part of the village, which is also the most populated. Another important residential area is the one located along the road N.154, commonly denominated as 下街 *Xiàjiē*, where the Shuiwei Village Activity Center is located.

Other residential areas include two well-defined groups of households located on the road N.15 and another couple of households located on the boundary that Shuiwei shares with the neighboring 二崙鄉 Èrlún Township.

The village elementary school, 陽明國小 Yangming Elementary School, is located on the road 154. Recently this school started to offer classes (not compulsory) in the local Hakka language. They did it because most of Shuiwei's inhabitants' surname is Zhong or Li. According to the Lunbei Township government, because of the strong presence of these surnames, Shuiwei should be considered a Hakka village. Apart from the highlighted areas, the rest of the village belongs to people who are not directly involved with the Christian faith. Actually in Shuiwei there are five temples and a couple of private shrines (私人堂 Sīréntáng) (Fig. 3.10).

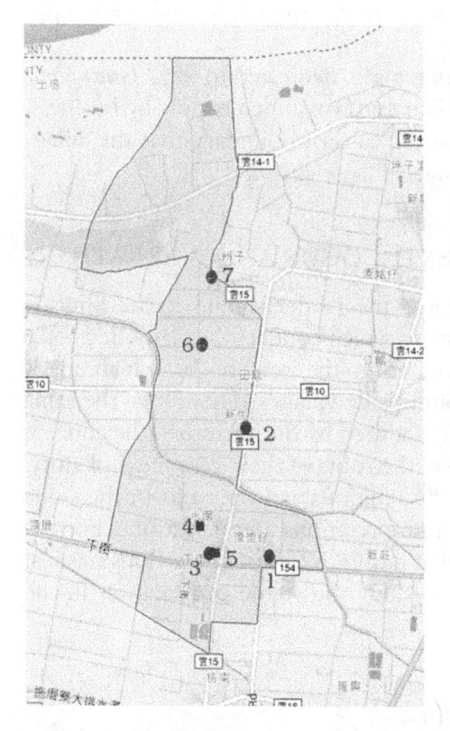

1: 土地公廟 Tudigong Temple

2: 媽祖廟 Mazu Temple

3: 無極金母宮 Wújí jīn mǔ gōng

4: 私人堂 Sīréntáng. Private Shrine

5: 私人堂 Sīréntáng. Private Shrine

6: 地藏王菩薩 Dìcáng wáng púsà

7: 真安宮 Zhēn ān gōng

Fig. 3.10 Temples' location in Shuiwei village. *Source*: Modified from Google Maps

Number one indicates a 土地公廟 *Tǔdìgōng* temple, one of the most common temples in Taiwan, located on the southeastern boundary of the village. Number two is a 媽祖廟 Mazu temple, another important and common deity in Taiwan, which is located on the eastern boundary of the village and inside a group of households called 新生 *Xīnshēng* (New Life). This household belongs to some Hakka immigrants from northern Taiwan (specifically from the northern county of 新竹 Hsingchu). Number three is a particular temple linked with the so-called 新興臺灣民間信仰 (*Xīnxīng táiwān mínjiān xìnyǎng*), which can be translated as New Taiwanese Popular Religion.[13] It was a branch of a main temple in Hualien, one of the eastern counties of Taiwan. According to my informants, this temple was dismissed in 2015.

Numbers four and five are private shrines, and number six is also a temple, 地藏王菩薩 *Dìcáng wáng púsà*. It is a temple commonly built near cemeteries, especially abandoned ones.[14] In fact, behind the temple, there is an abandoned cemetery.

Number seven is 真安宮 *Zhēn ān* temple, dedicated to 關公 *Guāngōng*, traditionally known as the God of War and worshiped mainly by businessmen. Also this temple is located on the eastern boundary that the village shares with the neighboring township of 二崙 *Èrlún*.

3.4 Shuiwei in Context: Locus and Narration

I briefly described the context where the reader should locate Shuiwei village. Within this context, the reasons which connect the Catholic people to their place are not so different from the reasons by which many Taiwanese are linked with their countryside villages. They share the same sense of the importance of the land inherited by the ancestors, the concept of 故鄉 *Gùxiāng* I mentioned above, the roots of their Taiwanese identity, and so on. The differences lie in the religious activities and in the value attached to this place by different interpretations and narrations. For the people of Shuiwei, the main road that passes in front of their houses is just a road. For the people in charge to carry the statue of Mazu, as in the

---

[13] For those interested, refer to 鄭志明 (1999).

[14] In modern Chinese Buddhism, Dizang is especially popular as the sovereign of the underworld. Please refer to Ng (2007).

previous story of Mister Zhong, it represents something more similar to a boundary made of fire (Locus, Sect. 2.1).

The same thought was shared by the mother-in-law of a Vietnamese woman who came from a very Catholic Vietnamese family. She married into one of the families in Shuiwei traditionally linked to the practices of the Taiwanese Popular Religion. Among the narration that most part of the practitioners of the Popular Religion share about Christianity, there is the conviction that Christians forbid the ceremonies for the ancestors. As a consequence, a Christian wife will not take care of the family's ancestors. In Taiwan it is commonly believed that when an ancestor is not fed by his descendants, he will become a 餓鬼 *Ègui*, a hungry ghost that will wander hungry forever (please refer to Genos, Sect. 5.2.1).

The family-in-law of this Vietnamese woman was sharing this firm belief. The mother-in-law of this girl not only forbade her to take part in any Catholic activities but forbade her even to pass in front of the Catholic houses of the village. The interesting thing is that her husband was in friendly relations with all the Catholic families of the village. We had dinner together at the Shuiwei Catholic faithfuls' home many times, of course without his wife. Despite the mutual knowledge and respect, the narrative depicting a Christian daughter-in-law as contrary to tradition and as a danger to the ancestors (and thus for the family) was still stronger. This narration came from the context which interacts with Shuiwei. Historical reasons, cosmological notions, and everyday practices linked with this place contribute to create a particular narration which describes Shuiwei as a different place. The differences of behavior are regarded as immanent, and therefore each interpretation provides and attaches sometimes contrasting values to human actions and thus to their narrations.

A good example of how different narrations give different value to the same place is the story of the creation of a public park in Shuiwei village. This example will underline how Shuiwei as topos is principally made by narration. The narration about this park is strongly linked with the narration of the identity that the governments of Yunlin and Lunbei are trying to create and that I previously introduced.

During my fieldwork, the Yunlin County government decided to start a project which, in the intentions of the project creators, should contribute to the development of tourism in the county. The purpose of the project was to create a cycle path through the region. In order to realize it, it was

Fig. 3.11 Theme park in Shuiwei village

decided to use the old rail network of the sugarcane factory.[15] This bike path had to cross culturally attractive places, and each township was asked to indicate places linked with traditional culture or with amusement areas. Lunbei Township decided to transform one of the Taiwanese traditional houses into a park (Fig. 3.11). This option had the advantage of serving two purposes: on the one hand the Township government wanted to revitalize one of the villages in the township, creating an environment where tourists could get in touch with the traditional Taiwanese farming culture. On the other hand, since the village of Shuiwei was considered a Hakka village, the Township government tried to push forward its "Hakka project."

---

[15] The Taiwan Sugar Railways (台灣糖業鐵路 *Táiwān tángyè tiělù*) were an extensive series of railways, concentrated mostly in southern and central Taiwan. The Sugar Railways were initially constructed during the Japanese rule in the early twentieth century. In the projects of Japanese colonial empire, Taiwan should have become one of the leading sugar producers.

Since Shuiwei is considered by the Township government as a Hakka village, they chose the Zhong Catholic family's ancestral home, already uninhabited for years. The choice was dictated not only by aesthetic reasons but also by the fact that all the owners of the house were living in the village. Therefore it was possible to contact them without losing too much time. The Zhong family members and the other inhabitants of the village were very happy with this project, which they considered a way to restructure their old home at the expense of the local government. In addition, the project involved the improvement of the whole area around the house.

The final project included the transformation of the Zhong's house into a museum with a refreshment point for tourists who would arrive by bicycle, a theme park, and a barbecue area. The area that was chosen to make the theme park was the one where the first Protestant church was built. This was an imposing structure made of bricks that also served as a kindergarten for the children of the village. The symbols chosen for the park drew on the Christian faith and Gospel passages. Apart from the presence of the church (which was now in ruins), a large cross was placed in relief on the floor of the square, one of the benches was made in the shape of a cross, and a pergola had to recall the phrase of the Gospel: "I am the vine, you are the branches. Whoever remains in me and I in him will bear much fruit, because without me you can do nothing" (John 15:5).

The construction of the park, which became an important meeting point for the village, was accompanied by a revival of stories about it and about the history of the Christian community of the village. The Presbyterians began to remember the original feature of the church and tried to reconstruct the "genealogy" of the pastors and presbyters who worshiped in that church. The Catholics started to remember the construction of their church and the time when their children used the Presbyterian church as a kindergarten. In other words, the construction helped the rediscovery and the reconstruction of their own history.

After a few weeks of work, the County government, the Township government, and the Village government organized a ceremony for the inauguration of the park. The contrast between the different ideas each part had about the park has been the more interesting part of the ceremony. The authorities of the township stressed the Hakka origins of the village and the special role of the bike path that in their view should link the various Hakka villages in the area. The authorities of Yunlin County (it was election time and even the Yunlin governor came to the inauguration) stressed that the project of the bike path was designed to rediscover and strengthen local (therefore Taiwanese) cultural heritage. But before the authorities could talk, they had to attend the blessing of the park by the priest and a few Christian songs performed by the Christian community of Shuiwei village.

Through a concrete place, the theme park, the township, the county, and the village developed three different narrations. At the same time, the three different narrations created the park as a "Christian place," a "Taiwanese place," and a "Hakka place."

Topos is certainly an element that develops itself on different levels. I am sure that the Christian community of Shuiwei recognized itself in the effort made by the governor to create Taiwanese roots. Anyway, if we link the concept of topos with locus, it is clear that topos is strongly related to the everyday life and experiences linked to that place. And this happens because the historical experience of a place, if stimulated by the introduction or by the revival of symbols linked with it, raises a myriad of stories which will help to create/consolidate the memory about that place and therefore its narration.

References

Allio, F. 1998. Procession et Identité: Mise en Scène Rituelle de l'Histoire Locale. *Cahiers d'Extrême-Asie 10*, 1–18.

Altan, C. T. 1995. *Ethnos e Civiltà. Identità Etniche e Valori Democratici*. Milano: Feltrinelli.

Andrade, T. 2008. *How Taiwan Became Chinese: Dutch, Spanish, and Han Colonization in the Seventeenth Century*. New York: Columbia University Press.

Boretz, A. 2011. *Gods, Ghosts, and Gangsters: Ritual Violence, Martial Arts, and Masculinity on the Margins of Chinese Society*. Honolulu: University of Hawai'i Press.

Caltonhill, M. 2013. Beigang 北港(and bengang 笨港, wanggang 魍港and vasikan 貓兒干). http://taiwanplacenames.blogspot.com/2013/10/beigang-and-bengang-and-wanggang.html?m=0. Accessed February 6, 2016.

CRNTT. 2005. 扁「國師」替台鐵看風水被批怪力亂神. http://hk.crntt.com/crn-webapp/doc/docDetailCreate.jsp?coluid=7&kindid=0&docid=100046291&mdate=0911123624. Accessed April 20, 2016.

Dell'Orto, A. 2003. *Place and Spirit in Taiwan: Tudi Gong in the Stories, Strategies and Memories of Everyday Life*. London: Routledge.

Eberhard, W. 1986. *A Dictionary of Chinese Symbols: Hidden Symbols in Chinese Life and Thought*. London & New York: Routledge.

Feuchtwang, S. 1974. Domestic and Communal Worship in Taiwan. In *Religion and Ritual in Chinese Society*, ed. A. P. Wolf, 105–130. Stanford University Press.

——. 2003. *Popular Religion in China: The Imperial Metaphor*. London: Routledge.
Freedman, M. 1967. Ancestor Worship: Two Facets of the Chinese Case. In *Social Organization: Essays Presented to Raymond Firth*, ed. M. Freedman. Chicago: Aldine Pub. Co.
Gates, H. 1987. Money for the Gods. *Modern China* 13 (3), 259–277.
Granet, M. 1968. *La Pensée Chinoise (1934)*. Paris: Albin Michel.
Lazzarotti, M. 2008. The Ancestors' Rites in the Taiwanese Catholic Church. Master's thesis, National Taiwan University, Taipei, Taiwan.
Li, Y.-y. 1976. Chinese Geomancy and Ancestor Aorship: A Further Discussion. In *Ancestors*, ed. W. H. Newell, 329–338. The Hague: Mouton Publishers.
Lin, W.-p. 2009. Local History Through Popular Religion: Place, People and Their Narratives in Taiwan. *Asian Anthropology* 8 (1), 1–30.
Lunbei Township, O. 2009a. Welcome to Lunbei Geography. http://www.lunbei.gov.tw/english/content/index.asp?m=1&m1=15&m2=92&gp=83. Accessed April 21, 2016.
——. 2009b. Welcome to Lunbei Special Products. http://www.lunbei.gov.tw/content/index.asp?m=1&m1=4&m2=22. Accessed April 21, 2016.
Makeham, J., and A.-c. Hsiau. 2005. *Cultural, Ethnic, and Political Nationalism in Contemporary Taiwan: Bentuhua*. New York: Springer.
Ng, Z. 2007. *The Making of a Savior Bodhisattva: Dizang in Medieval China*. Honolulu: University of Hawaii Press.
Paolillo, M. 2007. Paesaggio 'Misurato' o 'Qualificato'? Lo Spazio Prospettico Occidentale, lo 'Spazio Psico-Fisiologico' di Florenskij e la Percezione dello Spazio nella Tradizione Cinese. In *La Cina e l'Altro*, ed. A. Palermo, 435–460. Napoli: Il Torcoliere.
Seaman, G. 1982. Spirit Money: An Interpretation. *Society for the Study of Chinese Religions Bulletin* 10 (1), 80–91.
Wang, S.-h. 1974. Taiwanese Architecture and the Supernatural. In *Religion and Ritual in Chinese Society*, ed. A. P. Wolf, 183–192. Stanford: Stanford University Press.
Yearbook, T. 2014. Taipei: Government Information Office, 2014.
周明鋒. 1994. 臺灣簡史. 臺北:前衛出版社.
施正鋒, 劉益昌, and 潘朝成. 2003. 台灣平埔族. 台北: 前衛政經文庫.
朱詠薇. 2005. 台北車站改大門: 白虎昂首消災？. http://news.tvbs.com.tw/entry/424300. Accessed April 20, 2016.
林瑋嬪. 2000. 人觀, 空間實踐與治病儀式: 以一個台灣西南農村為例. 國立台灣大學考古學刊 56, 44–76.
林瑋嬪. 2005. 台灣廟宇的發展: 從一個地方庄廟的神明信仰, 企業化經營以及國家文化政策談起. 國立臺灣大學考古人類學刊 62, 56–92.
鄭志明. 1999. 臺灣新興宗教現象:傳統信仰篇. Taipei: 南華管理學院宗教文化研究中心.

CHAPTER 4

Epos

4.1 Stories of Shuiwei

Around the end of the nineteenth century, three brothers of the Zhong family were the bosses of the local criminal community. Their power in Shuiwei village was so big that they provided a shelter even to many murderers. The murderers found refuge within the Zhongs' households by changing their surname and, at least in appearance, becoming part of the Zhong family. The brothers' influence was felt even in places many kilometers away from Shuiwei, such as Erlun or Siluo, where they regularly went to collect their protection fees (紅包 *hóngbāo*).

During the same period, a Presbyterian Church was founded in Siluo. The Presbyterian pastor was a missionary from England, who owned a bicycle by which he paid visit to the faithful. At that time, in the surrounding territory, there were only a few bicycles, and therefore a bicycle was considered a kind of status symbol. The 大哥 *Dàgē*, the older of the three Zhong brothers, was very curious about this bicycle, which in Chinese is called 鐵馬 *Tiěmǎ* or "iron horse," so he decided to go to ride "a horse that doesn't eat grass.[1]" Because of his inexperience, he fell many times. Seeing this, the missionary jumped on the bicycle and started to ride it, impressing Mr. Zhong. From that time, whenever Mr. Zhong went to Siluo to collect his *hóngbāo*, he tried to ride the missionary's bicycle. In order to rest and escape the heat, he would enter the church. In this way he started to hear the pastor's sermons. Unexpectedly, he became more and more interested in the Christian faith. He was especially touched by the Bible verse: "Peace I leave with you; my peace I give to you. Not as the world gives do I give it to you. Do not let your hearts be troubled or afraid" (John 14:27). Meditating on this verse, he realized that, although he was very rich and respected, he lacked peace in his life. As a consequence, he converted and turn away from crime. After his brothers heard about his conversion, one of them—鍾欽先生 Mr. Zhong Qin—agreed with him, and he also received the baptism. The third brother did not convert and continued his previous way of life. Reflecting their new faith, the two converted brothers built a church made of wood in Shuiwei. During the harvesting season, the church was used as a place to dry the rice produced by the two families. One time the two converted families—the eldest brother and Mr. Zhong Qin—started to quarrel because each family wanted to put the rice inside the church earlier than the other. Following this episode, the relationships between these two families became more and more tense. One day a drug seller, who was Catholic, arrived in the village. While he was selling his medicaments, he noticed some symbols of the Christian faith. Encouraged by this, he started to preach his Catholic faith. In contrast with his brother, Mr. Zhong Qin converted himself and his family to Catholicism.

Zhong Zhimei. Presbyterian. Summer 2008

4.2　Epos

Epos is the symbolic transfiguration of historical memory. This element is thus linked with concepts such as history and myth, and it should be considered one of the most important narration (and identity) builders. Altan looks at epos as a group of people who remember their past by

---

[1] The Presbyterian who told me this story, referring to the first brother, called him 大哥 *Dàgē*, which in Chinese means "older brother." In some contexts this word may mean "boss," and it is used to indicate the head of criminal organizations.

looking at its positive aspects. He considers epos as something that gives not only prestige but also a sense of dignity and belonging. Through epos, a people can recognize itself and ennoble or complain about its own past.

Altan's primary aim was the analysis and understanding of the core of the symbolic values that define the sense of participation of the individuals in the community. Consequentially, he underlines that the most important characteristic of epos is the representation of the past as a common value. He believes that this reality necessarily belongs to any ethnic group (Altan 1995, p. 22).

Another key aspect pointed out by Altan is the close link between the discipline we call history or historiography (which is exquisitely rational in its planning of knowledge) and epos, which is its symbolic transfiguration in the form of myth. The Greeks placed history under the protection/inspiration of the muse Clio, as a specific cultural operation. Clio comes from the verb *Kleion*—to exalt, to celebrate. Only with Herodotus did they begin to use the term *Historia* from the verb *Historein*, which means to investigate, to research, and to report. In this case, the myth preceded, in the role of mythology, the rational practice of which it is the transfiguration. Altan believes that the most significant and authentic forms of epos can be found in ethnographic and historical literature in the guise of myths of origins, of the golden age, and of those that followed: the exploits of the founding heroes and those who invented the techniques and nurtured their people. The central role of myth as epos is to sacralize the historical memory of a social group that recognizes itself in this myth and at the same time celebrate itself through this myth, revealing the nobility of its origins (Altan 1995, pp. 22–23).

I consider Altan right in recognizing that history is a concept that people use to memorialize the common past. There is certainly a strong connection between history, myth, and narration. At the same time, I believe that in order to build a sense of belonging through a shared past, a people doesn't necessarily have to look only to the positive aspects of its history. It would be enough to think of what the Holocaust meant for both the German and the Jewish and how these negative experiences molded the sense of belonging to these communities. In the same way we can consider as epos the whole historical context, certainly shaped by a sense of abandonment, which created—and is still creating—the modern Taiwanese narrative and sense of identity. This happens because epos is a historical narrative extrapolated by a specific historical time in order to become a narration untouched by historical changes (which Altan calls *Meta-history*).

This non-historical narrative is always tied to poetic, religious, and political dimensions (Altan 1995, p. 22).

However, my research is linked not only with understanding the foundation of a social group identity but also with other aspects of this fascinating kaleidoscope. Therefore I will link epos not only to the mythical origins of Shuiwei village as a Christian village but also to the narration of the mythologized stories that the Shuiwei people made in order to tell their own history. Many of the concepts linked with epos are certainly linked with other elements that will be discussed in the next chapters. In my analysis of ethos, I will underline how the sacralization of the history of the village follows patterns linked with the history of the local Catholic church and its developments. This link with the history of the local Church is present in the "myths of origins" of the inhabitants of Shuiwei village and especially in the ways the stories about it are created and narrated.

Many of the developments of the history of the local Catholic church can be traced in documents written by Catholic missionaries. During the time that goes from the latter half of the nineteenth century to the first half of the twentieth, the Dominicans were the only missionaries working in Taiwan. They had the obligation to write reports about the developments of their evangelization work. From this obligation came the *Correo Sino-Annamita* (letters from the missions in China and Vietnam), *Misiones Dominicanas* (Dominican Missions), and *Ultramar* (Overseas), regular magazines printed in the University of Santo Tomas (Manila) (Borao 1993). These documents, together with many others, constitute the core of the historiography of the Catholic church in Taiwan, at least the one linked with the Dominican missionaries.

In the next pages, I will try to show that this history is a particular epic constructed by the Catholic church. To this epic is tied and established—and takes sense—Shuiwei's epos. Shuiwei's epos comes from the interweaving of the stories narrated and transmitted through different generations with the history of the Catholic church in Taiwan.

Significantly, especially among the Catholics, the younger generations of Shuiwei village are the ones who are writing down the stories about their family. These young people started to collect pictures and other documents that testify their origins. They are thus, by writing their history, bringing *Kleion* to *Historia*. The interest of these youths for their roots is linked to two main reasons. On the one hand, they are the first generation that left the village in order to get a better education and a job in one of the big cities of Taiwan. Moving away from the village, they moved away from the source of the myth or, better, from the narration which creates the myth. There is, thus, a strong connection between the creation of stories and the experience of living side by side in the same locus. They started to use other means to maintain the myth of their locus: writing their family genealogical records, collecting pictures, and inquiring about their family roots.

The second reason of this renewed interest in their roots is linked to the fact that one of the "children" of Shuiwei became the Bishop of the Diocese of Chiayi.[2] Because of this big event, the Catholic community of Shuiwei discovered its importance. As a consequence, they started to care about their roots by writing down their history.

4.3 SHUIWEI CHRISTIAN COMMUNITY, BETWEEN MYTH AND HISTORY

The story by which I started this chapter should be considered the "myth of origin" for both the Shuiwei Catholic and Presbyterian community. This story was told to me by the "patriarch" of the Presbyterian part of the Zhong family: Mr. Zhong Zhimei, an old man in his 80s. Significantly, he told me this story while we were drinking a coffee made by the Catholic priest, sitting in the backyard of the Catholic church with the Presbyterian pastor.

The fact of having a common founder, or at least founders linked by close family ties, is manifested in the sense of unity that comes out when the Christian faithfuls of Shuiwei talk about themselves or about other Christian denominations. It is possible to read it in this passage from my fieldwork notes:

> I was sitting, as almost every evening, in the garden of Fengrong when the postman came for his usual after-dinner walk. Mr. Chen, the postman, was called "presbytery" by all the inhabitants of Shuiwei. As the name could easily suggest, he was one of the presbyteries of the local Presbyterian Church. He was living in Shuiwei, and his wife was one of the teachers of Shuiwei kindergarten when this was managed by the Presbyterians. As many times happened, the topic of that night was my research about the religions around the Lunbei area. After telling me one of the many versions of the story of how

---

[2] Thomas Chung (鍾安住) has been appointed as Auxiliary Bishop of Taipei on October 31, 2006. On March 1, 2008, he has been installed Bishop of the Diocese of Chiayi (CRBC 2008).

Christianity arrived in Shuiwei [the story by which I started this chapter], he started to explain that the Christian community in Shuiwei came from the same root. And that, at the end of the day, "we [Presbyterians and Catholics] are the same Church, we share the same belief in Christ. You are called Old Christians (舊教 *Jiùjiào*) and we are called New Christians (新教 *Xīnjiào*), but we are the same (我們是一樣 *Wǒmen shì yīyàng*)."

The same point of view is shared also by Catholic believers. This is Hong-ying, a woman in her 50s who married a man of the Zhong family:

When I came to live in this village after the wedding, I met some problems. Before building our own house we were living together in the old house [the Zhong ancestral house, where she was living with her parents-in-law and the family of her brother-in-law]. You know, to live together is not always the best, especially for the last arrived daughter-in-law. Among the persons who mostly understood my difficulties and have been closer to me, there are at least two Presbyterians. You know, in this village Presbyterians and Catholics always shared good relationships. I personally think that we have some differences, but the most important aspects of our faith are in common. We are a family (我們是一家人 *Wǒmen shì yījiārén*). I never considered them as belonging to another Church. We live and work together…(smiling)…After all, we share even the surname!

This sense of unity or, using their words, the feeling to be one family, 一家人 *yījiārén*, is manifested also in the missionary activities that the two communities held together. Unlike many other places in Taiwan (at least those of which I am aware),[3] the Presbyterians and Catholics not only live together peacefully but share many pastoral activities. Almost every week, the two communities do apostolic work together by visiting a community of aboriginal people which work and live not too far from the village of Shuiwei. Most of the aboriginal people in Taiwan share the Christian faith. When they move to another place in order to get a job, for historical and cultural reasons, they usually don't take part in the activities of the local Christian communities that mostly consist of 漢 *Hàn* people. In order to welcome them and to let them feel the presence of the Christian community, Shuiwei's faithfuls go to visit them at their place. Apart from

---

[3] In 2010 I joined as a volunteer with the Ecumenical and Inter-religious Office of the Diocese of Chiayi.

this, there are also many shared activities for both the Catholics and the Presbyterian kids, such as the joint prayer at the beginning of each new school year. On Christmas Eve, Presbyterian families visit the Catholic families singing Christmas carols. From these events, and from many daily meeting and joint activities, it is possible to recognize how the myth of origins could affect the awareness of a peculiar sense of community and thus the activities and the stories—and consequentially the history— created by this particular context. The sense of belonging to one family helps to let the Christian community consider the differences between Catholics and Presbyterians less relevant, especially in comparison to the differences between Christians and non-Christians.

The story I introduced at the beginning of this chapter shows that the first converted was one of the Zhong brothers who headed the local mafia (Sect. 4.1). From him, the huge Presbyterian community of Shuiwei developed, which encompasses the Zhong family and other families who converted over the years. Among them the bigger family groups are the Li, which belong to the same lineage of Lunbei to which belong also the Catholic branch of the Li families, and the Chen family.

Historically the Shuiwei's Presbyterian community was linked with the mission of Siluo, which was the first place around Shuiwei to have a permanent Church. As we learned in the story at the beginning of this chapter, an English missioner was taking care of this Church. In the village of Shuiwei, the converted built several churches. From the one mentioned by Zhong Zhimei in his story to the big church made of bricks that I described in Topos (Sect. 3.4).

After 1949, this Presbyterian community has been involved in the big changes linked to the arrival of many people from the mainland who preceded the arrival of many missionaries from abroad (especially the USA and Canada). In Lunbei a new church was built in 南陽 Nán yáng village, just behind the Catholic church. Since that time the Presbyterian community of Shuiwei started to attempt the Sunday service in Lunbei. The church made of bricks was used as a kindergarten, and it was abandoned when the Township government opened a public kindergarten in 下街 Xiàjiē. This kindergarten is the Activity Center of Shuiwei village.

A few years ago, the arrival of a new pastor in the Church of Lunbei set off a series of changes, so that the Presbyterian community of Shuiwei divided itself into two parts. One part continued to attempt the Sunday service in Lunbei, while the other started to take part in the activities of the Church of 橋頭 *Qiáotóu,* in the neighboring township of Mailiao (see Logos, Sect. 7.3.1).

As for the Catholic community, the majority of the Shuiwei's Presbyterian community is composed of farmers, but there are also important economic activities which are renowned all around the county of Yunlin, such as the 欣昌錦鯉養殖場 Sing Chang Koi Farm, which specializes in farming goldfishes. This farm is very famous in Taiwan and also in the international goldfish market. When my wife and I arrived in Lunbei, we met two entrepreneurs coming from England who were living at the Sing Chang Koi Farm. They spent almost one year at the Sing Chang Koi Farm to learn how to farm and take care of the goldfish. Apart from this big enterprise, other Presbyterian members of the Zhong family opened cram schools and mechanics' workshops, some found work in commerce, and so on.

4.3.1   Shuiwei Catholic Community: At the Roots of the Myth

As we learned from the story of the "three brothers": two brothers (the eldest brother and Mr. Zhong Qin) decided to become Presbyterian. This conversion caused an important separation in the Zhong family that will be described in the following pages.

This separation was followed by another one, which involved the two converted brothers. Within the mainstream of Christianity, the big brother and Mr. Zhong Qin have chosen different religions. Although this separation did not create a climate of hatred between the two communities, it helped to build another important symbol in the construction of epos among the Catholic part of the Zhong family, the first converted: Mr. Zhong Qin (Fig. 4.1).

Nowadays Mr. Zhong Qin is an important symbol not only for the Catholic part of the Zhong family but also for the whole Catholic community of Lunbei. The importance of Mr. Zhong Qin lies in the fact that he is regarded as the founder of Catholicism in the Lunbei area. The story of his conversion underlines that Mr. Zhong Qin converted to Catholicism without the help of any missionary. This is unique in the evangelization of Taiwan, and the Shuiwei Catholic community is very proud of it. If the story of the three brothers can be considered as the "myth of origin" of the whole Christian community in Shuiwei, Mr. Zhong Qin could be

Fig. 4.1 Mr. Zhong Qin, who began the Catholic community of Shuiwei village in 1905

considered the "myth of origin" of the Catholic part of the Zhong family and for the Catholic community in Lunbei.

In 2005 the Catholic community of Lunbei (which, as we will see, since 2002 includes the community of Shuiwei) celebrated the 100th anniversary of the conversion of Mr. Zhong Qin. Since his conversion represented the beginning of the Catholic community in Shuiwei, he was considered the founder of Catholicism in the whole area of Lunbei. Through this celebration the conversion of Zhong Qin acquired a great importance not only within the Zhong family but among the whole Lunbei's Catholic community.

In that occasion the image of Zhong Qin was reconstructed through the few images (a very old portrait of himself and another one with his second wife) found in the homes of the faithful. Also the image of the wife has been "revalued" and put—together with the husband—inside the church of Shuiwei and in the house of many members of the Zhong family. Figure 4.2 describes the interior of the church in Shuiwei. These portraits are hung on the wall just beside the church main door.

Linked with the celebration of the 100th anniversary is the reconstruction of the family tree of the Zhong family. Zhong Kunmao, the young man who did it, told me: "Usually all the families in Taiwan have their family tree, but the old people of my house are not so interested in collecting their history. For me it is important to know and to collect the history of my family." Kunmao told me that contrariwise to the Taiwanese tradition, the old generation of Catholics in Shuiwei have no idea about the root of their family tree. Usually, this kind of information is taken in great account in Taiwan. Almost every family has a book, called 族譜 *zúpǔ*, where

Fig. 4.2 The images of Mr. Zhong Qin and his second wife

information is written about the province of origin in Mainland China and how many generations of the family have been resettled in Taiwan. In the Taiwanese context, in fact, the importance of the family lineage and history is strongly related to the cult of ancestors, perhaps one of the most important features in Chinese culture.

All this information is missing in the Catholic community. The family tree significantly starts with Mr. Zhong Qin.

This situation will be discussed more in depth when talking about other elements. Anyway, I want to introduce now the idea that the sense of "indifference" for their family history shared by the older generations of the Zhong family is linked with their conversion to the Catholic faith. More specifically, this "indifference" is related with the approach to evangelization chosen by the Dominican missionaries who, from 1859 until the end of the Second World War, were the only Catholic missionaries working in Taiwan.

Perhaps at this point, it is better to slow down and let *Historia* follow *Kleion* or, in other words, let the historical documents help us to frame, within a precise historical time, the history of the Catholic community of Shuiwei. In order to do this, I consider it necessary to give to the reader some brief information about the history of the evangelization of Taiwan, which will be helpful to better understand the unification process of the Shuiwei Catholic community with the parish of Lunbei.

4.3.2 A Brief History of the Taiwanese Catholic church

In 2009, the Taiwanese Catholic church celebrated its 150th anniversary. Linked to this important occasion, the Bishops' Conference of Taiwan organized several activities: new books on Catholic faith and on the history of Catholicism in Taiwan were published, old churches were restored, but the most important was a pilgrimage of a statue of the Holy Mary that reached every parish of the island. During the inaugural Mass for the 150th anniversary, the Cardinal of Kaohsiung, Paul Shan, asked for a new effort of evangelization with a request to reach the quota of 10,000 new baptisms during that year. The 150 years have been counted from 1859, the time when the Dominicans arrived in the village of 萬金 Wanjin (屏東縣 Pingtung County), where is located the 萬金聖母聖殿 *Wanjin shèngmǔ shèngdiàn*, the Catholic Basilica in Taiwan of the Immaculate Conception. The first missionaries to arrive on the island were the Spaniard Dominicans, who came to Taiwan from the Philippines.[4] In fact, the first encounter between the Dominicans and the local population of Taiwan could be dated back on 1626. It is because of this first contact that historians and other scholars agree on dividing the work of the Dominican missionaries in Taiwan into three phases (Verbist 2004; Fernandez et al. 1994; 古偉瀛 1998). The first phase of evangelization took place under the Spanish occupation of the northern part of the island (1626–1642) and ended with the destruction of the Catholic church by the Dutch.[5] Only after 200 years, during the last years of the Manchu, a second evangelization process (1859–1895) started, which was followed by a

---

[4] The arrival of these first missionaries should be read within a more geopolitical structure of relationships between European governments (especially Spain and Portugal) and started in the fifteenth century with the Treaty of Tordesillas (1494).

[5] The Dutch East India Company merchants were present in Tainan since 1624. They used Taiwan as a colonial trading center for goods shipped between Asia and Europe.

third period under Japanese rule (1895–1945). In all these periods, the evangelization project had been carried out by the Dominican fathers. After the Second World War it is possible to recognize a new phase of the history of the Catholic church in Taiwan. In 1949 the Nationalist government of China (Kuomintang) moved from Mainland China to Taiwan. At that time, many religious orders and priests came to Taiwan after leaving Mainland China because of the Communist persecution, changing in depth the process of evangelization.

As mentioned above, only in 1859 were Dominicans able to return to and settle down in Taiwan. The characterizing event of those years in China was the Second Opium War (1856–1860). On June 26, 1858, the Treaty of Tianjin between the Chinese empire and the Western colonial governments was ratified. This treaty turned out to be less negotiation and more diktat. "By the terms of the agreement, a large portion of China would be opened to British trade. The Chinese would pay $5 million in war reparations, Christian missionaries would be allowed to proselytize unhindered throughout the country, and eleven more ports would be opened to foreign ships" (Hanes and Sanello 2002, p. 222).

A majority of the Chinese people felt humiliated by the defeat suffered by the Chinese empire under the Qing Dynasty and, more important, the unequal treaties of peace that followed the Chinese defeat. One of the consequences linked with these treaties has been the several popular rebellions such as the Taiping (1850–1864), the Boxer Rebellion (1899–1901), and even the downfall of the Qing Dynasty in 1912, which meant the end of dynastic China. In fact, since the Opium wars, the Chinese government and Chinese people considered Christianity a foreign religion and, more important, imported by colonial powers by war and weapons (李若文 1997).

To this situation are linked many difficulties against which the Dominicans had to battle during the last years of the Qing Dynasty. These difficulties were the greatest obstacle to the mission's progress. The missionaries had little defense. They were too far removed from Beijing, and for them it was useless to appeal to the Treaties of Tianjin (Fernandez et al. 1994, pp. 77,99). This situation was a consequence created by the two Opium wars between China and the European countries. The missionaries explicitly described the "rancor that they [Chinese people] harbor in their hearts against anything that smacks of Europe and the Europeans" (Fernandez et al. 1994, p. 99).

Starting from these historical considerations, it is easy to understand the strong feeling of hostility by which the Taiwanese people (at least the largest part of them) received the first Spanish missionaries coming from the Philippines. They have been arrested by the local Mandarins, kidnapped, robbed; their houses and churches destroyed, looted, and burned by the local population (Fernandez et al. 1994; 古偉瀛 1998; 江傳德 2008; Ku 2000). Even today it is possible to recognize the hostility that many people continue to express toward the Christian faith and the Christians. During my fieldwork, I heard people refer several times to the Christian faith as something belonging to the West (西方宗教 *xīfāng zōngjiào*), something belonging, thus, to another tradition and another way of life.

Even in Lunbei, where the presence of the Catholic church is much more accepted than in other communities I visited, the owner of one of the lands neighboring with the parish put on the wall of his house a mirror facing the church. The meaning of putting a mirror outside the house facing "dangerous" structures or places (such as a road) is linked to the Daoist belief that ghosts and spirits—which mean dangerous entities—will be scared if they see themselves in the mirror. This idea of danger is linked with the fear of something that changes (or attempts to change) a predetermined order. For example, as we previously described in Topos, the traditional house in Taiwan is built according to the concepts of dragon and tiger. These concepts are related also with the construction which is beside the house. The dragon side should be higher than the tiger one. When this rule is disregarded (e.g. with the construction of a higher building on the tiger side), it is possible to put a mirror on the side of the house that faces the disharmonious element. The presence of the mirror will help to ward off all the bad luck coming from inauspicious situations. In Lunbei (but also in metropolises such as Taipei or Hong Kong), it is possible to see mirrors almost everywhere, on particular crossroads (Fig. 3.4), on balconies, and even on the doors of some apartments. Therefore, the church of Lunbei is, at least for some of its neighbors, a potentially dangerous place.

4.3.3 How Catholicism Arrived in Shuiwei

As I already introduced, Dominicans arrived first in the southern part of Taiwan in 1859. Only a few years later, around 1869 (古偉瀛 1998, p. 24), they moved toward the central and the northern part of Taiwan, establishing small communities especially in the current provinces of Chiayi, Yunlin, and Changhua (古偉瀛 1998; Fernandez et al. 1994; 江傳德 2008). The missionaries created a net of churches, chapels, and small communities that, because of the shortage of missionaries, could be reached in a day's walk.

Apart from the shortage of missionaries, this tactic was conceived to protect the missionaries from robberies, assaults, and other dangerous circumstances they can encounter on the road, especially at night (Ku 2000, p. 30).

In this way Fr. Francesco Herce in 1886 wrote to his Provincial Father in Manila:

> I am convinced that it would not be wise for us missionaries to be separated from each other by distances greater than a day's journey. I say this because we are exposed daily to dangers, dangers that may threaten both our souls and our bodies. These dangers would be minimized if we could get together more often, and that would be impossible if we lived too far away from each other.
>
> (Fernandez et al. 1994, p. 160)

Therefore we can see how from 鹿寮 Luliao in Yunlin County to 台中 Taichung there were many mission centers near one another.[6]

The missionary was not the only person to move around these centers. Often the missionary lived in a place where the believers who lived in the nearby villages joined him for the celebration of the Sunday Mass.

Whenever possible, in order to keep the faith and, above all, to give a deeper Catholic education to these young communities, the Dominicans left a catechist in the communities just founded. The importance of these catechists was so great that the Dominicans considered them as "the only one recourse to do our work" (Fernandez et al. 1994, p. 141). According to a letter written in 1872, the missionary work was led in this way:

> [The] catechists first try to win the natives over, to make them feel more kindly disposed toward us [the Dominican fathers]. At this time, the missionary must keep himself in the background, not intruding, not forcing himself on the natives. After a time, after the catechist has done his work, the missionary may step in and begin harvesting the grain from the seed that the catechists had sown.
>
> (Fernandez et al. 1994, p. 141)

---

[6] For those interested, please refer to the map at http://ace.uoc.edu/items/show/1082.

The evangelization of the central part of Taiwan started in 1869, when a man who lived in Zhu-a-ka (竹仔腳 nowadays 彰化縣員林鎮永靖鄉 Changhua County, Yuanlin City, Yongjing Township) went to Kaohsiung and met the Dominican superior Fr. Andres Chinchon, asking him to send a missionary to his place. Since there were no available missionaries, in 1872 the superior sent a catechist, Placido A-Sieng-Ko, to Zhu-a-ka where he opened a catechism class. The environment was very hostile to the Catholic faith, and in addition Placido A-Sieng-Ko retired because of his age. The new catechist, 林水龍 Lin Shuilong, could not continue the work of Placido. As a result, the first missionary station in central Taiwan had been closed (古偉瀛 1998, 25-6; 江傳德 2008, 118-9). This failure marked the first approach to the central part of Taiwan made by the Dominican missionaries.

We have to wait until 1875 when, in a very similar situation, a man from 羅厝莊 *Luócuò* (nowadays 彰化縣埔心鄉羅厝村 Changhua County, Puxin Township, Luocuo Village) who often went to Southern Taiwan for business, listened to a priest's sermon in Kaohsiung and became interested in the Catholic faith. He shared his experience of faith with his family and with some neighbors and in 1875 asked Fr. Chinchon to send a priest to their community. In 1877 Fr. Vicente Gomar was sent to Luocuo where, since the place was not too far from Zhu-a-ka, he bought land and established the first permanent mission in central Taiwan (古偉瀛 1998, p. 26; 江傳德 2008, p. 119-20).

Since the distance from Luocuo and the nearest mission station (臺南 Tainan) was four days away by foot (Ku 1998:27), the Dominicans decided to open another mission station in between. Therefore, in 1876 a mission station was opened at 沙崙仔 Sha-lun-a (nowadays 嘉義縣大林鎮中坑 Chiayi County, Dalin City, Zhongken), and Fr. Jose Nebot and a catechist were put in charge of it (古偉瀛 1998, p. 27; 江傳德 2008, pp. 127–132).

Here, since the historical data that describes this period and these places are incomplete, I have to (metaphorically) close the books and the articles about the history of the Church in Taiwan and to begin to use part of the material I collected during my fieldwork. This material comes from interviews with the parishioners of the Churches of Shuiwei, Lunbei, Raoping (Chu-a-ka, nowadays also 莿桐鄉 Citong Township, Yunlin County), and Siluo, from the archives of these Churches and from interviews with parish priests and with the bishops of the Diocese of Chiayi.

The historical reconstructions I collected are melded with the narration of them and above all with the ineffable and fluctuating experience of narration. These documents have a historical data foundation, and I personally found and read many churches archives, but passing through the kaleidoscope of the narration these data, although they conserved the same core, developed different images of historical facts and their development.

As we saw above, in central Taiwan there were two churches, in Luocuo and in Sha-lun-a. Sha-lun-a was the central point between Luocuo and Tainan, and the priest in charge of evangelizing the surrounding territories arrived at 斗六 Douliou (Yunlin County) and Siluo (Yunlin County) where he started a catechumenate (古偉瀛 1998, p. 28; 江傳德 2008, p. 133-4).

The priests in charge of these two parishes regularly traveled, by foot or by bicycle, between these two places in order to keep their communitarian way of life and for exchange pastoral experiences. Since there was a stream that should be crossed, the 濁水溪 *Zhuóshuǐ* Stream (which marks the boundary between the counties of Changhua and Yunlin), they had to take a bamboo raft in 樹仔腳 Chu-a-ka.

Over time, as they had done this trip many times, they became good friends of the captain of the bamboo raft and started to talk with him and his family about the Gospel. This fortuitous meeting, the fact that they really needed a place near the stream where to spend the night if the stream was overflow during the typhoon season, and the fact that they already started to evangelize many places in the surrounding areas (such as Siluo or Douliou) helped the Dominicans to make the decision to build another mission station in this place in 1880. In 1890 Chu-a-ka faithfuls went to Luocuo asking the parish priest of that time, Fr. Francisco Giner, to come to their place. They rented a little house made of bamboo that served as a chapel and as a mission station. This was probably the first church in Yunlin County.

During this period, the Shuiwei Catholic community was linked with Chu-a-ka and with the activities of the Dominican fathers in Yunlin and Changhua. According to the parishioners' accounts and their historical data, the conversion of Mr. Zhong Qin had happened in 1905, since this time the history of Shuiwei community started to be linked with the Catholic community in Chu-a-ka, which was the nearest church to Shuiwei village. After the conversion of Mr. Zhong Qin, Fr. Angel Rodriguez, the priest in charge of Chu-a-ka, established a catechism station in Shuiwei. The Catholics of Shuiwei started to attend the Holy Mass in Chu-a-ka, which is about 20 kilometers from Shuiwei village. According to the memories of the old believers, on Sunday three different groups of believers left the village in order to attend the Mass: the first group was the women and children. Because they walked slower, they left home when the sky was still dark, around four o'clock in the morning. The second group of people consisted of the men and the younger generations. Since they walked faster than the women, they left home around five o'clock. The last group was the elderly people, not because they could run faster than the other groups but because they rode bicycles. The sky was already completely clear, around eight o'clock or even earlier. The three groups arrived in Chu-a-ka almost at the same time, and after the Mass, a meeting with the priest, and a good rest, they went back home.

In 1934 a missionary station was established in Shuiwei, and Mr. Zhong Qin offered to Fr. Vincent Prada, who was taking care of Chu-a-ka parish, to build a little church on his land. Fr. Prada sent a catechist, Mr. Zhang Maorong (a Presbyterian converted to Catholicism), to preach the Catholic faith in the village. Since that time, and since the construction of a little church, sometimes the Sunday Holy Mass was celebrated in Shuiwei village.

As it will be underlined in the next chapters, because of this changing of faith, the relationships among the extended Zhong family became cooler in a certain sense. Catholic people were forbidden by the Dominicans to take part to the traditional ancestral ceremonies at the family temple. They were also forbidden to get married with non-Catholics. Because of this, many Catholics in Shuiwei married women from the Catholic village 二林Erlin (Changhua County), starting a cross-marriage tradition and building a small community of the Zhong family in Changhua. Since Shuiwei village is the first village in Lunbei that accepted the Christian religion, until now, the majority of Protestants and Catholic believers still live in this village (廖淑玲 2005). Anyway, the Catholic faith is well represented also in Lunbei. On the next pages, I will explain how the history of Shuiwei melded together with the one of Lunbei parish.

4.3.4 *Modern Times: Shuiwei and Lunbei Catholic Communities*

With the arrival of the troupes of Chiang Kai-shek, and the numerous refugees from the mainland in 1949, started what I called the fourth period of evangelization of Taiwan. In 1950, the government of the People's Republic of China decided to expel all the foreign missionaries from China. Chinese priests, and a few Chinese bishops, sought refuge in Taiwan in order to escape from the persecution. Many congregations also came to Taiwan and started to build hospitals, schools, churches, dispensaries, and so on. Missionaries who came from China already knew Mandarin Chinese and were already used to the Chinese lifestyle. After 1950, thus, the history of the Taiwanese Catholic church met a big change. A good number of foreigners or Mainlander priests arrived in Taiwan.

The number of the Dioceses increased as well as the number of the parishes and, of course, the number of missionaries. Just to give a concrete example of how much the situation of the Catholic church in Taiwan changed in this short time, it could be useful to mention that 14 Dominican Friars, 4 autochthonous priests, and 10 sisters, with 13,253 faithfuls, were working in Taiwan on March 5, 1948 (Verbist 2004; Borao 2009, p. 33). A few years later, in 1956, there were 306 foreign Catholic priests and 95 Chinese Catholic priests in Taiwan.

Catholic churches have been built not only in the big city but also in many villages. From 1955 to 1959, the number of believers increased from 48,000 to 182,000 people. In 1969, there were in Taiwan more than 300,000 Catholic Christians; one-third of them were aboriginal people or Chinese from the mainland (穆蒙 Motte 1971, p. 165).

The Diocese of Chiayi, where the parish of Shuiwei is located, was founded in 1952. The first appointed bishop was 牛故主教 Bishop Niu Ku, a bishop who came from Mainland China's 湖南省 Hunan province. Because of his presence, many priests and missionaries who had been expelled from Hunan and other provinces of Northern China came to the Diocese of Chiayi, some of them passing through the Philippines. In 1953 six priests from the Philippines came into Chiayi Diocese: from the 兌啞教區 Diocese of Duizhou, Fr. Sun Jishan and Fr. Zhang Xiangming; from 陽穀教區 Yanggu Diocese, Fr. Gao Shuren; and from the 青島教區 Diocese of Qingdao, Fr. Liu Daoquan, Fr. Tian Bin, and Fr. Zhao Zhonglu.

At the beginning, these above-mentioned priests were living in Douliou, bringing on a community life under the leadership of the bishop. Bishop Niu every Saturday assigned to the priests the place where to celebrate the Holy Mass. Some of them were sent—by bicycle—to Shuiwei to celebrate the Holy Mass. After this first moment, Fr. Liu Daoquan and Fr. Tian Bin became parish priests of the parish of Lunbei, where, in the meantime—and with the help of these new priests—some families had converted to Catholicism.

In 1957, five priests came from Bishop Niu's province Hunan (an Italian Franciscan named Fr. Ti Ximen (Simone) and four Mainlanders, Fr. Guo Xianguang, Fr. Guo Qinsan, Fr. Guo Feiji, and, a little later than the others, Fr. Guo Pandeng), because they were invited by Bishop Niu to take care of the parish of Lunbei. Fr. Simone, a Franciscan, bought a piece of land in Lunbei and built a church. It is worth mentioning here that in these years the situation inside the Catholic church in Taiwan was very confusing. Many priests coming from Mainland China continued to be linked with their previous bishops in China and did not consider themselves subject to the authority of the local Taiwanese bishops. This could explain why the Franciscan order in Taiwan was not aware that a priest belonging to their order was in Lunbei and that he had even bought a piece of land.

After that, Fr. Simone left in 1958, the other fathers who came with him continued to take care of the new parish of Lunbei, while Fr. Liu Daoquan continued to follow the community in Shuiwei. This situation continued till 1968, when two new churches were built in place of the old ones, one in Lunbei and one in Shuiwei. At that time Bishop Niu nominated Fr. Liu Daoquan to be in charge of both churches. He celebrated the Holy Mass in Shuiwei on Saturday night and the Mass in Lunbei on Sunday morning. Fr. Tian Bin also maintained this practice when he became parish priest of Lunbei in 1974. Only years later, around 2002, because Fr. Tian had become too old to handle two churches and because his health progressively got worse, the bishop reunified the two parishes. Therefore, to present day the Holy Mass is celebrated in Lunbei on Saturday night for both Lunbei and Shuiwei.

As many historians have (穆蒙 Motte 1971, p. 167), I described the period after the Second World War as a "golden period" for the Catholic church in Taiwan, with a considerable number of missionaries working all over Taiwan in big and small villages. This period of "abundance" of missionaries is confirmed by the narrations of Shuiwei faithfuls. When I talk about missionaries, I mean not only priests and friars belonging to the many religious orders which are present today in Taiwan but also the many nuns who take care of the kindergarten, hospitals, and schools. They, according to the words of Zhong Yinghui (an almost 40-year-old woman now living outside Shuiwei), were also taking care of the Catholic education of the children:

> When we were kids, every summer a nun came to stay with us for one month. I remember that one year one of the bishop's sisters came, but usually it was another nun. During the morning we prayed and then the nun read us some pages of the Gospel, or she gave us some lessons of catechism. All the Catholic kids of the village must take part, therefore all the children of the Zhong and

Li families met each other every morning. We all were like a family (我們是一家人 *Wŏmen shì yījiārén*), it was a lot of fun (很好玩 *Hén hăowán*).

At present, after 100 years and over 5 generations from the conversion of Mr. Zhong Qin, two-thirds of the Shuiwei village are involved in the Christian (one-third Protestant and one-third Catholic) faith. During my fieldwork, the Holy Mass was celebrated in Lunbei, while the church in Shuiwei was used as catechism class for the children or as classroom for study group activities. Moreover, every day at 8 pm, many of the elderly people of Shuiwei go to the church to pray the Holy Rosary. At the beginning of my fieldwork, a very important role was played by the parish priest. He was a Taiwanese man who was often invited to the activities organized by the Township government, and by many temples, because of his ability to make Italian coffee or because he was a member of the Yunlin County Bird Association. One year after our arrival (2008), he left Lunbei and went to take care of another parish, and the priest of Siluo took care of the Lunbei parish.

Recently the parish council decided to rebuild the church of Lunbei. The old one will be demolished and a new one will be built in its place. Since the church has been demolished, from January 1, 2016, the Mass is celebrated in Shuiwei for both communities.

4.4 THE CHINESE RITES CONTROVERSY AND THE DOMINICAN IN TAIWAN: HISTORY OR EPOS?

With the above-mentioned history of Taiwan, I tried to show how the Catholic church in Taiwan never reached a hegemonic position on the cultural horizon of the island. Due to the small number of missionaries and many historical and cultural misunderstandings, Taiwanese people felt that the Catholic religion, as well as Christianity, was not autochthonous but brought from outside. And this is still true for many Taiwanese people (Lazzarotti 2008, p. 69).

At the same time, it is not uncommon to find priests or other religious individuals who still complain about the "Taiwanese Idols" and about their own believers who attend the rites of the Church as though they still went to the temple. Western missionaries (and, for that matter, Western-educated Chinese clergymen) have been looking at the pantheon of the popular Chinese religion as if it was the pagan religion of ancient Greece and Rome or the religion of the heathen Canaanites descried by the Biblical prophets (Bresciani 2006, p. 109).

The description of the other as something anyway linked with negative values influenced and built the view of the other as a stranger and an enemy. This interpretive background melded the negative value of judgment that is immanent to almost all the narration that Taiwanese people make in order to describe Christianity, and it is present in the narration that Christians make about the local customs linked with the Taiwanese Popular Religion.

This fact is well explained by Eco when he affirms that "having an enemy is important not only to define our identity but also to provide us with an obstacle against which to measure our system of values and, in seeking to overcome it, to demonstrate our own worth. So when there is no enemy, we have to invent one" (Eco 2012, p. 46).

Until 1949 Dominican missionaries have been the only Catholic missionaries present in Taiwan. The evangelization project of the Dominican missionaries prompted a clean cut from local culture and practices. This approach has deep roots in centuries of experience of evangelization in China. The Dominicans' experience was created and molded by the encounter with the local population but also by the contrast they had with the Jesuits, the missionaries who started the Chinese mission. The contrast between these two religious orders about the way to evangelize the Chinese empire reached unbelievable levels of accusation and mistrust. Scholars refer to their clash as the Chinese Rites Controversy. This controversy erupted in the seventeenth century and was not resolved until the twentieth century when Pope Pius XII issued an instruction entitled *Plane compertum est* which allowed Chinese Catholics to take part in civil ceremonies honoring Confucius and the familial dead (Minamiki et al. 1985, p. 197).

By definition, the term "Chinese Rites" does not refer to any indigenous Chinese ritual but to three specific customs. First, periodic ceremonies performed in honor of Confucius, in temples or halls dedicated to the well-respected Chinese philosopher. Second, the veneration of the familial dead, a practice found in every social class and manifested by various forms of piety including prostration, incense burning, food serving, and so on. Third, the missionary use of the terms 天 *Tiān* (heaven) and 上帝 *Shàngdì* (lord of heaven) to convey the Christian concept of God (Chan 2000, p. 29).

This controversy, which has marked all the missionary works in China, has deep and complex theological and doctrinal roots. It involves concepts such as idolatry, idols, and heresy that, as I above mentioned, continue to be present in the vocabulary of many missionaries in Taiwan. Dominicans, in opposition to Jesuits, rejected these practices, thereby characterizing them as "pagan," "idolatrous," and "superstitious." They opposed Matteo Ricci's indulging position and prohibited believers from maintaining their ancestors' tablet and venerating them.[7] Chinese people who wanted to embrace the Catholic faith were obliged to burn down their ancestors' tablet and any image of Confucius present in their home.

One of the practical consequences of this missionary approach was prohibition of the believers to participate with their family in the traditional ceremonies for the ancestors which were (and still are today) performed during the lunar New Year or on other occasions. The system of evangelization carried out by Dominican missionaries had a great impact on the life of the Taiwanese people who converted to Catholicism. These restrictions often influenced the social and family structure of the converted. Chinese people particularly stressed the "communitarian," the familiar and social dimension of the religious life. Therefore the change of faith, linked with all the prohibitions that a faithful had to accept, made a big change also in the familiar and social structure of the communities that embraced the Catholic faith. In the next chapter (Genos), I will describe in detail how this method of evangelization melded the contemporary situation of Shuiwei and especially of the Zhong family. Now, it is important to note that in molding the social context, these prohibitions, and above all the practices linked with the new religion, molded the narrations about Shuiwei. And consequentially they molded Shuiwei as a place full of agencies, as a locus concretely able to interfere with the people who live inside and outside its boundaries. The narration about Shuiwei, and about the people who inhabit it, has roots in the concept of epos created by the immanent—and negative—value of judgment linked with the Dominicans' missionary approach. The missionary approach that has developed following the dispute with the Jesuits did not change much even after the Second Vatican Council. The aim for acculturation promoted by the Second Vatican Council was concretely applied in Taiwan by allowing the Catholic believers to keep their ancestor's tablets at their home. The Taiwanese Catholics were also allowed to take part in the ceremonies for the ancestors. The veneration of the ancestors was also allowed inside the churches and

---

[7] Matteo Ricci, SJ (1552–1610), known by the Chinese people as 利瑪竇 Lì Mǎdòu, was an Italian Jesuit priest and one of the founding figures of the Jesuit mission in Mainland China.

the ritual of the Mass. The Bishops' Conference of Taiwan introduced the possibility of putting ancestor's tablet inside the church to represent the souls of the deceased faithful. The Dominicans, once again, opposed this permission because according to the Popular Religion tradition, the souls of the deceased should be venerated only by the family of deceased. Strangers cannot venerate ancestors belonging to other families. As one priest told me, "when you don't want to do something, you will find all kind of excuses to not do it!" It is possible to see here, in this last example, how the tensions, and especially the epos, generated from the Rites Controversy is still vivid and present in the Dominican way of evangelization.

I defined epos as the symbolic transformation of historical memory, as a way to memorialize the common past. From a certain point of view, however, epos is not only the symbolization that a specific group of people make of its own past. From another point of view, epos comes also from the mythicizing of the past of a neighboring group of people, especially if this process of mythicizing is based on the underlying, immanent differences between the two social groups.

4.5 Epos, Stories, History, and Everyday Life

I already discussed at the beginning of this chapter how epos could be considered the symbolic transformation of the historical memory of a group of people. This transformation finds its more appropriate expression in the narrative about a common and shared past or, in other words, about a precise historical time. The symbols created, or re-semantized, during this process and the related historical narrative (then also epos) are embodied in the many episodes of the Shuiwei people's everyday life. These episodes and the composition of the social fabric of the village become symbols (certainly silent but under the eyes of everyone) of Shuiwei historical experience. These symbols, when stimulated by the questions of the anthropologist, are expressed in a myriad of stories that in turn create the village's historical background, creating then the epos.

I will give just a few brief examples that will help me materialize the concepts I expressed above. First I would like to explain how the social fabric of the village can show the historical roots of the village. In the village of Shuiwei, the Catholic population includes four generations. Eldest people, who in the case of the 李 Li family were the first generation to convert, are now more than 80 years old (Introduction, Sect. 1.2.3). Their children already started to have grandchildren. If we analyze the composition of the village using the married couples as a parameter, it is possible to observe an interesting phenomenon. The composition of the couples belonging to the older generation (people in their 80s or 70s) shows that both the husband and the wife are Catholics and come from traditional Catholic families.[8] The generation of their children (both males and females) is much more varied. Some are married to women from traditional Catholic families, but most of them have wives (or husbands) who come from non-Christian families. Anyway, all the spouses had to convert in order to become a member of the Zhong family. This trend is also followed in the third and the fourth generations, which in most instances have completed their education outside the village.

This situation reflects the historical patterns which the village has passed through. And this happened because the history of the village met with the history of the Taiwanese Catholic church. This meeting has created a particular local history that shows itself in the composition of the married couples within the Catholic community.

Elderly people have a lot of stories about this situation. They told me that when they got married, the priest, a Dominican, acted as matchmaker. He forbade the Catholic believers from marrying persons from non-Catholic families. As I already introduced in the previous pages of this chapter, the Dominican missionaries had to move around a lot of places to visit the Catholic communities. They were always connected with other missionaries around the island. Taking advantage of this situation, the missionaries introduced families who had children in the age of marriage to the "right" Catholic partner.[9]

I described this situation in my field note:

---

[8] It is important to note that in traditional Taiwan, marriage was arranged by matchmakers who negotiate between sets of people referred to as wife-takers and wife-givers. The bride and groom rarely had much to do with the marriage negotiations. This, of course, has changed dramatically since the mid-1980s. See Watson (1982) or the work in Taiwan of Margery Wolf (1972).

[9] It is important to note that, according to the Chinese tradition, the sons continue to live in the ancestral village and inherit the fields and the house. Women are traditionally considered to belong to another family since their birth. The reasons are many, but they can be embodied in the phrase "they (the women) will pray other people ancestors" "她們要拜別人的祖先." I will discuss this aspect further in the next chapters.

Today I discovered that the wife of Zhong Jing-Yi was not Catholic before their wedding [Jing-Yi belongs to the third generation of Zhong Catholics. See Genos, Sect. 5.4]. As usual here in Shuiwei, she has been baptized on the day of her wedding. During the wedding Mass she also received the sacrament of Eucharist. Since I heard that it was forbidden by the Dominican missionaries to marry non-Catholic women, I asked to Jing-Yi how he managed to get a non-Catholic wife. He told me that at that time it was allowed, but the wife should accept the Catholic faith and receive the baptism. Besides, he told me, when they got married the priests were not Dominicans. In fact, Fr. Tian Bin was already in charge of the parish. Jing-Yi told me an interesting story about the wedding rules during the Dominicans' time: "When I was a kid, I remember very well the fathers [missionaries]. I also remember that they were much more strict than our current priest. Once, one of our uncles let his daughter to marry a Presbyterian who lived – and still lives – in our village. At that time, it was not allowed for Catholics to marry people of other religions, not even a Presbyterian. The priest was so angry that he forbade our uncle to receive the Holy Communion. I don't remember how long this prohibition of taking the Communion lasted, but I think it lasted for a very long time."

One of the consequences of this practice (also linked to the fact that in the extremely androcentric Chinese society it was, and in many aspects still is, the bride who usually moves into the household of her father-in-law) was that, at that time, many of the daughters of the Zhong family married men of the village of 二林 Erlin in the neighboring county of Changhua, which is relatively close (although separated by the 濁水溪 stream *Zhuóshuǐ*) to Shuiwei. This exchange continued also, even if in a reduced manner, during the third generation, creating a network of contacts and relationships that united and characterized these two villages.

Regarding the third generation, both sons and daughters of the Zhong family could marry non-Catholics. The requirement for brides was that they had to convert and be baptized. This is still a requirement for the fourth generation, but the fundamental difference is that young couples usually choose not to live in the village or in their parents' homes because of their work.

We will come back again to this interesting phenomenon, which is linked with the concept of genos, but we can see here how the history of the village openly reveals itself in its social fabrics.

References

Altan, C.T. 1995. *Ethnos e Civiltà. Identità Etniche e Valori Democratici*. Milano: Feltrinelli.
Borao, J.E. 1993. The Aborigines of Northern Taiwan According to the xviith Spanish Sources. *Newsletter of Taiwan History Field Research* 27: 98–120.
———. 2009. Dominicos Españoles en Taiwan (1859–1960): Primer Siglo de Historia de la Iglesia Católica en la Isla. *Encuentros en Catay* 23: 1–46.
Bresciani, U. 2006. The Future of Christianity in China. *Quaderni del Centro Studi Asiatico* 1 (3): 101–111.
Chan, D.A.S. 2000. *Weaving a Dream, Reflection for Chinese Filipino, Catholics today*. Quezon City: Jesuit Communications.
CRBC. 2008. Bishop Thomas Chung. https://www.catholic.org.tw/en/bishopthomas.html. Accessed July 3, 2017.
Eco, U. 2012. *Inventing the Enemy and Other Occasional Writings*. Boston: Houghton Mifflin Harcourt.
Fernandez, P., F.B. Bautista, and L. Syquia-Bautista. 1994. *One Hundred Years of Dominican Apostolate in Formosa (1859–1958): Extracts from the Sino-Annamite Letters, Dominican Missions and Ultramar*. Taipei: SMC Publishing Inc.
Hanes, W.T., and F. Sanello. 2002. *The Opium Wars: The Addiction of One Empire and the Corruption of Another*. Naperville: Sourcebooks, Inc.
Ku, W.-y. 2000. Conflicts, Confusion and Control: Some Observations on Missionary Cases. In *Footsteps in Deserted Valleys: Missionary Cases, Strategies and Practice in Qing China*, ed. K. De Ridder, 11–38. Leuven: Leuven University Press.
Lazzarotti, M. 2008. The Ancestors' Rites in the Taiwanese Catholic Church. Master's thesis, National Taiwan University, Taipei.
Minamiki, G., et al. 1985. *The Chinese Rites Controversy from Its Beginning to Modern Times*. Chicago: Loyola University Press Chicago.
Verbist, S.N. 2004. Special Issue on the Catholic Church in Taiwan: 1626–1965.
Watson, J.L. 1982. Chinese Kinship Reconsidered: Anthropological Perspectives on Historical Research. *The China Quarterly* 92: 589–622.
Wolf, M. 1972. *Women and the Family in Rural Taiwan*. Stanford: Stanford University Press.
李若文. 1997. 晚清教案研究的回顧與展望. 中華民國史專題論文集—第四屆討論會.
古偉瀛. 1998. 十九世紀台灣天主教(1859–1895)——策? 及發展. 臺大歷史學報 22: 091–123.
廖淑玲. 2005. 掌中葡背. Yunlin County Government.
江傳德. 2008. 天主教在臺灣. Wendao chubanshe.
穆蒙 Motte, J.S. 1971. 中國天主教史. 臺中:光.

CHAPTER 5

Genos

5.1 Narrating Genos

During the Japanese occupation, the government decided to forbid Taiwanese people to bury their dead close to residential areas. Our ancestor, Mr. Zhong Qin, who had been the first to convert to Catholicism, died during the Japanese occupation. His sons and family, rather than bringing him to the common cemetery, decided to bury him secretly near their home. Since they were afraid that it would be discovered, they did not even build a tomb.

This is why until now, we don't have any traditional grave for Mr. Zhong Qin and his wife. What we have here are two stones with their names engraved on it. We know that they are here and this is enough.

A-Mao, Catholic believer. Spring 2008

The choice of the name is a very important matter for us [Taiwanese people]. Five brothers of our family decided to concretely show their faith. They agreed that to their first-born males should be assigned Christian names.

Because of this now we have 路加 *Lùjiā* (Luke), 若瑟 *Ruòsè* (Joseph), 瑪竇 *Mǎdòu* (Matthew), 保錄 *Bǎolù* (Paul), and 米格 *Mǐgé* (Michael).

Feng-rong, Catholic believer. Summer 2010

The first time I heard someone talking about 米格 Mǐgé (Michael) I did not understand if they were talking about a person, a Soviet warplane, or about a person whose father loved so much the Soviet warplane.[1]

                              Mr. Cheng, non-Christian. Summer 2008

The Zhong family in Lunbei is believed to come from an ethnic group in China, the Hakka. They are Hakka people, but unlike all other Hakka in Taiwan which come from the province of Canton, they come from the Fujian province, precisely from the Zhaoan county, which is located in the municipal region of Zhangzhou, in the Fujian province. There is a story about the Zhong family and their origins.

    Long time ago the Chinese emperor was struggling against some enemies who wanted to occupy the Chinese empire. Since the situation was difficult he asked help from the people. He promised that he would give his daughter in marriage to the man who would help him to defeat his enemies. Only a dog showed up and agreed to fight for the emperor. The dog was able to defeat the enemies and presented himself to the emperor in order to marry his daughter. As promised, the emperor consented the marriage, but he ordered the dog to stay 30 days under a large bell. After that, the dog would become a man, which surname would be Zhong (鍾 *Zhōng*) that in Chinese means bell. The twenty-ninth day, the princess, who wanted to make sure that the dog was really transforming, raised the bell to have a look. As a result of this action, the process of transformation was stopped and the dog became a man with a dog's head. Even with the head of a dog, the dog hero married the Princess. They had several children. They put the first on a plate, therefore the child's surname was盤 *Pán* (Plate). The second one was put in a basket, therefore his surname was 籃 *Lán* (Basket). The third one was born during a storm, therefore they decided to give him the surname 雷 *Léi* (Thunder). The funny part of this story is that the ancestor of the Zhong family is a dog. Maybe it is because of this that when they pray for their ancestors, they still prepare food for the dog which it is put on a very small and short table.[2]

                        Li Ri-quan, non-Catholic. Local politician. Autumn 2008

After the Mass, my family and I followed the procession of the Zhong family to the tombs of their ancestors. The bishop blessed the tombs and a stick of

---

[1] The person, a non-Catholic in Lunbei, was referring to the Soviet warplane MiG, which in Chinese is translated with the same characters—and clearly with the same sound—of the name of the Catholic faithful Michael, 米格 Mǐgé.

[2] This story is present, with some minor changes from the version I heard, in the book of 朱介凡 (1989).

incense was offered to all the members of the family. Someone put the stick of incense in my hand. Surprised, I smiled at him, asking, "Does this mean that I am part of the Zhong family too?" The other believers smiled and said: "There are no problems, we are all children of God!"

My own field notes. Spring 2010

5.2 Genos

Genos is the element that Altan relates to kinship, lineage, and dynasty. Through genos the power is transmitted from one generation to the other (Altan 1995, p. 23). According to Altan, genos is one of the fundamental symbols of society which certainly reflects the patterns of aggregation of the history of mankind.

> What the genos transforms into a symbol is the set of rules that regulate the relations based on the offspring of families (lineages), and the set of kinship relations that follow from them (clans and ethnic groups with their specific ordinances, rituals, celebrations and festivities to honor the dead). All these phenomena start from the fundamental taboo of incest. This set of social realities, which have their own implicit rationality consisting in the fact that, especially in the past, they made possible the coexistence of large social groups, are the subject of a symbolic transfiguration. This transfiguration gives them an absolute value in many communities, a value that diminishes and narrows down in modern complex societies.
>
> (Altan 1995, p. 23)

Following the intuition of Altan, in this chapter, I will link genos with kinship and especially with the research about Chinese kinship. In the context of Chinese studies, this aspect has been analyzed by many distinguished scholars, although under different points of view. Traditionally the research about Chinese kinship agrees that in Chinese traditional society, descent is patrilineal, and each child is given his or her father's surname (Freedman 1958, p. 42). According to Steven Sangren (2009), Chinese patriliny is not only a product of kinship but involves many important (I would say constitutive) aspects of the Chinese culture such as ancestor worship, funerary practices, marriage rituals, ethno-biological ideologies, gender categories, and, especially, pervasive values like filial piety. Patriliny thus encompasses a complex nexus of discourses and institutions (Sangren 2009, p. 256).

I consider the argument of Sangren as one that is worth taking into consideration in order to better understand Chinese kinship and consequently Chinese society. Starting from Marxian and psycho-analytic theory, Sangren argues that Chinese patriliny is a mode of production, not only of the material means of subsistence and social forms but also of persons and desires. According to him, desire is an effect or product of social processes, including especially family processes or domestic cycles. These processes take culturally variable forms: in the Chinese case, as patriliny. Patriliny is thus a culturally particular process of production of institutions (e.g. social roles, families) and of desire simultaneously (Sangren 2009, p. 256).

Patriliny is also one of the most important Confucian values: 不孝有三無後為大 "There are three things which are unfilial," says Mencius, "and to have no posterity is the greatest of them." Among the philosophy of Confucius and especially in the interpretation of it, patriliny is also linked to other concepts, such as the way the state/subject, teacher/student, and husband/wife relations should be performed. I think that this point of view could help us understand the importance of patriliny and filial piety in Chinese society, and it gives us an idea of how Chinese kinship divisions and terms are deeply linked with a myriad of cosmological concepts and daily and practical acts (ancestor worship, inheritance, division of the house, etc.). More specifically, the idea of patriliny stressed by Sangren helps us to more fully understand the kinship situation in Shuiwei village. It is possible, in fact, to recognize two forces that through their action have shaped the social structure of Shuiwei. On the one hand, it is easy to recognize the Chinese traditional way of thinking (and acting), which is still linked with the concept of patriliny mentioned by Sangren. On the other hand, the new concepts brought by the Catholic faith challenged and implemented a new mode of production which incremented other desires and a non-traditional development of the social structure of Shuiwei.

5.2.1 *Genos, Kinship, and the Chinese Family*

In traditional Chinese culture, the family (家 *jiā* or colloquial 家庭 *jiātíng*) is considered the basic unit of society, and individuals are only one part of the family. According to David K. Jordan, who did extensive research in Taiwan, the traditional Chinese family was a patrilineal, patriarchal, prescriptively virilocal kinship group sharing a common household budget (Jordan 2006). Patrilinearity is linked with the fact that the blood relationship between the father and son is the most important element of society. High respect for family and paternal authority became a specific feature of Chinese civilization (Lang 1946, p. 9). Filial piety was proclaimed "the root of all virtue" 夫孝,之本也 *Fū xiào, dé zhī běn yě*. Linked to this concept of 孝*xiào* and to patrilinearity is the observance of ancestor worship. In popular belief ancestors depended upon the living for this reverence (usually seen as provisioning them with sacrificial food, literally feeding them), and therefore the failure to produce (or, if necessary, adopt) male offspring was considered an immoral behavior or, if accidental, a great misfortune. As previously showed, this kind of ritual implies that the ancestors are not entirely dead, but their souls continue to live and watch over the life of their descendants. Thus, the rites are based on the idea that those who perform them help both the living and the dead. An ancestor is presumed to be endowed with a supernatural power, which he may use to help his descendants. Therefore it is necessary for the descendants to worship and feed him, otherwise he will become a wandering ghost, as happens with those who have no descendants (Lang 1946, pp. 18–19). Of course, this will cause a lot of troubles for the family.

I would like to give a concrete example of this by introducing a piece from my field notes. The field note is about Mr. Li, who was a man around his 50s when we met him for the first time. He was one of the few private drivers in Lunbei Township. We used his car service several times, especially when we just had arrived in Lunbei and were without a car. Mr. Li had an accident a few years earlier. Because of this, his left arm had been cut off just below the armpit. One day his wife told us how this mishap happened. I transcribe here her recount:

> When we got married we were living in my husband's parents' house. Our kids were always sick, and I asked my mother-in-law if we should ask advice from the temple, but she said that it was not necessary. After a while we moved to this house and things seemed to be going better. Just a few months later my husband had this accident when he was working. A heavy metal sheet fell on his arm, cutting it. After this accident my mother-in-law changed her mind and we went to the temple. The shaman told us that all the misfortunes around my husband and his family were caused by his elder brother. This brother died when he was a child. My husband has never seen him and did not know anything about him. My husband's brother wanted to let the family know about his existence because nobody fed him since he was a kid. When I asked why he singled out my husband, the shaman told me that this brother cannot ask his parents because it was not respectful (因是不孝的 *Yīnwèi shì*

bùxiào de). Moreover he was the fifth son, but when he passed away my husband became the fifth son. As our tradition, my husband was called "the fifth" (老五 *Lǎo wǔ*), therefore the brother felt that my husband, who took his place within the family, should provide food for him. Now, every time we worship our ancestors we make a special portion of food for him. We also call him to eat before the other ancestors. Otherwise since he is the smaller, they will not let him eat.

Another important aspect of Jordan's definition of Chinese family is that family is a prescriptively virilocal kinship group. An old Chinese proverb stated that "the ideal family had four generations living under one roof" 四代同堂 *Sìdài tóngtáng*. In old China, the patriarch of a family which met this Confucian ideal was eligible to receive an official letter of congratulations from the Emperor. This form of cohabitation is very common also today in the Taiwanese countryside, even if the younger generations tend to move to the major cities.

It has been convincingly argued that the common budget is one of the most important defining characteristics of Chinese families. One effect of this custom is to define who is in or out of a family by means other than kinship (Jordan 2006). Sharing a budget is a strictly economical way of viewing what families shared, but sharing went beyond that. In the religious sphere, families tended to share luck. A family in which one member was chronically sick while another had bad habits and a third tended to make bad investments might seek to treat all of these as symptoms of a single ill, the inharmony of the family as a whole (Jordan 2006). Traditionally, Taiwanese families practiced partible inheritance. They usually divide the estate equally among all sons, who inherit the house and continue to live on the family land. The importance of this practice is demonstrated by the fact that according to many scholars (Ahern 1973), the inheritance of property creates the obligation to venerate their own ancestors.

It is possible to say that the idea of family and these kinship concepts are influenced by Confucian, religious, and cosmological conceptions, such as ancestor worship or the basic division of the Han supernatural beings (gods, ancestors, and ghosts). Their influence is very deep and concretely build up the social division of territorial unities (e.g. villages), 族譜 *Zúpǔ* family genealogical records, and so on. These relations are easily visible, especially during funerals. The particular kind of clothes, which the participants of the funeral must dress, the 五服 five degrees of mourning attire (*Wǔfú*), defines not only the proper attire but also the proper mourning ritual one should observe when a relative has died (see Ethos, Sect. 6.3.2). In fact, all these above-mentioned concepts are deeply linked with each other and more important are permeated with kinship concepts.

5.2.2 Chinese Kinship and the Importance of Ancestors' Rites

In the previous pages, it has been mentioned how, for many Taiwanese people, the concept of family also includes the members who have already passed away. They can be ancestors as well as ghosts, as in the example of Mr. Li. Their presence exerts a strong influence on the living and on the practical activities of the family. One example of the events where these relations are manifested is in the practices linked with the veneration of the ancestors. These rituals are very important in order to understand the family structure. Actually, some scholars maintain that it is through this kind of ritual that family structure is experienced, which means that the ritual reproduces kin positions (Ahern 1981; Jordan 1999).

The link between people and their ancestors creates different familiar structures named, according to the relation with the ancestor, family, lineage, or clan. A lineage is an *organized group* of descendants of a single, specific ancestor. The ancestor is referred to as an "apical" ancestor because he is at the "apex" of the genealogy by which the lineage membership is determined, and the descent links to this person are known (or written in a genealogy where they can be looked up). A clan is a property-holding group made up of descendants of an apical ancestor, but the details of the descent lines from that ancestor are unknown. In some cases the ancestor is clearly mythical, and in some societies the apical ancestor may even be non-human (Jordan 2006).

As I already mentioned, the structure of these groups is related with the worship of an ancestor. Ancestors' rites are very important in order to keep the unity of the family, as well as the unity of the lineage and of the clan. For a man the worship of the ancestors at the home altar refers to his male ancestors and their wives.

Usually, the ceremonies for the ancestors are performed in the house of the son (not necessarily the oldest) in charge of preserving and caring for the ancestral tablets. The ancestor's tablet is a rectangular piece of wood on which the name of the deceased is written. Generally some basic information, like who made and offered the tablet, the surname of the lineage, and the date at which the tablet was completed, are written on this tablet. These pieces of information are commonly written in three vertical lines (Lazzarotti 2008, p. 118). To take care of the ancestral tablet is considered a very important task. Inside the tablet lies one of the deceased souls (Lazzarotti 2014, p. 111). On the anniversary of either the deceased's birth or death, food, incense, and paper money are offered to the ancestor (represented by the tablet).

The whole family is required to meet together to pay respect to the ancestors and share a lunch or a dinner together. Sometimes it happens that a lineage or a clan decides to choose a piece of land between those inherited from ancestors and build a 宗祠 *Zōngcí*, an ancestral shrine where all the ancestors' tablets (usually those that go beyond the third generation) are put and venerated together. These ancestral shrines are very important in order to keep a certain cohesion within the lineage or the clan. During my fieldwork, I noticed how these places are used as identity builders and as a way to transmit the traditions and values to the new generations. Identity and values which are linked and produced, as Sangren pointed out, by the idea of patriliny.

The ancestors' rituals that usually include offerings of food, wine, and incense are exclusively performed by men. Usually women should stand behind the men (their husbands, their brothers, and their sons) during the performance of the ritual. However, women must bow down or prostrate themselves to ancestors when the men do so.

Traditionally a woman was quite explicitly removed from the family of her birth (her 娘家 *niángjiā*) and affiliated to her husband's family (her 婆家 *pójiā*), a transition always very clearly symbolized in local marriage customs, despite their variation from one region to another. One of the first consequences of this particular situation is that it is easier for women to convert to Catholicism. In fact, it is a common opinion that they will anyway pray for ancestors belonging to a different lineage. Ahern also points out this fact when interviewing her informants: they told her that a daughter "does not belong to us. From birth on, girls are meant to belong to other people. They are supposed to die in other people's house" (Ahern 1973, p. 127).

From another point of view, if it is true that the rituals are performed exclusively by the men, it is important to note that it is women who are in charge of remembering each of their husband's ancestors' celebration days. Apart from that, it is the women who concretely prepare the food for the ceremony, buy the incense, and so on. Their importance is thus fundamental. In relation to this situation, it is possible to read an anecdote told to me by the parish priest of Lunbei. He told me that in recent years there has been an increasing number of women who wanted to marry Christian men. The reason for this phenomenon, according to the priest, is that since there are no ancestors to worship, they would be released from all obligations and all the work that the ceremonies of ancestors involve.

5.3 Christianity in Taiwan and the Reconstruction of Genos

Connecting these cultural elements with the history of Catholicism in Taiwan previously described (even if we can talk here about all Christianity in Taiwan, since the historical patterns are almost the same), it is easy to understand why Taiwanese people have been in strong opposition to conversions to Catholicism among their relatives. The request for abandonment of all traditional practices, which were considered pagan and idolatrous by the Dominican missionaries, certainly contributes to the deep chasm between the converted and their relatives. As we have seen, the historical situation that accompanied the return of the Dominicans to Taiwan has helped to create and develop an interpretation (coming from both sides) which stressed the negative elements of the other. While the Taiwanese people considered the missionaries as Western devils, the missionaries branded the local religion and traditions as idolatry, paganism, superstition, and so on. Once the dialogue was set in this way, any possibility of cultural integration was clearly put aside. The newly converted were obliged to burn their ancestors' tablets and the images of Confucius present in their houses. They were also forbidden to perform any ceremonies in honor of the ancestors. The consequence of this approach was the separation of new converts from their families, lineages, and clans. Because of these prohibitions, new converts suffered small and large persecution and, in some cases, even martyrdom (Fernandez et al. 1994, p. 76,129). But apart from these persecutions, the removal from the family and from the practices of ancestor veneration was considered by the unconverted as an act of renunciation of filial piety and in a wider context as a waiver of Chinese identity.[3]

---

[3] The awareness that conversion involved a renunciation of the Chinese identity, or at least a deep division between the converted and his/her original family and culture, was felt and

This approach caused a series of practical consequences which certainly influenced the family relations among the converted. It has been mentioned that the converted were ordered to burn the ancestral tablets and that they were forbidden to participate in the ceremonies for the ancestors, which are celebrated at least once a year by the family, the lineage, and by the clan. This caused a significant disruption of relationships within the family and the converted within their lineage or clan. Near Shuiwei there are at least two parishes, 鹿寮 Luliao parish (元鄉, 雲林縣 Yuanchang Township, Yunlin County), in the Diocese of Chiayi, and the one of 田中鎮 Tianzhong Township (彰化縣 Changhua County) in the Diocese of Taichung, where the Dominican missionaries bought the lands surrounding the church. The land was used in order to let the newly converted build their homes. In this way, living together, the newly converted were helping and defending themselves. In Shuiwei this never happened because Christianity became the major religion in the village, since the contemporary conversion of the two brothers and their families.

I already described in epos how the missionaries' prohibitions and tactics of evangelization changed in some ways the kinship concepts among the Catholic community in Shuiwei. I will suggest that the process of separation of the converted from their families and lineages went hand in hand with the effort that the missionaries put in creating a Catholic concept of family. Dominicans tried to make a semantic translation of some of the main symbols of the Taiwanese Popular Religion. The main idea that underlies this semantic translation is that the Universal (Catholic) Church is a family and that Jesus should be considered the first ancestor (Lazzarotti 2008, p. 126).

5.3.1 *The Catholic Community of Lunbei*

The Catholic community which attends the Lunbei services is nowadays formed by a few big families: the 鍾 Zhong and the 李 Li who live in Shuiwei and the 李 Li and the 韓 Han who live in Lunbei. More recently, apart from these families, there are a number of others and a few faithful

---

taken under big consideration by many missionaries who worked in China. An exemplar figure is Richard Wilhelm, a German sinologist, theologian, and missionary. He lived in China for 25 years. He admitted that during his entire 20-year stay in China, he was very proud to have never baptized a single Chinese (Jung 1989, p. 375).

converted. There are also a couple of Vietnamese brides who were Catholic believers before coming in Taiwan. Lunbei's Li family and the Han families are somehow related, since they converted at the same time and especially because Mr. Li Chuanli (who now is in his 60s) married the elder sister of the Han family. These relationships could be better understood through the reading of these two families' genealogical records.

Both Li and Han families converted after 1949; their conversion is linked with the work of evangelization carried out by the new missionaries who arrived from Mainland China (Epos, Sect. 4.3.3).

Mr. Han, who was coming from Yunlin's township of 古坑 Gukeng, was a pharmacist. His three sons followed in his steps: the elder is a pharmacist, the second is a dentist, and the third is a doctor specialized in traditional Chinese medicine.

Apart from the two daughters of Mr. Li and the last daughter of Mr. Han, all the sons of the second generation married no Catholic woman. In order to get married, all the wives of the second generation, and also the one belonging to the third, were baptized during the Mass at each of their weddings. In Figs. 5.1 and 5.2, it is possible to see the kinship schema of the two families. The small gray circle within the images symbolizes the people linked to the family who did not convert to Catholicism, while the small gray square symbolizes the people who converted after their wedding or sometime after they got in contact with their partners' families.

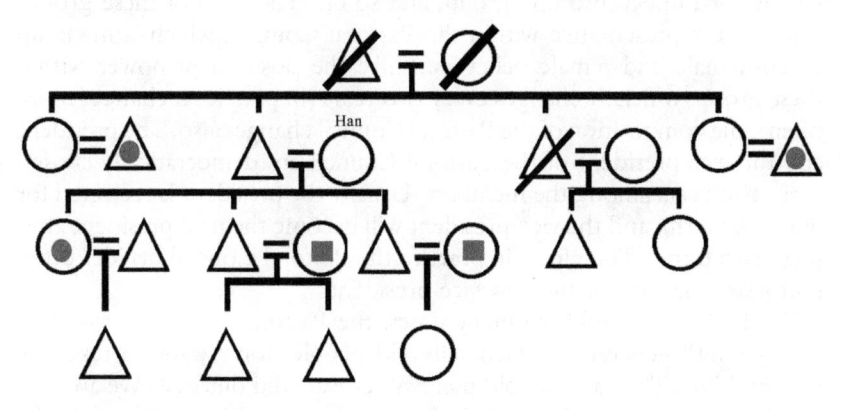

Fig. 5.1 The kinship structure of the Li family of Lunbei

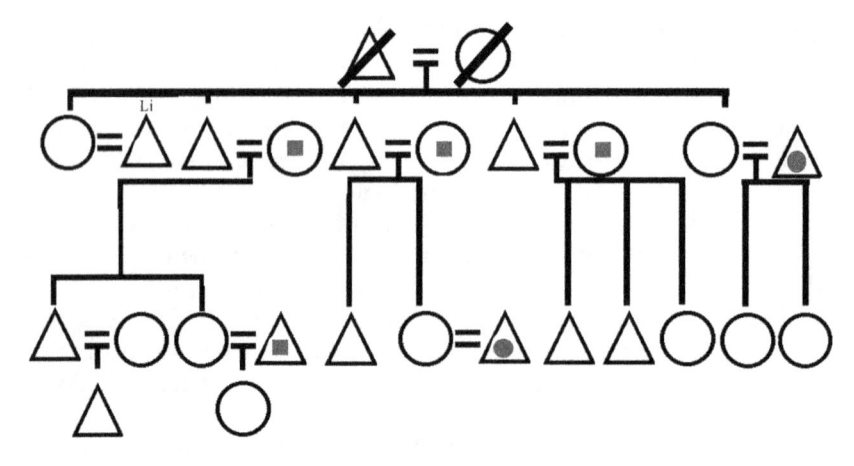

Fig. 5.2 The kinship structure of the Han family of Lunbei

All these families and a consistent number of other people who converted more recently are part of the parish of Lunbei (Epos, Sect. 3.3.3). The parish community is divided into small groups. In general, the composition of these groups follows the presence of the families in the territory of the parish. Therefore the Zhong families of Shuiwei are divided into four groups, the Li families of Shuiwei into one group, the Han families of Lunbei into one group, and so on. The head of these groups is also the representative within the Pastoral Council, which is made up of both male and female believers. Since the position of power within these groups officially changes every two years (in practice it changes more often), the composition of the Pastoral Council changes also. The president and the vice-president of the Pastoral Council are democratically chosen every two years among the members. Usually the president is reelected for one more term, and the vice-president will become the next president after these two terms. Therefore, in practice the Pastoral Council decides every four years who will be the new vice-president.

As the believers told me many times, the Pastoral Council is made by the "young" generations. Generally old people don't want to take any responsibility. They always told me: "We already did our best. We are old. It is better that our children (who have in between 40 to 60 years) take care of the parish."

What I noticed during the time I spent in this community is that within the parish community, there is no tension among the members to reach any prominent position. The faithful are always willing to take part in the activities organized by the parish, but they don't yearn to reach prominent positions. This is perhaps related to another aspect of this community I noticed during my fieldwork. Since there are so many opportunities to meet with other parishioners and because the groups I mentioned above are mainly composed of family groups, it follows that the Pastoral Council is seen as a kind of "family gathering." Almost all the topics discussed in the Pastoral Council have already been discussed among the different family groups and between each other. In this sense I would say that the Pastoral Council is a sort of "bureaucratic" extension of the families that form these groups.

It is with an understanding of this background that we must read the situation of the Catholic community of Shuiwei village and consequently the narrations made about it.

5.3.2 The Catholic Community of Shuiwei

The Catholic community of Shuiwei is mainly composed of two familiar groups or, in Freedman's words, lineages. The 李 Li lineage, which is indicated in Fig. 5.3 by the numbers 19 and 20, is composed of four households. The rest of the community is composed of the Zhong lineage.

Figure 5.3 shows in detail the distribution of the Zhong lineage in the part of Shuiwei (indicated in Fig. 3.9 as a kind of red isosceles trapezium resting on the smaller base; see Topos, Sect. 3.3.3) which is considered by its inhabitants and by the other non-Catholic people as the "proper" Catholic area.

The elements marked with the number 2 indicate Protestant households. The numbers 3, 4, and 7 indicate, respectively, a Christian public park, the ancestral home of one branch of the Zhong lineage, and the location of the Catholic church. Apart from them, we can see that there are 15 Catholic households in this specific portion of the village. The family living in the household number 9 does not belong to the Zhong lineage. In fact this household is inhabited by the 林 Lin family. Mister Lin married a woman of the Zhong Family who was living in her parents' house because all her brothers moved to another city. Actually this land is considerably important for the Zhong family because it is the land where Mr. Zhong

Fig. 5.3 Position of the Catholic households in Shuiwei. *Source:* Modified from Google Maps

Qin and his wife (the first converted to Catholicism) are buried, which is indicated in the map by the letter T in a red circle.

Of these 15 households, 13 belong to the Zhong lineage and 2 to the Li lineage. It is important to note that the households indicated by the number 8 are the only non-Christian households within this particular area. Even if this household is inhabited by people whose surname is Zhong, it doesn't belong to the Catholic branch of the Zhong lineage. However, this household certainly belongs to the extended Zhong lineage. Within the 15 Catholic households, 13 are living off farming or farming-related activities (sellers of agricultural products like pesticides, fertilizers), and of the remaining 2, one is a carpenter and the other a plumber. Very often they have some other side activity managed by the wives, such as selling food or other products.

Among the Li family in Shuiwei, the first family members (now more than 90 years old) were converted during the Japanese occupation of

Taiwan, before 1945. At that time the only missionaries working in Taiwan were the Dominicans. The first converts were the three brothers, but while the first and third brothers regularly attended Church activities, the second one and his elder son's family (who was living with his father) did not take part in any activity, not even the weekly Mass. Only after the second brother passed away (Ethos, Sect. 6.3.2) did his elder son and his family start to take part in the Saturday Mass.

The third brother lives not far from the other two, whose traditional houses 三合院 *Sānhéyuàn* (Topos, Sect. 3.2) are neighboring. There are other Catholic Li families in the village, but while one is still linked to the same lineage, the other one (two brothers) comes from another lineage, since they were living in Changhua County. Their mother, who was originally from Shuiwei, moved back to the village after the death of her husband.

5.4 THE GENEALOGY OF THE ZHONG FAMILY

As I earlier introduced, the first person who converted to Catholicism was Mr. Zhong Qin, who was baptized in 1905. According to the genealogical record of the Zhong lineage, he had 12 children, 3 of whom were males.

The genealogical record is a very important document, called 族譜 *Zúpǔ*, for almost all the Taiwanese families. I already mentioned (Epos, Sect. 4.3) that the *Zúpǔ* of the Zhong lineage has been compiled by Zhong Kunmao. From this document it is possible to collect much information about the change of kinship among the Zhong lineages. First of all, the family tree starts with Mr. Zhong Qin, and the only link with the Zhong clan is the name of the father of Mr. Zhong Qin, 鍾牛港 Mr. Zhong Niugang, and the one of Niugang's wife, 廖漢 Liao Han. This fact has a special meaning, especially if we read it among the "Hakka revival" that the Lunbei Township government is trying to impose on the people of Lunbei. To this Hakka revival is linked one of the stories by which I started this chapter. I already explained more in detail this process of ethnic (and identity) colonization in Topos (Sect. 3.3.2). The Township government is trying to rediscover/rebuild the Hakka roots that are certainly present in the Lunbei area. Many researches have been done by the Township government, and according to them, both the Li and the Zhong lineages are in fact Hakka people. The efforts of the Township government and other cultural associations barely seem to touch the Zhong and the Li lineages in Shuiwei. When I introduced to them the researches made by the Township government, their answer was "yes, I know that some people from the Township government said that we are Hakka. Maybe it could even be, but we don't care. We are Christians (我們是基督徒 *Wǒmen shì jīdūtú*). This is the most important thing." The other Zhong households who inhabit the villages surrounding Shuiwei mostly agree that they are Hakka.

There is another sign of the division that happened between the Catholic part of the Zhong lineage and the rest of the Zhong lineage to which Zhong Niugang belonged. One of the Catholic women of one of the Zhong families, Zhong Zunxin, married a man whose last name was Zhong. This kind of marriage between persons sharing the same family name was traditionally forbidden. People with the same family name were considered belonging to the same lineage and thus, in some ways, relatives. Especially in pre-modern Taiwan, persons with the same surname were coming from near places or neighboring villages. Therefore people were afraid of consanguinity, or as they say, 怕有血亯關係 *Pà yǒu xiěyuán guānxì*. Anyway, these kinds of marriages, even if completely legal nowadays in Taiwan, are still seen by most of the people as strange and strongly unusual, especially by the elder generations. The peculiarity of the case I just introduced is that both the Catholic and the non-Christian communities consider the Catholic part of the Zhong lineage as out of the lineage. This has been confirmed to me by the members of the Catholic community and by the husband of Zhong Zunxin. He told me that at the beginning his parents were a little bit surprised, but since the future wife was coming from the Catholic community, they finally agreed.

From this anecdote it is possible to bring forward an interesting point that I will explain later in the text. The missionaries replaced the ancestor worship with other kinds of rituals all focused on the importance of Jesus. Their interactions with the local culture had two outcomes. On the one hand, the Catholic part of the Zhong lineage, no longer tied to the Zhong lineage by the ancestor's ceremonies, became an independent lineage. On the other hand, by introducing a new—and only—ancestor, Jesus, the missionaries concretely helped the changes within the family structure. In this way, somehow revisiting the idea of patriliny stressed by Sangren, the Catholic community became a sort of clan.

Another element that leaps out from the Zhong lineage *Zúpǔ* is the fact that beside all the names (both male and female), the Christian name—

the name that is chosen for the child at the time of baptism—is present. Apart from this, the most interesting element is the fact that contrariwise to all the family trees compiled in Taiwan, the Zhong *Zúpú* is bilateral. It contains also the female members of the family. The Zhong *Zúpú* tells us not only the name of the female on the Zhong family but also with whom they are married and a record of their descendants. In this way the *Zúpú* of the Zhong lineage also contains and records part of the genealogical trees of different surnames, thus belonging to other families and lineages.

It is very unusual to see genealogical records written in this way. Personally I am aware only of this one. When I asked the reason for this choice, this is what I was told:

> Kunmao: When I started to collect information about our genealogical tree, I felt that women were part of our family also. My aunts, my sisters, my cousins ... how I can consider them as separated from my family? They and their families often come back here in Shuiwei. We often meet each other for Christmas or during the Mass. We grew up together, we are part of the same family. Besides, we all are sons and daughters of God.
>
> Marco: Did someone of your family complain about it?
>
> Kunmao: No! Nobody complained. Besides, this is our family's *Zúpú*, so we can manage it as we want.

From a sociological point of view, the links between the village and the family's faith play a fundamental role in order to define the kinship of the Zhong family. The women who already left the village often come back and take part in the religious ceremonies. Very often all their families attend the weekly Mass, even if they are not Catholics. The Mass became a sort of "family meeting," where everybody can see who is back and how their family members grow up. This feeling is shared also by the other familiar groups that compose the parish of Lunbei.

From this genealogical tree, it is possible to recognize the influence of the Catholic faith on the concept that the Zhong families of Shuiwei have on their kinship relations. Women are part of the family, and they should be recorded in the genealogical tree as well as the men. As it is possible to read in the words of Kunmao and how I will explain better in the next few pages, the Catholic concept of universal brotherhood plays a very important role here.

I would like now to make a more systematic and precise description of the kinship schemes I created through the reading of the genealogical tree of the Zhong family.

In the following schemes, I tried to summarize the genealogical records of the Zhong family. In doing this, I took into account only the male descendants of the family. I did it for several reasons. First of all, because in this way I can consider in a more direct and concrete way the link between the land and the male part of the family that, as we mentioned earlier, is entrusted with the task of providing offspring to ancestors. In these schemes, I represented only the number of family members who are currently living in the village. All these are marked by a number which shows on Fig. 5.4 the household that a specific family member is living in.

On Fig. 5.4 I painted the different branches, or in Chinese terms 房 *fáng*, of the family with different colors.[4] In this way it will be easy to trace them in the map. Therefore, the first branch of the family is black, while the second and the third branches are, respectively, dark blue and red. Green represents the Presbyterian households present in the village, while the two light blue polygons show the position of the Li family household. The Catholic church is described by a little yellow cross. This church had been built by the members of the first branch of the family (the black one), specifically by the father of the current bishop of the Jiayi Dioceses, who is marked by B in the first branch kinship scheme. The sign T shows the position of the tombs of Mr. Zhong Qin and his wife. The rest of the surface of the area, the one not characterized by colors, is occupied by agricultural land.

In Sect. 5.4.1 there are four kinship schemes that I have made following the genealogical record made by Zhong Kunmao. The first one represents the kinship relations of Mr. Zhong Qin. I divided the following schemes according to the traditional Chinese division of the family lineage. Therefore each son of Mr. Zhong Qin is the starting point of a branch. It can mean a genealogical group or a conjugal group. It is perhaps the term that more closely resembles the Western idea of the family.

---

[4] 房 *fáng* is one of the basic concepts to understand Chinese kinship (陳其南 1990).

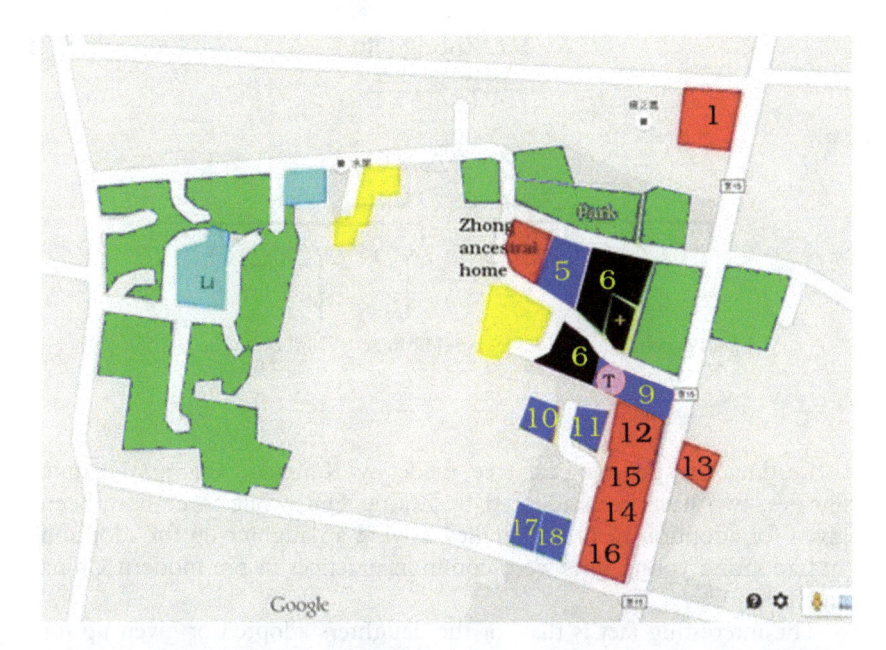

Fig. 5.4 Catholic kinship situation. In black is represented the first *fáng*. The second and the third are, respectively, dark blue and red. *Source:* Modified from Google Maps

5.4.1 Mr. Zhong Qin Kinship Scheme

From the Mr. Zhong Qin kinship scheme, it is possible to extrapolate many interesting pieces of information.

Mr. Zhong Qin had 2 wives and 12 children. The first wife died young, and he remarried. He had three sons and nine daughters.

Mr. Zhong Qin
鍾欽 老先生

First Branch
第一房

Second Branch
第二房

Third Branch
第三房

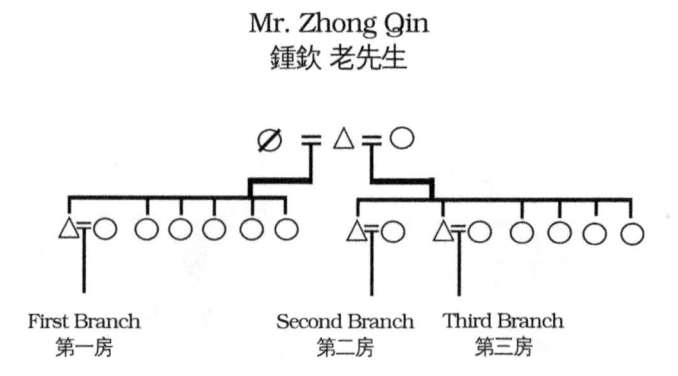

Reading the genealogical tree made by Kunmao, among the nine females, two have been adopted by Zhong Qin, while three have been given for adoption to other families. Giving a daughter up for adoption and adopting young girls were common practices in pre-modern China and Taiwan.[5]

The interesting fact is that, of the daughters adopted or given up for adoption, they are all those he had with his first wife. All the daughters he had from the second wife married exclusively Catholic believers. Only the last daughter married a Presbyterian faithful. According to Kunmao and the elders of the Catholic community of Shuiwei, this means that Mr. Zhong Qin converted after the second marriage.

---

[5] This practice has been the object of research of Arthur P. Wolf (Wolf and Huang 1980) who focused on the adoption of girls of poor families. Also Margery Wolf discussed such arrangements (童養媳 *Tóngyǎngxí*, called in Minnan language shim-pua) in her 1972 book. Within social anthropology research of Chinese marriage, shim-pua marriage is referred to as a "minor marriage" because the daughter-in-law joins her future husband's household when both are minors, in contrast to Chinese major marriage, in which the bride joins her husband's household on the day of the wedding. For those interested, please refer to Arnhart (2005) or to Wolf (2005).

5.4.2 First Branch

The first branch, or *Fáng*, of the Zhong family is represented by the black color in Fig. 5.4. This branch starts with 鍾夐 *Zhōng Tiāndé*, the first son of Mr. Zhong Qin.

First Branch
第一房

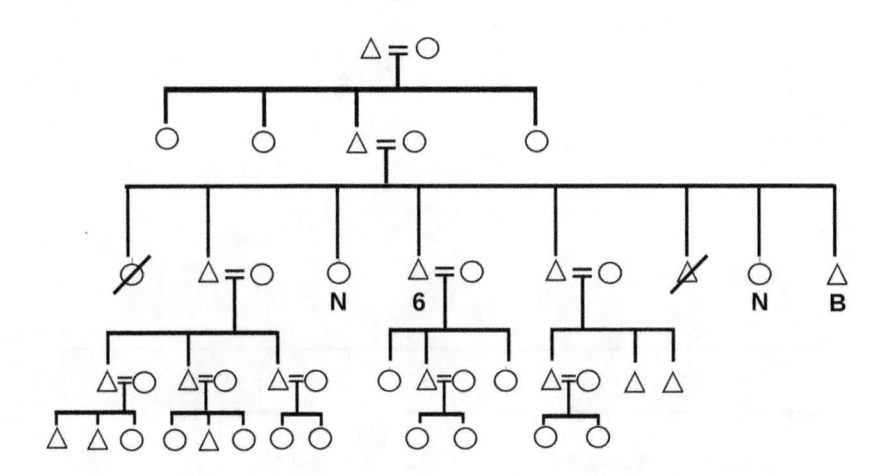

He and his wife had only one son. This fact helped to create the current situation, which we can see in Fig. 5.4. The following generation shows that there is one bishop (鍾安住主教 Bishop Thomas Zhong, the B in the scheme) and two nuns (the two N). In Fig. 5.4 it is possible to recognize that the Catholic church has been built on the land belonging to this first branch. The church, which I have introduced in Topos, Sect. 3.1, is symbolized by a yellow cross beside the number 6. The only person of the first branch who lives in the village is one of the elder brothers of the bishop, who in Fig. 5.4 is indicated by the number 6. The other brothers live in 臺南 Tainan, one of the big cities in Southern Taiwan.

5.4.3 Second Branch

The second branch of the Zhong family starts with 鍾夐義 *Zhōng Tiānyì*, the second son of Mr. Zhong Qin. As I already introduced in one of the stories by which I started this chapter, all firstborn males of the third generation have proper Catholic names. J refers to Joseph, L to Luke, Ma to Matthew, P to Paul, and M to Michael.

From the point of view of traditional Chinese culture, the choice of these names is a little bit unusual. The choice of the personal name is a very important matter for Taiwanese people because it is believed that the choice of name can influence a person's life. This is so important that people usually consult specialists (算命 *Suànmìng*) who can help with determining the right name and who can predict with "scientific" precision (看生 *Kàn shēngcháng*, 流年 *Liúnián*, 八字 *Bāzì*, 紫微斗數 *Zǐ wēi dòu shù*) the future of the child, her/his misfortunes, and so on.

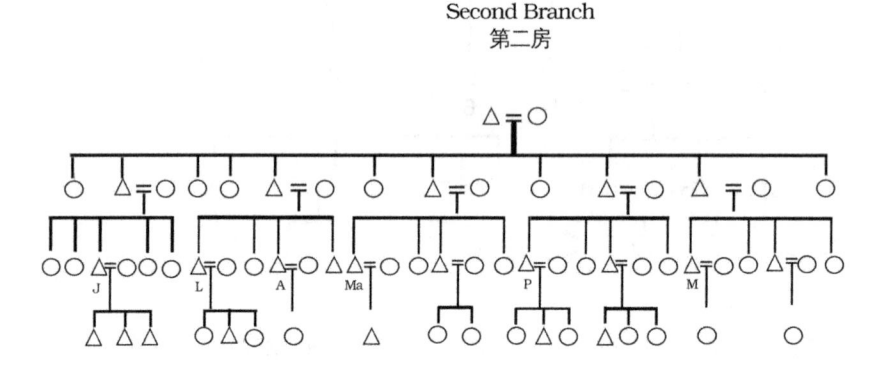

Second Branch
第二房

Another important point is that Chinese writing is unique in that every character is formed by a precise number of strokes. Therefore, in choosing the name, it is important to pay attention to the number of strokes which will form the name's character. A bad choice could have adverse influences in the beholder's life. Furthermore, the choice of the character (which sometimes can be led just by its sound) is a way to wish the child success or fortune in a specific field like study, health, and so on. The name, or the better choice of the name, represents not only the identity of a person but also a meaningful way to link the beholder of it—thanks also to other elements, such as the choice of the right time of the childbirth—to a precise and concrete cosmological order. Indeed, when someone is living a particularly unlucky or critical situation, they have the chance to change their names (改名 *Gǎimíng*), to start a completely new life.

As it is possible to realize also from the story of Mr. Chen that I described in the first paragraph, the Catholic names have certain meanings only inside the Catholic community. These names sound strange, or at least a bit unusual, to the non-Christian people. These names were not chosen following the common tradition; rather their choice belongs to a complete "other" tradition. The names of saints have been considered more important than their number of strokes. The meaning of this is a renouncement of the previous belief system and the full acceptance of the new one.

There is another important element about the Chinese names that should be taken into account: the so-called generation name 字輩 *Zì bèi*. The generation name is one of the characters in a traditional Chinese name. Even if the Zhong family doesn't have its own generation name, some of the surrounding families still have it. For example, the Catholic part of the Li family in Shuiwei still uses the generation name. These generation names are quite common in Taiwan. It is so called because each member of a generation (siblings and cousins of the same generation) shares that character. Usually a lineage has a record of its generation names, commonly called in English a "generation poem" and known variously in Chinese as 班次聯 *bān cì lián* or 派字歌 *pài zì gē* or others. These poems represent the sequence of the characters that should be used as generation names. Families sharing a common generation poem are considered to also share a common ancestor and have originated from a common geographical location (Bao 2012, p. 212). In other words, the sequence of generations is named in a way that a poem is formed. From this point of view, the choice to adopt Catholic names for their firstborn sons acquires a special meaning, especially if we consider that the first branch of the family used this 字輩 *Zì bèi* system. In fact all the male of the third generation have the character 安 *Ān* in their name. The same tradition continued also for the fourth generation. All the males have the character 寬 *Kuān* in their name.

From the point of view of genos, the choice of the names means to cut (almost) all ties with a lineage (the original Zhong lineage) and to become fully a member of another one (the Catholic one).

5.4.4 Third Branch

The third branch of the Zhong family starts with the third son of Mr. Zhong Qin, 鍾明泉 *Zhōng Míngquán*.

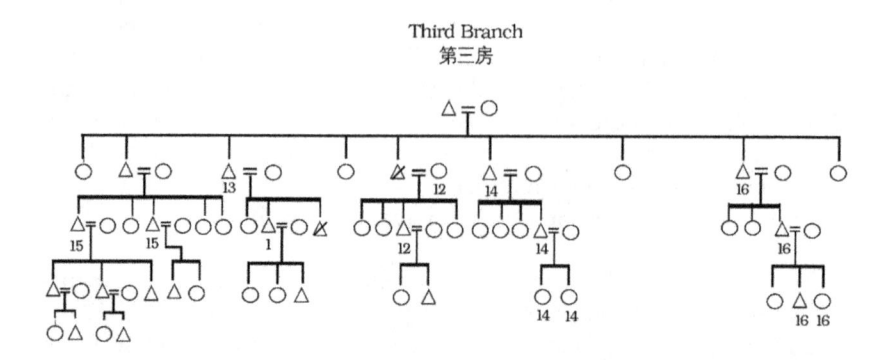

Third Branch
第三房

This branch of the family is the one that has more descendants living in the village than the other branches. Confronting the kinship scheme with Fig. 5.4, it is possible to note that the Zhong ancestral house belongs to this branch. All the members who are now living in the village still remember the time when they lived together in the traditional Taiwanese household. With the gradual enlargement of the family and especially in conjunction with the golden period of the Taiwanese economy (around the 1990s), each family decided to build their own home and to leave the ancestral household.

5.5 Reconstructing Genos

The transformation into symbols of a specific set of kinship rules is what Altan considers as genos. Also the kinship relations that spring from these sets of rules such as lineages, clans, and their specific ordinances, rituals, celebrations, and festivities in honor of the dead (Altan 1995, p. 23) are symbolized by genos. Among the specific situation of Shuiwei, it is possible to realize how much the Catholic faith influenced and molded the symbolization of these sets of rules, helping to create a unique and original genos shared by the Catholic community of Shuiwei. The influence of the

Catholic faith is manifested in the genos of the Zhong family and in the Shuiwei Catholic community on different levels.

On the one hand, it manifests itself as a phenomenon of division among the original lineage and clan and the Catholic part of the Zhong family. This happens because, as mentioned above, the prohibition of participating in the ceremonies for the ancestors of the Zhong lineage has effectively caused a separation between the Catholic community and the rest of the lineage.

On the other hand, the Catholic faith represents a unifying force within the Catholic community and especially within the part of the Zhong family that shares it. This unification process is certainly due to the need to strengthen family ties after the separation with the rest of the family. At the same time, it reveals the profound change in the cosmology and in the everyday life practices which a conversion to a new religion usually brings with itself.

5.5.1 From Ancestors to Ancestor

As mentioned above, the ancestors worship is considered of primary importance in the Chinese cultural world by many scholars (Ebrey et al. 1986; Watson and Rawski 1988; Liu 1999; Jordan 1999). Actually, it is toward the idea of ancestors that the Taiwanese Catholic church acted as a powerful semantic change in order to provide the converted with a new key for the interpretation of religious concepts.[6] The missionaries put forth a strong effort in order to carry forward the idea to let Jesus become the first, true ancestor. Through venerating and worshiping Him, the faithful becomes part of the Catholic (universal) family spread around the world.

It is possible to recognize this effort in the changes that have affected the traditional household. I already mentioned how the external changes in the Christian households (Topos, Sect. 3.2.1, Figs. 3.2 and 3.3) represent one of the most obvious and visible symbols that help outsiders to identify Shuiwei village as a "different place," as I have heard many times in the stories about this place.

These changes represent the immense changes implemented by the missionaries through new rules and new religious practices. With the interdiction to participate in the lineage's annual activities aimed at paying respect to the clan's ancestors, the people of Shuiwei broke apart from

---

[6] Please refer to Lazzarotti (2008), especially Chap. 4.

Fig. 5.5 Schema of the traditional home altar

the Lunbei's Zhong clan. It is easily understandable that such a rupture facilitated stronger corporate relationships between the Catholic families. These external changes manifest a separation between the Catholic and the non-Catholic members of the Zhong lineage. At the same time, however, the part of the Zhong family that adopted the symbols of the new faith developed a new and strong identity (Lazzarotti 2013). In this new identity is celebrated the elevation of Jesus as the true ancestor and the edification of the Celestial Jerusalem and the household of God (Lazzarotti 2008).

As I mentioned earlier, the conversion to Catholicism required the elimination of ancestral tablets. This "physical" elimination of the tablets made possible another important and significant change in the rearrangement of the main hall of the house: the 正廳 zhèngtīng. The zhèngtīng is located in the central part of the U compound (Topos, Sect. 3.3, Fig. 3.1). This room is occupied by the home altar, usually a rectangular shaped table, where the home deities and the ancestors' tablet are placed. This room can be considered the social and ritual heart of the house. In the zhèngtīng, guests are received, and traditional ceremonies of the ancestor worship are performed (Lazzarotti 2013, pp. 278–279).There are several rules for the setup of the home altar (Fig. 5.5). According to these rules, the image of the god of the home must be put at the center of the shrine, while the ancestors' tablets must be on the left part of the shrine (Lazzarotti 2008, p. 117).

Usually, sticks of incense are burned every day and put in the incense pots located in front of the deity painting or stamp (or also statue) and in front of the ancestor's tablet. Traditionally these daily activities are performed by the elder men of the family. Apart from these daily activities, in this room other anniversary rites take place on the death date of each major deceased member of the family. During these events, food could be offered, and the members of the family who take part in the ceremony usually share a common meal. This room and the home altar are very important places where the family gathers together, during major festival periods such as Lunar New Year and Middle Autumn Festival and on important family occasions such as births, weddings, and funerals. In other words, there are several moments during the year when a family must gather together in front of the home altar.

These celebrations increase the sense of belonging to a familiar group and enforce the family bonds. At the same time, since the members of the family participated in the ceremony in ritual order based on age and generation, they actively learn their position among the family and among their family lineage. Sometimes, if too old, the elder male let some other men of the family perform these rituals. Anyway there is a strong gender and generational importance among the rituals performed in front of this altar. Even though the role of the women is very important (they should take care of the food, remember the anniversaries, etc.), the performance of these rituals is a task of the male. As for the external changes I mentioned above, in the Catholic households, the *Zhèngtīng* also went through important changes. Figures 5.6 and 5.7 show some of the important and structural changes that happened in the home altar.

The position of the table on the zhèngtīng is the same as in the house of the practitioners of the Taiwanese Popular Religion, but the composition of the altar brings with itself many interesting meanings.

The image in Fig. 5.6 is one of the oldest images that the Dominican missionaries started to distribute among the first Taiwanese converts.

It represents images from the Bible and from the Catholic tradition (it can be recognized in the top left corner as the picture of the Last Supper), and it was used in order to teach catechism to the newly converted. The missionaries used the images in order to explain and let the faithful understand what they were unable to explain with words.

The rearrangement that the Catholic believers made of this room and of the table used as home altar acquired a particular importance. In the Catholic households, this room still keeps a certain importance. In this room and in front of this altar, many families in Shuiwei still pray the rosary every morning. Here we can notice how, at least among the ritual, the renouncement of the ancestors' rituals established a gender equality. They

Fig. 5.6 Old version of the Catholic home altar

pray the rosary, but this kind of prayer does not require a disparity of roles between men and women.

The most important change we can note contrasting Fig. 5.5 with Figs. 5.6 and 5.7 is that, in the Catholic altar, there is no ancestor's tablet or incense burners (one for the deity and one for the ancestors).

The image of the deity is replaced by images taken from the Christian tradition, and on the table, there are statues of Jesus or Holy Mary, flowers, and candles. Both Catholic altars show the above-mentioned sentence 萬有真原 (*Wàn yǒu zhēn yuán,* The true origin of all things) and some sentences related to Christian faith.

In a more detailed way, we can see how Fig. 5.7, a relatively new image, is a Chinese version of the Holy Family (Joseph, Mary, and the little Jesus), perhaps linked with the effort that the Catholic church made in Taiwan in 2001. On that occasion, the Catholic church celebrated the "congress of the new century and of the new evangelization" in order to define the

Fig. 5.7 Modern version of the Catholic home altar

pastoral work for the new century. In this congress, the importance of the layman believers on the life of the Church was stressed. The attention was therefore put on the family as the witness of faith, charity, and hope. The result of this congress was that Catholic families were asked to allow a corner of their house for "Christian symbols," in order to create a religious atmosphere in the family (Meldrum 2005).

Because of these new directives, sacred images have been created by Catholic artists with a special look to the concept of the localization of the Catholic faith. Therefore, many traditional sacred images such as Holy Mary and Jesus or the above-mentioned Holy Family have been adjusted to Chinese tradition and represented as Chinese persons. Before this, in Shuiwei village the only sacred images for the house altar were pre-Raphaelite images like the one described in Fig. 5.6.

5.5.2 Family Ceremonies

One of the most important features of the Taiwanese Popular Religion is that ancestors and ghosts still share the same living space as their descendants. This fact, added to the series of Confucian precepts related to the concept of filial piety or 孝 *xiào*, led Chinese people to create elaborate and important rituals. The goal of these rituals is to put together the idea of strengthening family ties and the desire to exorcise the bad luck. Through these rituals related to death and the ancestors, people learn their position within the family, which includes both the dead and the living.[7]

The Qingming Festival (清明節 *Qīngmíng jié*, often translated as Tomb Sweeping Day or Clear Brightness Festival) is one of the most important festivals in Chinese culture and also in Taiwan. Traditionally this was the only festival regulated by the solar calendar. The day before, people fast and are forbidden from lighting fires. On the day itself, eggs are boiled, colored, and eaten. It is also the feast of resurgent life, dedicated to remembering the dead. The family graves are cleared of weeds, burial mounds are repaired, and sacrificial vessels are laid thereon (Eberhard 1986, p. 120).

This holiday involves all the family. Since most cemeteries are located in the countryside on hillsides or the outskirts of town, apart from completing the Qingming Festival rites, many families will take advantage of the fine spring weather by going on a family outing. These trips have become an important part of the Qingming Festival as a time for families to enjoy time together. In Chinese culture, this festival is so important that in Mainland China the government decided to insert this festivity among the ones when small passenger cars can take the highway for free (People's Republic of China 2012).

In Taiwan, especially in countryside townships like Lunbei, which are affected by an intense process of migration toward the big cities, the Qingming Festival is one of the few days of the year when all the family gathers together. The Qingming Festival is an opportunity for the family to remember and honor its ancestors at grave sites. Both young and old clean the graves and cut the grass, pray for their ancestors, and offer them libations. Under many points of view, the Qingming Festival combines the people's respect for their ancestors and for nature (Williams 1976, p. 16) and the reaffirmation of the Chinese ethic of filial piety. Today, the

---

[7] The idea that Chinese people learn their social relations through rituals is shared also by Ahern (1981).

Qingming Festival is a time not only for worship and maintaining the tombs of ancestors but also for a tangible expression of filial respect for the teachings and virtues of forebears.

Only after the Second Vatican Council (1962–1965), the Catholic church allowed the faithful to perform the cult of ancestors at home and in these ancestors' related ceremonies. Catholic believers were allowed to take part in the ancestors' ceremonies performed by their families and were allowed to keep their ancestor's tablets (if just converted) or to remake new ones.

Also in Shuiwei the Qingming Festival is one of a few occasions in the year when all the members of the Zhong family come back to the village. Usually early in the morning, each branch of the Zhong family gathers separately and pays respect to the branch ancestors (actually only the second (blue) and the third (red) lines of the family have their dead buried in the fields within the village). Each lineage brings to the tomb offerings and libations, and the ceremony ends soon after some prayers. Following this first moment, all the different branches of the family gather together in the village's church where the bishop celebrates the Requiem Mass for the souls of the deceased family members. This tradition started when Bishop Zhong had been ordained priest in 1981. After the Mass, the family members form a procession. A group of young people had the task of carrying the cross, which is followed by two candles and several flower compositions. After them comes the bishop and after him all the rest of the faithful. During the procession, the faithful do not observe any particular age's or branches' division. The procession ends in front the graves of Mr. Zhong Qin and his wife. Then, the bishop gives some prayers, offers fruits, and blesses the tombs with holy water. A stick of incense is given to each family member, who places it in the ground near the graves. Next, the whole family goes back to the church where a rich lunch is already waiting.

5.5.3 We Are All Brothers and Sisters: The Holy Mary Pilgrimage

I already introduced the idea that the encounter between the Zhong lineage and the Catholic faith (through the Dominican missionaries) within a precise historic and social context developed two tendencies: one centrifugal, by which the Zhong families of Shuiwei had separated themselves from the original clan, and the other centripetal, which could be considered a unifying force among the Catholic part of the family.

The evangelization strategy of the missionaries encouraged a semantic translation of some of the main symbols of the Taiwanese Popular Religion. The main idea that underlies this semantic translation is that the Universal (Catholic) Church is a family and that Jesus should be considered the first ancestor (Lazzarotti 2008, p. 126). This kind of tactic became evident during the celebration of the 150th anniversary of the Catholic church in Taiwan, which was celebrated in 2008–2009 (Fides 2009a). One of the many activities planned by the Bishops' Conference in Taiwan was a pilgrimage, across all the parishes of the island, carrying the statue of the Virgin Mary located on the church of Wan Jin 萬金 (Pingtung County, Wanluan Township), which had been the place where the Dominican missionaries started the evangelization of Taiwan.

The pilgrimage was organized by the Bishops' Conference so that each parish could host for at least a few hours the statue of the Virgin Mary (Fides 2009b). Each parish had the task of picking up the statue in the previous parish and escorting her to their own church. This is also what the Lunbei faithful did. They organized a procession of bicycles which accompanied the Madonna during her passage. The procession started in Siluo and ended in the church of Lunbei, where the majority of believers and many curious people were waiting. When the procession stopped in Shuiwei, it had been the first time, at least for me, to hear firecracker explosions in the village. In fact, a long line of firecrackers was placed along the roads where the procession was planned to walk through. This kind of firecrackers is quite common, and it is principally used during Taiwanese Popular Religion deities' pilgrimages or other temples' activities.

When the Virgin Mary arrived in Shuiwei church, she was welcomed by all the children of the village and, after some prayers and songs, the procession again took the road to Lunbei, where the statue was supposed to stay for the night. The parishioners organized shifts to pray the rosary. The day after, the Virgin Mary continued her pilgrimage, which ended in Taipei several months later.

The parish of Lunbei hosted this pilgrimage twice. Apart from the ceremony I already described, the statue came back during the township celebrations of 元宵節 *Yuánxiāo jié*, usually known as Lantern Festival. Yuánxiāo is celebrated on the 15th day of the first month of the Lunar New Year, which marks the last day of the Lunar New Year celebrations. On that occasion, the statue of Holy Mary took part in the local allegorical parade organized by the local Township government. Within allegorical compositions on floats made by the different villages and also a deity from the local temple (三太子 *Sān tàizǐ* or Third Prince, because he was born the third son of General 李靖 Li Jing), two trucks carrying the statue of Mary and a life-sized crucifix took part in the procession. The faithful from Lunbei and from neighboring parishes participated in the parade, following the trucks. Also, many priests and Bishop Zhong took part in this parade. While one of the trucks played church music, from the other, a faithful continuously introduced the Catholic church and the fact that Holy Mary, along with Jesus, was blessing all the people on the road. When the parade ended, the statue returned to the parish where it was supposed to spend the night.

Apart from this special occasion, as I already mentioned, the pilgrimage reached all the parishes of the island. Gadgets linked with the 150th anniversary and with the procession have been created and sold in order to cover the expenses of the activities for that year. Caps, gilet, bandannas, and other objects became very common among the Catholic faithful all over the island. In those days, it was very easy to recognize a Catholic believer, even in crowded places such as Taipei City.

This event was intended to reinforce the cohesion of the Taiwanese Dioceses and to give new strength and encouragement to the Taiwanese faithful and especially to let Catholics show their faith. On another level, with the slogan "Holy Mary and the Lord travel together to bless the 150th anniversary of Taiwan 聖母與主同行福臨臺灣150年 *Shèngmǔ yǔ zhǔ tóngxíng fúlín táiwān 150 nián*" (Fig. 5.8), the Church hierarchy wanted to make clear that Jesus was the center of the Catholic faith, also because in Taiwan the difference between Catholic and Protestants Churches is not so clear. Therefore, people tend to indicate the Catholic church as the Church where the Virgin Mary is worshiped.

A more detailed analysis of the symbols displayed at this event can be read in the intent by the Taiwanese Catholic church to let all the faithful around the island feel like part of the unique family represented by the Church. It is important to note that the name Mary is commonly called is Saint Mother 聖母 *Shèngmǔ* in Taiwan. The faithful often refer to her with the devoted and familiar term 聖母媽媽 *Shèngmǔ māmā*.

The figure of Holy Mary as the mother of all faithfuls acted as the catalyst for all believers who rediscovered and reevaluated their positions as brothers and sisters among the family represented by the Church. From another point of view, it is possible that the integration of a female

Fig. 5.8 The poster of the 150th anniversary

ancestress in the big family represented by the Catholic church acted as a template for the integration of women into the Zhong's *Zúpú*.

5.5.4　*Ancestors, Jesus, and the Zhong Clan*

Ancestors are always very present in the life of many Taiwanese people. I heard many people telling me "We buried our ancestors in our fields because they should continue to care for their proprieties." Ancestors should be notified of any change in the family: marriage, pregnancy, business, and so on. The relationships between supernatural beings and those who are still living are physical and direct, for the most part of Taiwanese people. The dead and the living—spirit and human—share the same time and the same living space, and, maybe most importantly, they also share the same bodily preoccupations or needs.

As Francis Hsu noted in his *Under the Ancestors' Shadow*,

> The attitude of the living toward the dead and that of the living are functionally one. The relation of the living with the dead is essentially modeled upon that of the living with the living. By glorifying the dead, it both idealized and sets the standard and pattern for kinship relationship. (Hsu 1948, p. 245)

There is a Chinese proverb which says, "The same service to the dead as to the living; to the absent as to the present" (事死如事生 *Shì sǐ rú shì shēng*) which implies an equality of relationship between the dead and the living and that—more importantly—links together these two categories of people (Lazzarotti 2014, pp. 114–115). The "physical" elimination of the ancestors' tablets from the home altar and the prohibition to take part in the ancestors' ceremonies of the Zhong clan created a separation between the Catholic and the non-Catholic part of the lineage. As already mentioned, people who converted to Catholicism had to burn their ancestors' tablets and all the images of Confucius and other deities present in their house. Even more important, the elimination of the ancestors' tablets has created a division between the Catholic community and the supernatural part of the family (if in Taiwan it makes sense to use the word supernatural).

The renunciation of having ancestors' tablets symbolizes a separation with this belief system but also the acceptance of the new one where Jesus represents the first and the true ancestor for all the Christians all over the world. The first consequence of this change is the disappearing of all the mediators between human and gods and between human and the supernatural. The only medium is Jesus, who is the first ancestor (because he is the first who rose from the dead (1Cor 15:20)) and the head of the Catholic community (Col. 1:18).

The ancestors of the Zhong family are still remembered for the anniversary of their death, but no rituals are performed at home. If traditionally the family should provide food and all the members of the lineage linked with that particular ancestor should take part in the ceremony (I will explain it more in detail in Ethos, Sect. 6.3.2), the Catholic part of the Zhong family invites the priest to remember the ancestors during the Mass. This is the one of the few moments when the Zhong faithfuls pray for their ancestors. The place which concretely represents the presence of the ancestors thus moved from the house to the church.

Another moment is during the Qingming Festival. For what concerns this festival, the presence of the bishop is of central importance. The Catholic community started to perform these kinds of ceremonies with the Mass only when the current bishop was ordained as priest. Only when Zhong Anzhu became bishop did the Catholic part of the Zhong family realize that they were an important community among the Taiwanese Catholic church. This discovery has helped them to emphasize their sense of genos. Only recently they cleaned the area where the tombs of Zhong Qin and his wife are buried. A small garden with flowers and trees was created around the two tombs. Apart from this, they started to draft their genealogical record.

Without common ancestors, the Zhong Catholic community of Shuiwei has detached itself from the Zhong lineage and clan. The introduction of a new ancestor, Jesus, let the Catholic community become a sort of clan. Jordan defined a clan as a property-holding group made up of descendants of an apical ancestor, but the details of the descent lines from that ancestor are unknown. In some cases the ancestor is clearly mythical and, in some societies, the apical ancestor may even be non-human (Jordan 2006).

The Catholic communities pray for the same ancestor, do the same activities, gather together for the Mass, just as a traditional clan. This sense of belonging to the same clan is implemented by the Catholic doctrine that considers all men and women as children of the same father. From this point of view, we can consider also the Li and the other families that compose the Catholic community of Lunbei as part of this clan.

Among this clan, even if the influence of the concept of patrility is still very present, the gender relationships and the relations between different generations are in some ways reconceived. In the Catholic community, women hold important positions (the current head of the Pastoral Council of Lunbei parish is a woman); the elders tend to leave all the positions within the parish to the younger generations. To the idea of this clan based on their faith, we can read also the attempt made by the Bishops' Conference to expand this clan to embrace all the Church as a community of believers made by brothers and sisters. Just as the faithful told me in the last story by which I began this chapter.

REFERENCES

Ahern, E.M. 1973. *The Cult of the Dead in a Chinese Village*. Stanford: Stanford University Press.
——. 1981. *Chinese Ritual and Politics*. Cambridge: Cambridge University Press.
Altan, C.T. 1995. *Ethnos e Civiltà. Identità Etniche e Valori Democratici*. Milano: Feltrinelli.
Arnhart, L. 2005. The Incest Taboo as Darwinian Natural Right. In *Inbreeding, Incest, and the Incest Taboo: The State of Knowledge at the Turn of the Century*, ed. Arthur P. Wolf, and W. H. Durham. Stanford: Stanford University Press.
Bao, Y. 2012. *The Richness of Chinese Names. Masteroppgave*. Ph. D. thesis, University of Oslo.
Eberhard, W. 1986. *A Dictionary of Chinese Symbols: Hidden Symbols in Chinese Life and Thought*. London & New York: Routledge.
Ebrey, P.B., and J.L. Watson, et al. 1986. *Kinship Organization in Late Imperial China, 1000–1940*, vol. 5. Berkeley: University of California Press.
Fernandez, P., F.B. Bautista, and L. Syquia-Bautista. 1994. *One Hundred Years of Dominican Apostolate in Formosa (1859–1958): Extracts from the Sino-Annamite Letters, Dominican Missions and Ultramar*. Taipei: SMC Publishing Inc.
Fides, A. 2009a. At the close of celebrations for the 150th anniversary of the evangelization bishop of kaohsiung calls everyone to open wide the missionary doors. http://www.fides.org/en/news/25430-ASIA_TAIWAN_At_the_close_of_celebrations_for_the_150th_anniversary_of_the_evangelization_Bishop_of_Kaohsiung_calls_everyone_to_open_wide_the_missionary_doors#.VjCS1d8SppQ. Accessed February 1, 2017.
——. 2009b. Brief overview of the church and celebrations for the 150th anniversary of the evangelization. http://www.fides.org/en/news/25455-ASIA_TAIWAN_Brief_Overview_of_the_Church_and_Celebrations_for_the_150th_Anniversary_of_the_Evangelization#.VjCT9t8SppQ. Accessed February 1, 2017.
Freedman, M. 1958. *Lineage Organization in South Eastern China*, vol. 18. London: Burns & Oates.
Hsu, F.L. 1948. *Under the Ancestors' Shadow; Chinese Culture and Personality*. New York: Columbia University Press.
Jordan, D.K. 1999. Gods, Ghosts, & Ancestors: Folk Religion in a Taiwan Village. Published as a WWW document http://anthro.ucsd.edu/~dkjordan. Accessed August 8, 2017.
——. 2006. Traditional Chinese Family and Lineage. http://pages.ucsd.edu/~dkjordan/chin/familism.html. Accessed August 8, 2017.
Jung, C. 1989. *Memories, Dreams, Reflections*. New York: Vintage (Original work published 1961).

Lang, O. 1946. *Chinese Family and Society*. New York: Archon.
Lazzarotti, M. 2008. The Ancestors' Rites in the Taiwanese Catholic Church. Master's thesis, National Taiwan University, Taipei.
——. 2013. How the Universal Becomes Domestic: An Anthropological Case Study of the Shuiwei Village, Taiwan. In *The Household of God and Local Households: Revisiting the Domestic Church*, ed. T.K.-P. le Roi, M. Gerard, and D.M. Paul, 301–314. Leuven: Peeters Publishers.
——. 2014. Modern Life and Traditional Death. Tradition and Modernization of Funeral Rites in Taiwan. *Fu Jen International Religious Studies* 8 (1): 108–126.
Liu, L. 1999. Who Were the Ancestors? The Origins of Chinese Ancestral Cult and Racial Myths. *Antiquity* 73 (281): 602–613.
Meldrum, W. 2005. A cardinal comes of age. http://taiwantoday.tw/ct.asp?xItem=1123&ctNode=2229&mp=2015. Accessed April 21, 2016.
People's Republic of China, T.C.P.G. 2012. 院于批交通部等部重大假日免收小型客通行施方案的通知. http://www.gov.cn/jrzg/2012-09/29/content_2235833.htm. Accessed June 17, 2015.
Sangren, P.S. 2009. 'Masculine Domination' Desire and Chinese Patriliny. *Critique of Anthropology* 29 (3): 255–278.
Watson, J.L., and E.S. Rawski. 1988. *Death Ritual in Late Imperial and Modern China*, vol. 8. Berkeley: University of California Press.
Williams, C.A.S. 1976. *Outlines of Chinese Symbolism and Art Motives: An Alphabetical Compendium of Antique Legends and Beliefs, as Reflected in the Manners and Customs of the Chinese*. Chelmsford: Courier Corporation.
Wolf, A.P. 2005. Explaining the Westermarck Effect, or, What Did Natural Selection Select For? In *Inbreeding, Incest, and the Incest Taboo: The State of Knowledge at the Turn of the Century*, ed. Arthur P. Wolf, and W.H. Durham. Stanford: Stanford University Press.
Wolf, A.P., and C.-s. Huang. 1980. *Marriage and Adoption in China, 1845–1945*. Stanford: Stanford University Press.
Wolf, M. 1972. *Women and the Family in Rural Taiwan*. Stanford: Stanford University Press.
朱介凡. 1989. 中華諺語志. 臺灣商務印書館.
陳其南. 1990. 家族與社會: 台灣與中國社會研究的基礎理念. Lian jing chu ban shi ye gong si.

CHAPTER 6

Ethos

6.1 Stories from Shuiwei

We were looking at pictures at Zhong An-fu's house. Among the many, one picture caught my attention. It portrayed a traditional funeral, but the thing which attracted my interest was the face of An-fu. He was dressed in the 喪服 *Sāngfú* traditional clothes, which means he was taking part in the ceremony. Behind him I recognized many of other Shuiwei Catholics, dressed in the same way. When I asked An-fu, he told me that it was his uncle's funeral. It was, thus, a Catholic funeral. "When our uncle passed away, he asked us to perform a traditional funeral. Since he wanted to show that our faith is different from the one of other people, he asked us not to use any incense stick. We did a very big funeral, everybody dressed in the proper clothes. Many people came to pay respect to our grandfather. He was very old and well-known around Lunbei. But we decided not to use incense sticks, even if other people felt this as strange or unusual."

Field notes. Autumn, 2009

Mei-hsia is an 尪姨 *Ang-i*. She has 陰陽眼 *Yīnyáng yǎn*; she can see what in Taiwan is called 另外個世界 *lìngwài gè shìjiè*: "another world." In other words, she is able to see the many spirits which cohabit with people in Taiwan. She inherited her power from her mother, and her daughter has the same power. She lived in Shuiwei village until her wedding, and, at the

© The Author(s) 2020
M. Lazzarotti, *Place, Alterity, and Narration in a Taiwanese Catholic Village*, Asian Christianity in the Diaspora,
https://doi.org/10.1007/978-3-030-43461-8_6

time of my fieldwork, she owned her own private shrine in 油車Youche, not too far from Shuiwei. Mei-hsia's daughter was living in Taipei, but when she was a child, she used to play with the children of the Catholic families, since they attended the same elementary school. Despite the fact that she was not Catholic, she took part in many Catholic activities, pilgrimages, and youth camps. Especially because of her daughter, Mei-hsia was in good relationships with the Catholic community of Shuiwei. I met her for the first time in the Lunbei church's courtyard, where I was taking a cup of coffee with Fr. Zhao. Mei-hsia came to bring vegetables to Fr. Zhao, who knew her very well. After we exchanged some courtesies, she told us a fact which happened just few weeks before.

> Did you hear that the old Miss Chen [a Presbyterian] passed away in Shuiwei a few weeks ago? I knew her very well, so I went to her funeral. The pastor was doing his ceremony, but I saw her. She knew me very well, so she asked me to do her a favor. She said «We are Presbyterians and I understand that this kind of thing is forbidden, but I would like that the kids bow at me [she was referring to her grandchildren]. Of course they don't have to say anything, but it would be fine if at least the kids can show to me their respect. Better you wait till the pastor will leave the room, otherwise he won't allow the kids to do it». So I did, at the beginning someone said that it was not possible, but at the end of the day they allowed the grandchildren to pay respect to their grandmother bowing at her.
>
> Field notes. Winter, 2008

Today I went to Liaolei house with Judy. My wife wanted to show her something she received from Korea. At her house I met Mr. Liao, who is a friend of Mr. Chen [Liaolei's husband] and a remote relative of Liaolei. Both Liaolei and Mr. Liao, as well as Mr. Chen, are non-Christians. Mr. Liao told us a story about a fact that happened just a short while ago. This is the transcription of the story and of the dialogue which followed it:

Mr. Liao: «Some days ago the former principal of Lunbei Elementary School passed away. Actually it has been a very sad thing because he committed suicide. I really don't know what happened to him, he was a good man. After the retirement he opened a stationery shop near the school. A few days ago he went in the Elementary school backyard and he cut his throat with a knife. Can you think about it? He was certainly sick, because you can hang yourself, but how can you cut your own throat? And do you know? On these days some people saw him walking around the school backyard».

Liaolei: «What do you mean? There is a ghost in the school backyard?»
Mr. Liao: «I just said that someone saw him, and it was the watchman of the school, who is a Christian...»

Field notes. Autumn, 2008

6.2 Ethos, Ritual, and the Taiwanese Daily Life

According to Altan, ethos is the sacralization of the norms and institutions, by religious or social origin, on which the sociality of a group of people is based. Epos and ethos are the two main pillars in the construction of ethnos, the symbolic complex lived by different people as a constitutive element of their identity and as a principle of social aggregation (Altan 1995, p. 21). If ethos and epos are not strong enough, the other components are not sufficient to fill the vacuum of identity that these two elements leave in the mythical symbolic complex of ethnic identity (Altan 1995, p. 24). In his analysis, Altan links ethos with the religious institutions in charge to maintain and legitimize the code of conduct of a certain society.

> The subject of ethos includes a series of symbolically transfigured cultural phenomena, related to the social relationships of a group. These cultural phenomena, in the form of precepts or taboos, include the rules that establish what is good and what is bad, right or wrong. These norms are usually felt as the core of a people's culture, taking in this way the value of categorical imperatives. Also the behaviors, the customs, and the institutions created to ensure the observance – through social control – of the above-mentioned rules, are symbolically transfigured in ethos. Moreover, we should consider as ethos also the totality of religious beliefs, which are important in order to guarantee the basis of an ethnic group. (Altan 1995, p. 24)

In his analysis, Altan considers both local or folk religions and those of universalistic inspiration. As a matter of fact, the dialectic between local cultural values and universal values brought by Christian missionaries opens several serious contradictions that have been of paramount importance in the history of evangelization in China.

The idea that ethos is linked with religion is also shared among a part of anthropologists who addressed the study of religion.

The anthropologist who undoubtedly has linked his name to the concept of ethos is Clifford Geertz. Since his first article on this topic on 1957, he developed a vision of ethos which found its more complete expression in his famous piece, "Religion as a Cultural System" (Geertz 1973, pp. 87–125). In this article, Geertz directly connects the concept of ethos, "the tone, character, and quality of their [a people's] life, its moral and aesthetic style and mood" (1973, p. 89), with the concept of world-view, "the picture they [a people] have of the way things in sheer actually are, their most comprehensive ideas of order" (1973, p. 89). Geertz considers ethos and world-view synthesized and represented by the sacred symbols. It is, thus, within religion that the world-view and the ethos are melded in a coherent experience, especially in a religious act or ritual.

> In a ritual, the world as lived and the world as imagined, fused under the agency of a single set of symbolic forms, turn out to be the same world, producing thus that idiosyncratic transformation in one's sense of reality to which Santayana refers in my epigraph. Whatever role divine intervention may or may not play in the creation of faith—and it is not the business of the scientist to pronounce upon such matters one way or the other—it is, primarily at least, out of the context of concrete acts of religious observance that religious conviction emerges on the human plane. (Geertz 1973, p. 112)

In other words, the rite attempts to match the world of ethos, synthesized by sacred symbols, with the image of the world in its entirety, bringing in this way ethos to *hólon* (Terrin 1999, p. 149). It is necessary, in this view of the rite, that there is a need for a global sense, a horizon full of common sense shared by all participants of the rite. Only in this way, in fact, can the rite be active in relation to life and incisive in relation to the praxis (Terrin 1999, p. 149). This universe of meaning is constituted by what Geertz defines as culture, namely, that complex symbolic system that gives order and meaning to our lives.

And it is precisely because man is constantly surrounded by a horizon full of common sense that the moods and motivations induced by religious practice seem supremely practical. The only way that it makes sense to adopt given the way in which things are "real." That is to say that this is the way by which these moods and motivations have been incorporated into everyday life, becoming, in some ways, dominant symbols of culture.

6.2.1 Ethos and "As if" World

Another interesting point of view on the link between ethos, ritual, and everyday life is presented by Adam B. Seligman, Robert P. Weller, Michael

J. Puett, and Bennett Simon (2008). Their goal is to go beyond the definition proposed by Geertz—they believe Geertz tames ritual practice by interpreting it according to a coherent world-view, instead of looking at its actual workings (Seligman et al. 2008, p. 20)—they argue that the ritual is about doing more than about saying something. Therefore, the authors argue that the ritual creates a subjunctive world where all the people's actions should be framed and interpreted. It is because the imaginative capacity of human mind that ritual creates "as if" worlds, the boundaries of which are defined by the performance of these rituals. According to them, creating a common subjunctive, the ritual is not anymore relegated to the "religious realm," but, considering it a particular form or orientation—the authors use here the word *frame*—it follows that it is the framing of the actions themselves that make them ritual.

> Whenever the expressions "please" and "thank you" are used, when we ask a casual acquaintance, "How are you?" both knowing in advance that we do not really expect an honest answer (…) we are enacting a crucial ritual for the maintenance of our shared world. [These rituals] create subjunctive universes (…) [They] permit the very existence of a shared social world, [holding] us in a universe that, without such performatives, would simply not exist. (Seligman et al. 2008, p. 8)

The ritual thus creates imagined realities which are shared on a social basis. More precisely, people are able to live and accept this imagined reality only because of the mediation of the rituals. It seems that the authors get the gist of one of the most central points in the understanding of the Taiwanese people complex approach to rituals and religion. When we discuss about Taiwanese rituals, we must take into consideration that the ritual, or it would be better to say the ritualization of people's everyday life, takes place by virtue of a system of belief and the way of life that "subvert" the Western concept of supernatural, making it (in some way) unusable. It changes the idea of supernatural by eliminating the classic Western divisions between culture and nature or between natural and supernatural. What in Western cultures are traditionally two distinct realms are not so clearly separated in most Taiwanese people's everyday life. This is, in my opinion, a very important premise to understand the analysis of ethos. Especially if we consider that the Chinese word for ritual, 禮 *Lǐ*, represents an explanation of ritual both as an act of worship 禮儀 *Lǐyí* and as a code of conduct 禮貌 *Lǐmào* (Seligman et al. 2008, p. 20).

There is, thus, a strong mixture mainly due to lack—or the redundancy—of the supernatural, a profound influence, clearly reciprocal, between what we might call the everyday life and the complex symbolism of the rite. In other words, there is a rich and always-present symbolism which concretely influences or at least gives a particular key to interpretation and the understanding of the everyday events. This ritualization of many aspects of people's everyday life, mainly caused by the merger of natural with the supernatural (at least in the Western way of thinking), leads people to cohabit with many entities, which in the Western tradition should be considered as supernatural. The result of this situation is that the subjunctive world created by the ritual is not an "as if" world, but it is the true world. The world constructed in this way is not a "subjunctive" world, but rather a "present indicative" one.

In the concrete situation of Lunbei, this constructed reality, this imagined world created by the rituals (in the sense explained above) commonly shared by Taiwanese people, is in contrast with the imagined world created by the Catholic tradition and by the observance of its rituals. These differences bring the people of Lunbei to recognize that the people of Shuiwei are living in another "as if" world. A world that they can recognize as different but of which they don't have a full understanding. I personally experienced several times, as a Catholic believer, this contrast between different ethoi.

When I moved to Lunbei, I lived for the first year in the district of 崙前 Lunqian, not far from the Catholic church. Our landlord, a woman about 70 years old, was not Christian. The episode I am going to introduce is intended to show how, for Taiwanese people, even the Western God is one god among the others. He shares, thus, the same living space and living time with human beings.

> Today our landlord came to our house, and I signed the rent contract. She spent some time watching a calendar that one of the faithful had just given us. On the calendar it had depicted Jesus the Good Shepherd, and the landlord, even before saying "hello" told us not to invite Jesus to live in our home (不要請耶穌住在這裏 *bù yàoqǐng yēsū zhù zài zhèlǐ*). I told her that Jesus was already living in the church, and that he probably would not have come to live here even if I had invited him. Reassured by my answer, she explained to me that once previous tenants brought their gods and their ancestors to live in this house. Since the house is so comfortable and the *fēngshuǐ* is so

good, when tenants went away, their ancestors refused to leave the house. In addition, they quarreled with the ancestors of the tenants who rented the house after them. They were so noisy that nobody could sleep.

This cohabitation between human and non-human beings (but maybe it would be better to say visible and invisible entities) let people continuously feel the presence of these entities. These non-corporeal entities share the same human needs, such as hunger, cold, heat, jealousy, anger, and so on. Therefore many Taiwanese people offer not only incense but also money, food, wine, cigarettes, and even wives or husbands to their ancestors and to the many ghosts who wander around.[1] Apart from this, the cohabitation also influences many other social aspects, such as how roads or even houses are built.

Our first house in Lunbei was a two-floor building, and like almost all the houses in the Taiwanese countryside, it was very big. My wife and I chose the largest room at the second floor as bedroom. The only missing thing was a place for the air-conditioner. I felt this to be very strange because the hot and humid Taiwanese weather requires air-conditioning. When I complained about this with Fengrong (a Catholic believer), he smiled and told me: "Is the room the one at the second floor? When you look at the house, the room is on the right side, it is correct? Well, the room you chose is not for people, but for ancestors. That's why there is no place for air-conditioning: they just do not need it!"

6.3 Different Ethos, Different Worlds?

In order to explain and fully understand the stories by which I started this chapter, I considered it necessary to introduce some basic ideas about the world created by most of the Taiwanese people, where almost all the aspects of everyday life are ritualized (at least in the Western way of thinking), and thus potentially subjected to the sphere of ethos. The world created by this kind of ethos is above all the social fact, which is able to create and shape the social links between different social actors.

In the narrative of the world made by most Taiwanese people, and within the narrative by which the world "reveals" itself to the Taiwanese, the ritual is omnipresent. Maybe it is not totally recognized by the Taiwanese people

---

[1] See Jordan (1999), especially chapter 8, and also Wolf (1976).

(Lazzarotti 2008, pp. xi–xii), but certainly (at least for Western canons) ritual is always present.

This fact entails several consequences. One of the most important is that it is not just the ritual that gives the idea of otherness or reveals the belonging to another cosmology. Often the Christians act differently even during events where everyone is used and would expect them to act in the opposite way. The daily encounters/clashes between different kinds of ethos contribute to the construction of the "other" on the schema of contrast. This contrast contributes to building the world where stories, as the three I mentioned at the beginning of this chapter, could find their places.

I would like to underline the importance of these daily clashes between different visions of ethos by taking as example an incident that occurred to a young woman I met during my fieldwork. She had just finished her college, and like many of her peers in Yunlin County, she was struggling to find a job. During the time of my fieldwork, she was living in Shuiwei with her parents. After she graduated, at first she tried to open her own business, but after some time she decided to be employed somewhere. She finally found a position in a convenience store where, apart from beverages, sweets, cigarettes, and betel nuts, the national lottery tickets were sold. She was very happy she found a job near her house, at least until her boss asked her to burn paper money and incense sticks twice a month. Every month on the 1st and the 15th day of the lunar calendar, many Taiwanese people burn paper money in large metal barrels and leave food on tables outside their homes or businesses. They do this in order to feed the hungry ghosts so that they will not cause any trouble for the offerer's family or business (Fig. 6.1).

She told her boss that as a Catholic believer she was not allowed to do it, but the boss said to her "don't worry, you don't have to say anything when you burn the paper money and you put the incense in the cup. You don't have to worship (the right term was you don't have to 拜拜 *bàibài*). Anyway, you must do it, otherwise if our customers see we are not offering anything to the 好兄弟 good brothers (*hǎo xiōngdì*, the "good brothers" is a very polite way to say ghosts) they will think that this place is plenty of bad lucks and will not come here to buy their lottery tickets."

Not being sure how to deal with this situation, she went to the parish priest to ask advice. The priest, knowing the situation of my friend and her family, advised her to keep the job. "Since these things [the ghosts] do not exist," he said, "you must not be afraid of them." Therefore, she continued

Fig. 6.1 Offering for the ghosts

to work in this place, but after a few weeks she decided to quit that job and moved to a city in the northern part of Taiwan, where she found another job in a factory.

Differences of ethos are leading to miscomprehensions and even to contrasts. I think that this contrast comes out very clearly in the anecdote I just exposed. Anyway, if we compare this episode with the incense episode told to me by Fengrong (Locus, Sect. 2.1), we can see that there is another way to conceive the differences of ethos. In both cases, the elements belonging to ethos are considered as common sense, and the behavior's differences are considered as cosmological differences. This interpretation is based on the fact that these differences are inserted in a frame of meanings which interpret the other as belonging to a different socio-cosmic system.

The interpretation of the woman's case is based on moral values. Ethos is strongly linked, and takes power, from cosmological concepts always linked with a precise conception on the world and consequently of human relationships. Therefore, we can say that if ethos forms the moral and ethical guidelines of the society, it should be considered as the first and strong parameter for the discovery of what is not similar to us.[2]

The woman's incident shows us how Taiwanese common sense suggests that it is necessary to burn paper money and put food and incense sticks on the table, because ghosts are real. The common sense (a very pragmatical one) of the owner of the shop added the reason that by not performing such a ritual, nobody would come to buy lotto tickets. Confronted with this mountain of common sense, she persevered to refuse because her common sense belonged to another world-view. At the end, failing to find a point of contact and peace, she preferred to leave the job. It is possible to recognize here an uncompromising attitude toward identity. An identity not built by "construction" but by "contrast" (Eco 2012).

In Fengrong's case, things worked in a different way. The main difference was played by the level of confidence and interaction that Fengrong has with the Taiwanese Popular Religion environment. Fengrong's anecdote had a different conclusion just because all the principal characters of the story were aware that the "other" belonged to a different ethos, to a different way of conceiving the world and the relations among its (natural and supernatural) inhabitants. Both parties were aware that the "other" was not part of their system of ethos, but this has not caused irreparable conflict. They were aware that differences can coexist in the same social fabric and, indeed, can dialogue.

The contrast between the ethos of the people of Shuiwei village and the massive presence of rituals in Taiwanese society is experienced also in less dramatic ways.

As we can see in Fig. 6.1, the offerings for the ghost are put on a table. The dimension of the table are not random, but they should reckon with precise measurements related to fēngshuǐ (Fig. 6.2). In Fig. 6.2 we can see in detail how the measuring tape is made to fulfill the fēngshuǐ requirements. The right and lucky dimension is showed by the red characters. The dimension of these tables, thus, is not accidental; likewise, the position that the table should have during the offerings to the deities is not left to chance.

---

[2] It is not by chance that the word ethos forms the root of *ethikos*, meaning "moral, showing moral character." Used as a verb in the neuter plural form *ta ethika*, used for the study of morals, it is the origin of the modern English word ethics.

Fig. 6.2 Taiwanese measuring tape

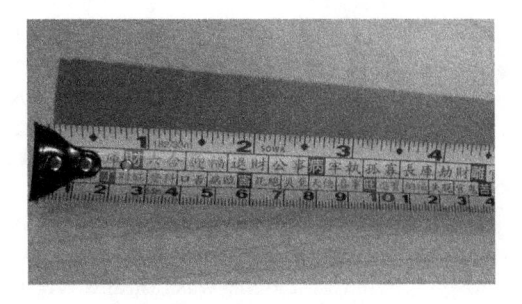

The table must be positioned parallel to the front door of the house or shop. If someone is using this kind of rectangular table to take a tea or beer with friends, the table should be placed perpendicular to the main door. If this precaution is not observed, it is likely that other incorporeal guests will consider themselves invited to that table.

The one who told me this was Fengrong. He told me that he was never able to remember this precaution, causing each time the protests of his friends—who continued to pay him visits and to share tea or beer with him anyway.

Ethos—or, better yet, the contrasts between ethos readable in public ceremonies—is one of the most important story makers. Of course these public ceremonies are not necessarily belonging to the Catholic tradition. Near Lunbei Township, there is the city of Huwei, where Saint Joseph Hospital is located. This hospital, founded in 1955, was the first Catholic hospital in Yunlin.

There are many stories shared by Christians and non-Christians about this hospital. One of the most meaningful stories is linked with a 乩童 Dangki performance or, better yet, with the failure of his performance.[3] It is common in Taiwan—especially in the countryside but also sometimes in Taipei—to see Dangki or Daoist priests inside the hospital.[4] This happens because when the doctor or the "official medicine" fails to provide a solution to the sick person, it is believed that the reason of the illness should be linked with "supernatural" causes. Therefore, in some occasions,

---

[3] The 乩童 Dangki (*Jītóng* in Chinese) is usually a medium who is possessed by a deity that through him will act in order to perform certain rituals.

[4] I have personally seen shamans in a hospital in Sanxia, Taipei County, now Great Taipei, and also Taoist priests in Taipei City's hospitals during the SARS period (2003).

a Dangki or a shaman is invited to make some exorcisms in order to clean the patient or the place from dangerous presences. Several people told me about a Dangki who wanted to enter Saint Joseph Hospital because he had been invited by a patient's family. The Dangki is usually a medium who is possessed by a deity that through him acts in order to perform certain rituals. The problem was that as soon as the possessed Dangki tried to enter the hospital, the deity which possessed him immediately went out from his body. People explained this event, saying that Saint Joseph was a Catholic hospital, where the deity was not allowed to enter.

6.3.1　Open Rituals

The first two stories of this chapter tell about funerals, while the third one is related with episodes linked with the interconnections of different—because they belong to different ethos and thus to different rituals—imagined worlds. It is not just by coincidence that I chose two stories related with funerals in order to explain how different ethoi, embodied in rituals, give different interpretations of reality. These different interpretations of the reality lead the different entities that take part to the ritual (missionaries, Christians, and non-Christians) to create the triangular shape of the dialogue I mentioned at the beginning of this work (Locus, Sect. 2.3.3).

Funeral rites have played an important role in the ritual acculturation of Catholicism (and Protestant Christianity as well) in China (Standaert 2011; Addison 1925). It is not my goal to describe the historical and cultural meaning of the acculturation process of the Catholic rites in China. I would like to discuss this phenomenon as I observed it in Shuiwei village.

I have chosen funerals as examples of the interaction of different ethoi especially because of the inspiration I received from reading the work of Nicolas Standaert (2011) about the role of funerary rites in the cultural exchange between China and Europe in the seventeenth century. As Standaert underlined,

> When Christianity was introduced into China it took the shape of an exclusive community, which is characteristic of all eastern Mediterranean religions. Rituals, such as baptism, Eucharist, and confession were responsible for creating such exclusion, because they were intended for the "in" group. It is noteworthy that they underwent hardly any significant change after their arrival in China, compared with the same rituals in Europe. (Standaert 2011, p. 228)

If these rituals helped to maintain the exclusiveness—and we could even say the peculiarity of the ethos—of the Catholic community, other rituals such as funerals should be considered as "open," because their performance is open not only to what Standaert called the "in" group but also—and in some cases especially—to non-Catholic people.

> Funeral rituals tend to be open rituals: though they can be limited to the in-group, usually they are inclined to be open to all people who were associated with the deceased or the relatives of the deceased. (Standaert 2011, p. 115)

And again:

> Therein funerals differ from other rituals, such as the Christian Eucharist or confession. The latter are "closed" or exclusive rituals, since they are only for the participation of in-group members; they are not so easily affected by people from outside the community and over the course of time, as was the case in China, largely retained their European characteristics. (Standaert 2011, p. 116)

One first consequence of this consideration is that the traditional concept of religious dialogue should be reconceived. I consider this triangular shape of the dialogical relationships as the best way to analyze and interpret the process that accompanied the meeting between these two cultural universes. In the performance of the ritual, with the two parts represented by the missionaries and the Catholic believers, the third vertex of the triangle may be assigned to the Taiwanese people who did not accept Catholicism (Lazzarotti 2010, p. 28). Especially because, as Standaert pointed out, "the Chinese who were not directly involved in the Christian community became a primary agent in the change that was to occur in the funerals celebrated by that community" (Standaert 2011, p. 116).

The first story, for example, is full of meanings linked with the above-mentioned contrasts between ethoi. The story tells us an apparently banal fact, but a further analysis can recognize different levels of reading and interpretation.

The incense sticks are commonly used in Taiwan in almost every place: in the temple where people pray to the gods, at home for the ancestors or for the deities present on the home altar, and even on the street during the offers for ghosts or during the deities' processions. The point of using an incense stick during a prayer shows that the person is concretely 求 *qiú*, demanding something to the gods or to other supernatural beings. In the Christian tradition, the faithful cannot—at least not officially—demand or request anything if not from God. This is the reason why many Catholic believers, especially if recently converted, don't want to use incense sticks to pay respect to their ancestors, even in the ceremonies performed inside the church by priests. This is the main reason why the uncle of An-fu asked to avoid the use of it: he wanted to give a clear signal to all non-Catholic people about the different faith shared by him and by his household.

In many churches in Taipei City, where the presence of foreign missionaries is higher compared to the situation in the countryside, I personally interviewed many parish priests on this argument. A good number of them have confirmed to me their difficulties in introducing the use of incense sticks during the ancestors' ceremonies performed in the church. The priests considered the use of incense sticks as a way to acculturate Catholic ceremonies to the local Taiwanese customs, but they met the opposition of the parishioners. I think this problem summarizes very well the idea that, as we already saw in the chapter about epos, rituals played—and still play—a very important role in the history of the contact between the Catholic church and the Chinese world. It has been already described how the Chinese Rites Controversy was dragged on for three centuries before the historical events let it appear outdated and then closed (Epos, Sect. 3.4).

To this historical background is linked another level of interpretation, which involves the need of Christianity to acculturate to the Chinese customs. This need for acculturation certainly has relations with the Chinese cultural background and especially with the preeminence of the Confucianism influence on concepts such as ethics or morals. As Erik Zürcher (1994, pp. 40–41) pointed out, Christianity was considered by Chinese people—and in many ways it is still considered—as a marginal religion in opposition to the mainstream religious ideology represented by the influence of Confucianism on ethical concepts. Because of this, from the beginning of the evangelization of China, the Catholic church started to incorporate some concepts (e.g. importance of ancestors, respect to the elders, filial piety) linked with the Confucian teachings.

6.3.2 Open Rituals in Open Life

The second story is linked with a more complex net of relationships. There are many levels of understanding linked with the story of Mei-hsia.

A first-level reading of this fact highlights the contrast of different practices. Presbyterians, as well as the most part of Protestant Christians, forbidden any activities linked with the practices of ancestor worship. Even the ritual bows before the picture of the deceased or before the tomb are forbidden. This is a big contrast with the non-Christian world, where the respect for ancestors and the deceased should be expressed in a visible and concrete way. In traditional funerals in Taiwan, the family of the deceased should kneel in front of the coffin, and inside the rich funeral ritual, they should cover on all fours a path that leads them to the coffin. The contrast coming from different practices is linked with the difference of cosmologies. According to the Bible, believers cannot worship or bow down before anything or anybody except God. In Exodus 20, 4–5, we can read "You shall not carve idols for yourselves in the shape of anything in the sky above or on the earth below or in the waters beneath the earth; you shall not bow down before them or worship them. For I, the LORD, your God, am a jealous God, inflicting punishment for their fathers' wickedness on the children of those who hate me, down to the third and fourth generation." This is the main reason, actually a commandment, why these practices are forbidden. Nevertheless, an analysis of cosmologies is still not enough to explain the interweaving of meanings present in the story of Mei-hsia. This happens because, as Geertz pointed out:

> Religious patterns do not become embodied in social forms directly, purely and simply, but in many devious ways, so that religious commitments and others commitments – to class, neighborhood, etc. – tend to balance off, and various "mixed type" individuals and groups arise, which can play an important mediating role. (Geertz 1976, p. 356)

In other words, despite the fact that some points of two ethoi seem incompatible, society is built by men and women, relationships, neighbors, friends, and so on. It is this habitual routine of everyday experiences and meetings which played an important role in this episode. Probably, if Mei-hsia had not been a part of the village (and she was a part of the village until her marriage), no one would take into account the fact that she pretended to be the spokesperson for the deceased. The fact that the request was verisimilar, especially because it was linked to the sense of filial piety—so important in Taiwanese society, as in all of Chinese culture—has certainly played a key role in the decision to allow children to bow before the coffin of their grandma.

There is, thus, another important level of reading of how people belong to a certain ethos. At a local level, ethos is not made only by the acceptance of cosmological concepts linked to specific religion and rituals. It is also influenced, more or less deeply, by the environment (education, friendships, daily contingencies, etc.) where a person lives. Therefore ethos, or better yet the adherence to a certain ethos, adapts itself to contingent situations. It is not something static and fixed. The respect and the filial piety which every Taiwanese—as well as every Chinese—person should show to the elderly, and especially to his or her parents, are one of the fundamental points of Confucianism. These Confucian values are the basis of the Taiwanese educational and social system.

These concepts—this ethos—are so important in Chinese culture that Christianity had to (and has to) adapt to them. Values such as filial piety (which in the Catholic tradition is very often related with the fourth commandment "Honor your father and your mother") and the role of women in society were accepted by the missionaries as translations of Catholic values and thus as a sort of platform where they could start the process of evangelization. These concepts were important even to the Dominicans, who decided to ban the practical acts related to them.

With the arrival of different congregations after 1949 and after the Second Vatican Council, the practices linked to these values have also been accepted and elaborated by the Taiwanese Catholic church. Through this long historical process, within the Catholic doctrines, small discrepancies were created, a sort of interstices where the Confucian values and their concrete and visible experiences (bows, incense, etc.) have found their space and their *raison d'être*.

During my fieldwork, I was able to take part in a Catholic funeral. The notes I made after the ceremony will help me to materialize the ideas I expressed above.

> This Saturday has been celebrated the funeral of Mr. Li. The funeral has been celebrated under a big tent [which is very common for funeral countryside in Taiwan] that was placed in front of the house. The audience of the funeral was composed by Catholics, Christians and by non-Christians.
>
> (Field notes)

Mr. Li was the first generation of the family converted to Catholicism; therefore all the members of the Li family linked in the way presented in the table in Fig. 6.3 were present at the funeral. The table, made by David

Generation	Main Line	Their Brothers	Their 1st Cousins	Their 2nd Cousins	Their 3rd Cousins
+4	2				
+3	2	5			
+2	2	4	5		
+1	1	3	4	5	
0	Ego	2	3	4	5
-1	2	3	4	5	
-2	3	4	5		
-3	4	5			
-4	5				

Fig. 6.3 Table from David Jordan (2006)

Jordan, displays a series of boxes arranged in a kind of diamond shape. The underlying design shows a column of boxes showing line of descent from the plus-four generations above Ego to the minus-four generations below him (Jordan 2006).

At each level a row of boxes extends to the side, representing same-generation collaterals set out beside one another. For example, to Ego's right comes his brother, then his first cousin, next his second cousin, then his third cousin. Above Ego is his father, and to his father's right is his father's brother (Ego's uncle), then his father's first cousin, second cousin, and third cousin. And so on.

Except in his direct ancestral line, a man's mourning obligations attenuate rapidly with genealogical distance. In broad outline this produces roughly (not in fact) the distribution of mourning obligations described in the table in Fig. 6.3 (Jordan 2006).

The sequence of the persons who must pay respect to the deceased at the funeral is linked to this order. Therefore, if the father of Ego passes away, Ego should be the first to pay respect, offering wine, a stick of incense, and fruit. Other people will follow starting at 2, 3, and so on. When the relatives who are obliged to pay respect to the deceased are finished, the master of ceremonies calls the friends, the co-workers, neighbors, and everyone who wants to show his/her condolences and who signed their names—and left a white envelope containing money—in a specific book. They should use an incense stick and put it in an incense burner placed in a small altar where a big picture of the deceased, usually surrounded by white flowers, which stands out.

> The funeral ceremony started with the Mass, the priest prayed for the deceased and blessed again the corpse. As soon the Mass ended the parents of Mr. Li dressed the 喪服 *Sāngfú*, the traditional mourning clothes, and a majorettes dance troupe entered inside the household courtyard, dancing and playing western musical instruments.
>
> (Field notes)

This kind of performance is very common in Taiwanese countryside funerals: usually there are companies that provide services such as dancing, singing, and providing tea or coffee and other snacks. Usually these performing groups (in some traditional funerals, the audience could even see performances of acrobats) are linked and work together with one or more Daoist priests and someone able to prepare the corpse (to clean and to dress it). The service also provides transportation with special cars, called 電子花車 *Diànzǐ huāchē*, to the cemetery or to the place where the body will be cremated. Anyway in the case of Mr. Li's funeral, because of his Catholic faith, only the musicians and the majorettes were employed to help with the execution of the ceremony.

> After the majorettes finished their performance and distributed some hot beverages, the ceremony started. The role of master of ceremonies was performed by one of the deceased nephews. This nephew had moved in northern Taiwan since he started to study at the university. Now he was married with children and working near Taipei. I met him every time he came back to visit his father's family, because he was used to attend to the Mass in Lunbei.
>
> (Field notes)

In traditional funeral performance, a specialist, who works together with the majorettes and the Daoist priest, plays the role of master of ceremonies. He should lead the people who take part in the funeral, telling the family and the guests when the right time is to pay honor to the deceased. The fact that a nephew of the deceased was chosen as master of ceremonies was already very unusual. Usually this master of ceremonies does not belong to the family. He is a professional performer specialized in moving the audience to tears.

> The ceremony started with a mistake. The Mass was really long as well as the majorettes' performance, the weather was fine and the temperature was rising. A group of nuns (there were two nuns in the Zhong family and one in the Li family) was attending the ceremony, the eldest of them was around eighty and they came on purpose from Jiayi. Maybe because of these reasons, Mr. Li's nephew, who was the master of ceremonies, looked at them and called them to pay respect to his defunct uncle. Immediately one of the non-Christian members of the Li family approached him to explain that what he was doing was very impolite. Therefore he started again calling the deceased elder son with his family to pay respect to their father, as prescribed by tradition.
> (Field notes)

From this episode we can learn some important points. Living together a system of meanings different to the one a person belongs to and that produces another kind of ethos gives new ways of interpretation of the surrounding reality. On a level, the nephew of Mr. Li gave priority to religion over kinship hierarchies, mixing in this way values belonging to different—but, as I tried to explain, overlapped—kinds of ethos. This happened because the particular situation of Shuiwei, and the narration that the peculiarities of this village help to create, has been built by a long coexistence of different ethoi.

6.3.3 Different Ethos and Shared Knowledge

This fact leads us to the third story. It is the only story where both the narrator and the listener were non-Christian. Among their dialogue and their stories, the particular situation of Shuiwei village—especially because of the long interaction (more than 100 years) between different ethoi—built up another interesting phenomenon.

The difference between the two world-views is partially constitutive of Locus. Especially because these differences are created not only by a singular contact but through a long interaction. The ontological alterity of the other becomes a symbol. This symbol can help to interpret unexpected or everyday events which life brings with it and that are not and which cannot be interpreted by people's common sense. In other words, people can use this alterity, which as we mentioned is linked with a long coexistence, to reinforce their narrations and their personal world-view. At the same time, this kind of narration helps to give a particular shape to this local community.

Almost everybody in Lunbei Township shares the knowledge that people who live in Shuiwei village act according to a different kind of ethos. Everyone knows that this ethos is linked to a cosmology and therefore to a certain belief and to an understanding of the world somehow different than the one shared among the majority of the Taiwanese people. These bits of knowledge form which we might call common feeling.

Non-Christian people use this common feeling, the different ethos of the Christians, in order to strengthen and give a solid foundation to their stories. For Mr. Liao, the fact that a Christian saw someone who passed away a few days ago was the unequivocal proof that what he was telling was true. In the context of Lunbei, to say "even a Christian saw a ghost," it is much more powerful than saying "someone saw a ghost." This is because according to Lunbei people's common sense, everybody could see (at least potentially) a ghost. On the other hand, this common sense suggests to them that a Christian cannot see a ghost because—as Mr. Liao and Liaolei know very well—there are no ghosts in their world-view.

This common sense is also used, among the people of Lunbei, to explain some inexplicable and strange events linked with the Christian community in Shuiwei. Also actions or particular and strange behaviors performed by Christian believers are interpreted through this above-mentioned common sense:

> Fengrong told me that his co-worker was absent from work for two days. The third day Fengrong paid a visit to him. When he arrived under his house he called him, telling him to come down to have some tea together. The co-worker came down, they spent the rest of the evening chatting and drinking tea, just as they have done many times before. Few days later, the mother of co-worker met Fengrong and told him that before that evening her son was continuously crying, for two days, without a specific reason. This situation

seemed too strange and they already decided to go to the temple when Fengrong arrived at their home. As soon her son heard Fengrong's voice, he stopped crying and everything was fine. After telling him this story, the mother said to Fengrong, "I think this happened because you are a Christian, it should be something linked with your faith."

Situations like the one I just wrote are very common in Lunbei. The difference of ethos, considered as common sense, explains and reinforces the narrative related to moments that are not explainable by the own symbolic system. I have acknowledged this situation through many personal experiences. One of them is linked with the fact that as (almost) every Taiwanese person knows, when a woman is pregnant she cannot touch certain things, like needles or scissors. Similarly she cannot move the bed and not even touch it with the broom when doing the cleaning. During pregnancy it is also forbidden to put nails in the wall. All these precautions are taken in order not to hurt the spirits that live in the house because they have the power to cause the loss of the baby.

When we lived in Lunqian, the sister-in-law of our neighbor had unfortunately lost her baby. My neighbor (a woman of 35 years) told us that her mother, making comments on this fact, said, "It is likely that she has touched scissors, or a needle. I told her to be careful several time, but…" Hearing that, our neighbor, referring to my wife, said, "My neighbor touched scissors and needles, hung nails on the wall and has even moved into a new house while she was pregnant, taking with her all the furniture, including the bed! Don't be superstitious. How can a needle affect a pregnancy?" Her mother replied, "Don't be silly! This does not matter. They are Catholic!"

References

Addison, J.T. 1925. Chinese Ancestor-Worship and Protestant Christianity. *The Journal of Religion* 5 (2): 140–149.
Altan, C.T. 1995. *Ethnos e Civiltà. Identità Etniche e Valori Democratici*. Milano: Feltrinelli.
Eco, U. 2012. *Inventing the Enemy and Other Occasional Writings*. Boston: Houghton Mifflin Harcourt.
Geertz, C. 1973. *Interpretation of Cultures*. New York: Basic Books.
———. 1976. *The Religion of Java*. Chicago & London: University of Chicago Press.

Jordan, D.K. 1999. Gods, Ghosts, & Ancestors: Folk Religion in a Taiwan Village. Published as a WWW document http://anthro.ucsd.edu/~dkjordan. Accessed August 08, 2017.
——. 2006. Wǔfú 五服: The Traditional Chinese Mourning Categories. http://pages.ucsd.edu/~dkjordan/chin/MourningGrades.html. Accessed February 02, 2017.
Lazzarotti, M. 2008. The Ancestors' Rites in the Taiwanese Catholic Church. Master's thesis, National Taiwan University, Taipei.
——. 2010. The Internal Structure of Dialogue. Two Taiwanese Case Studies. *Fu Jen International Religious Studies* 4 (1): 19–36.
Seligman, A.B., R.P. Weller, B. Simon, M.J. Puett, et al. 2008. *Ritual and Its Consequences: An Essay on the Limits of Sincerity*. Oxford: University of Oxford.
Standaert, N. 2011. *The Interweaving of Rituals: Funerals in the Cultural Exchange between China and Europe*. Seattle: University of Washington Press.
Terrin, A. N. 1999. *Il Rito: Antropologia e Fenomenologia Della Ritualità*. Brescia: Morcelliana.
Wolf, A.P. 1976. Aspects of Ancestor Worship in Northern Taiwan. In *Ancestors*, ed. W. Newell, 339–364. New York: Walter de Gruyter.
Zürcher, E. 1994. Jesuit Accommodation and the Chinese Cultural Imperative. *The Chinese Rites Controversy. Its History and Meaning, Steyler Verlag, Nettetal* 132: 31–64.

CHAPTER 7

Logos

7.1 Narrating Logos

We met Mrs. Li for the first time during a lunch break organized in the courtyard of the Catholic church by the priest and the (non-Christian) church neighbors. She opened a store in her house; Mrs. Li was specialized in preparing vegetarian lunch boxes that she sold along with other vegetarian products. Both she and her husband were Buddhists. Since her house-shop was right on the way from our house to the church, after that first meeting, we often dropped in to greet her and her husband.

One day we were talking about how she started this activity. After a while, the discussion moved on to the taste of her customers. In particular, on the requests of a Catholic faithful whose name was—believe it or not—Mrs. Li. "Every day Mrs. Li comes to my shop to buy our vegetarian lunch box. You know we are Buddhist, so we don't eat any meat or eggs. Vegetables such as onion and garlic or ginger are also forbidden. Mrs. Li told us that she became our customer because our lunch boxes are very healthy. Since her husband has problems with his teeth, she always asks me to overcook all the vegetables. In this way, her husband can eat the lunch box without any problems. I think it's great that a wife has these little attentions for her husband. Anyway, she is special also in another way. You know we are Buddhists. When a customer comes to my shop to buy our lunch box I always thank him or her, and I say 阿彌陀佛 *Amitofo* as a

© The Author(s) 2020
M. Lazzarotti, *Place, Alterity, and Narration in a Taiwanese Catholic Village*, Asian Christianity in the Diaspora,
https://doi.org/10.1007/978-3-030-43461-8_7

kind of blessing, as our Buddhist master told us.[1] Every time I say Amitofo to Mrs. Li, she answers 天主保佑 *Tiānzhǔ bǎoyòu* (God bless and protect you)."

Mrs. Li, Buddhist believer, talking about Mrs. Li, Catholic believer. Winter, 2008

Mr. Liao is a man of about 70 years. He is the owner of a store where he sells fertilizers and other products for agriculture. He already retired and one of his sons is managing this business. Nevertheless, Mr. Liao is often coming to the shop—their house is just at the back of the store—to spend time drinking tea and chatting with many old customers. Mr. Liao used to be a non-believer, but he converted to Catholicism after he married a Catholic girl. The whole family is Catholic now, and all his three sons have married Catholic girls. His grandchildren are now at university. I went to his shop every day because the kindergarten bus picked up and delivered my son there. Every time I went to pick up my son, I tried to have a friendly conversation with Mr. Liao, his son, and his daughter-in-law, who was one of the nieces of the Bishop Zhong. One day, when I was waiting in his shop for my son's school bus, Mr. Liao told me this story:

> Did you see the small pool in front of the grotto of our Lady of Lourdes I built in my backyard? When my grandson was more or less the same age of your son [in between two and three years old], he fell down in that pool. At that time I did not build the fencing around the small pool, I did it just after my grandson has fallen into the water. He fell down in the water, but he was able to stand on a rock in the middle of the pool. The body was under the water and only his head was standing outside. We were busy with customers and did not pay attention to him. Besides, as you can hear, the noise coming from the road was too loud [Mr. Liao's shop was located along the national road number 19]. He was calling us, asking for help, but since we were chatting with the customers, none of us had heard him. It had been one of our clients who first noticed his cries. I don't know how long he had been in the water, but I think quite a long time, because when we brought him out, he was really cold and exhausted. Can you think about this? A little kid around three years old was able to stand on a small rock for such long time

---

[1] The Amitofo mantra, or mantra of Amitabha Buddha, is a very popular mantra, for it is the main cultivation technique of the Buddhist Pure Land school founded by the Chinese monk Hui-Yuan. Please refer to Tanaka (1990).

into the water. I really think that it was a miracle. Also because he recovered very fast. After this fact, all our customers and the neighbors have begun to say that our Mary is very 靈 *Líng*.[2]

Mr. Liao, Catholic believer. Summer, 2011

One evening, as usual, I was sitting in Fengrong's courtyard when he told me a curious anecdote about his house. He told me that when he built his new home, he contacted an architect to oversee the work. When the project was finished and the ground prepared, they had to decide when to begin the work. As usual in Taiwan, the architect told Fengrong that they should look for a good day to decide when they could start the building of the house "we should look for a day" 我們要看一個日子 *Wǒmen yào kàn yīgè rìzi*. This means they should consult a special kind of calendar (Fig. 7.1), or to consult a fēngshuǐ specialist, and choose an auspicious day as the official starting of the building. Fengrong did not believe in such practices, and he knew very well that the expression "to look for a day" means that the building work could start even after several weeks or even a month after that "good day."

Playing with all these meanings, Fengrong answered, "We don't have to look for a day. We should decide a day and then start our work! (我們不要看一個日子，我們要訂一個日子後來開始工作 *Wǒmen bùyào kàn yīgè rìzi, wǒmen yào dìng yīgè rìzi hòulái kāishǐ gōngzuò*). Don't waste my time telling me that we are going to start next week and then disappear. Tell me a day, I will prepare all the materials, but we should really start the construction in that day!"

"So, you did not consult any fēngshuǐ master when you built this house," I asked him. "Of course not, even further there was something I did," answered Fengrong. Then he told me another anecdote linked with the construction of his house. "When I built my house, the first thing I did has been to find four big stones. I put one at each corner of the basement of the new house. I did so because in the Gospel is written «The stone that the builders rejected has become the cornerstone»" (Matthew 21, 42).

My own Field note. Summer, 2010

---

[2] 靈 *Líng*, as many Chinese characters, has several meanings. It is a character usually linked with the concepts of the mind, spirit, or soul. Within the context of the story told by Mr. Liao, it means efficacious, powerful.

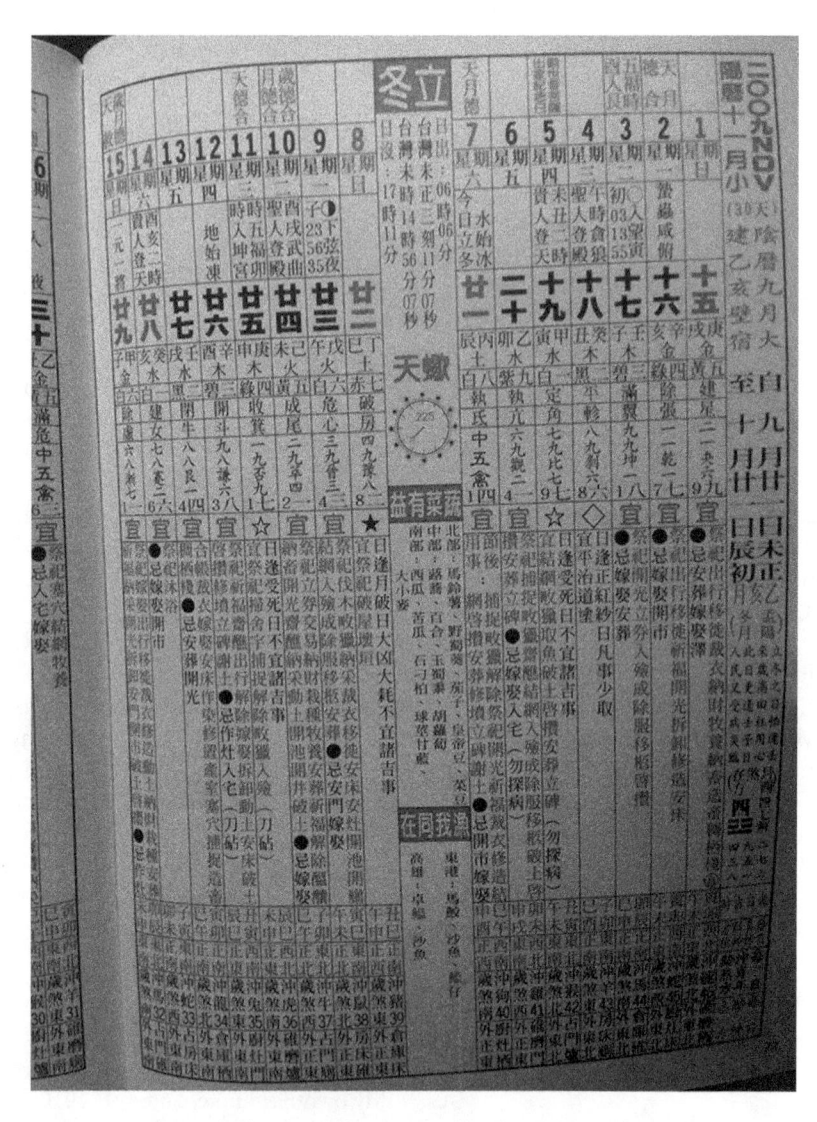

Fig. 7.1 Traditional Chinese Calendar. Under the Western date, some information about weather, and the corresponding date in the lunar calendar, there are indications about what to do and what not, what are the propitious directions or zodiacal signs, and the position of the spirit of the house in that day. *Source*: 農民曆系列. ACME Cultural Enterprise Co., Ltd.

It was already in the late afternoon when we decided to have a walk through the main road of Shuiwei. Looking at us, one of the faithful families called us, inviting us for dinner.

That day all the family was gathered together. Their daughters and their sons-in-law were sitting together in the courtyard. Also their elder son was present. Despite the fact that we were living in the same village, I did not meet him before. He was not going to the Mass and not taking part in Church activities. His wife, who was much more active in the Church than him, ran away some months before, especially because some contrasts with him, with his style of life, and also with his family.

> When we entered the courtyard, not sure who this man was, I introduced myself. When I told him my name, instead of telling me his name, he said: "I am their son [indicating his parents], I am a lost sheep" (Luke 15, 6).
> My own Field note. Summer, 2009

7.2 Logos

Logos is the element linked with the language. In this chapter I will consider language as both a system of communication between individuals and a social phenomenon. In fact, language is indissolubly connected with the members of the society where it is spoken. Their speech reflects inevitability many social factors. Altan quotes a passage from the Bible in order to demonstrate how old the historical evidence of the close links between language and ethnos is (Altan 1995, p. 26). In the biblical text, we read:

> If now, while they are one people, all speaking the same language, they have started to do this, nothing will later stop them from doing whatever they presume to do. Let us then go down and there confuse their language, so that one will not understand what another says. (Genesis 11, 6)

At the end of this story, Yahweh, jealous of the attempt made by the people to build a pyramid to reach the top of the sky, produced the confusion of their languages. In this way, Yahweh, dissolving the unity of languages, dissolves the unity of the people. Here the concept of language is associated with the value of language. It is throughout language that people can communicate and are able to act together.

As explained by Altan, the specific weight of language among the complex of ethnos varies from people to people. It depends on the importance that each of them gives to the values of poetic and literary production as moment of epos (Altan 1995, p. 26).

In this chapter I will try to integrate the trace of Altan with some reasoning proposed by the Italian thinker Antonio Gramsci. I will proceed on this way because my interest is not to understand the importance or the weight of language in the process of ethnic or national formation. What I consider crucial to my work is to understand how the language, as a social fact, can become an element that creates narration and, above all, which can be narrated. Language itself is an element that can be inserted into a story and in a narrative world.

7.2.1 Logos, Common Sense, and Daily Life

In his *Prison Notebooks* the Italian thinker Antonio Gramsci introduced the idea that language is public. He achieved this certainty by paying great attention to the problem of the evolution of the Italian language through time. Gramsci stresses that language is public because it is a "social product" and that it should be studied within a context formed by history.

> It seems that one can say that 'language' is essentially a collective term which does not presuppose any single thing existing in time and space. Language also means culture and philosophy (if only at the level of common sense) and therefore the fact of 'language' is in reality a multiplicity of facts more or less organically coherent and co-ordinated. At the limit it could be said that every speaking being has a personal language of his (or her) own, that is his own particular way of thinking and feeling. Culture, at its various levels, unifies in a series of strata, to the extent that they come into contact with each other, a greater or lesser number of individuals who understand each other's mode of expression in differing degrees, etc. It is these historico-social distinctions and differences which are reflected in common language (...). From this one can deduce the importance of the 'cultural aspect', even in practical (collective) activity. A historical act can only be performed by 'collective man', and this presupposes the attainment of a 'cultural-social' unity through which a multiplicity of dispersed wills, with heterogeneous aims, are welded together with a single aim (...). Since this is the way things happen, great importance is assumed by the general question of language, that is, the question of collectively attaining a single cultural 'climate'. (Gramsci et al. 1971, Q 10, §44, p. 1330)

Here we can read some of the cornerstones of Gramsci's thought. Language, as a collective term, helps people to think (to be a philosopher, in Gramsci's words). Consequently each speaking being has its own way to communicate that is, however, made intelligible by culture or, in Gramsci's words, by a "single cultural 'climate.' "

From these considerations it is possible to extrapolate some guidelines which will address our approach to the analysis of logos in the particular context of Shuiwei village. First of all, we can see how, according to Gramsci, language is not only a device of knowledge, but it is considered as a series of dimensions and functions linked with the complex of psychic and social life of all the people. Therefore, language (*Linguaggio* in original Italian) should be considered as a collective term.

Language—which for Gramsci is the manifestation of the thought and of the feeling of individuals and social groups—is the concrete form by which the socialization of people takes place within the economic, productive, functional network that characterizes their life. Within this view, language is closely related to another cornerstone of Gramsci's analysis: common sense. Language, in fact, repeats the character of sedimentation and the semantics and ideological layering of common sense. As consequence, through the language, through the choice of particular words, pass all the processes of composition and decomposition of hegemony. According to Gramsci this happens especially in the historic period when hegemony increases its complexity giving the start to multiple "outbreaks of radiation" of linguistic and cultural conformism (Gensini 2012, pp. 166–168).

Therefore, language is the detector, a kind of thermometer of the opinions of a certain individual or group, and also the point of attachment of any major restructuring of the common sense that a political entity intends to fulfill.

From this point of view, the ambiguities and encrustations of irrational thought that sediment in the language are social and historical products. What Gramsci considers as nonrational presences among the language is the phenomenon determined by sedimentation and interweaving of conceptions of the world belonging to various social groups and to their ways of expressing and feeling themselves. Therefore, these imperfections of the languages should be conceived as an element belonging to the historical—and local—dialectic which is susceptible to transformations (Gensini 2012, 176, my translation).

7.3 Shuiwei Logos: Between Hegemony and Daily Life

"Every time the question of language surfaces, in one way or another, it means that a series of other problems are coming to the fore: the formation and enlargement of the governing class, the need to establish more intimate and secure relationships between the governing groups and the national-popular mass, in other words to recognize the cultural hegemony." (Forgacs and Nowell-Smith 1985, Q29 §3, pp. 183–4)

These words of Gramsci could be applied to the concrete situation of the Shuiwei people and, more in general of Taiwan, in two main ways. The first one is considered from a social and political point of view. There are many connections between the concrete situation of the languages used in Shuiwei and the political situation of Taiwan. In fact, considering language as the manifestation of the social thought and of the feelings of individuals and social groups, it is possible, among Shuiwei's situation, to recognize different kinds of social groups and centers of power symbolized by language. These social groups are related with political or religious power at different levels: local, national, and over-national. Local Hakka and Taiwanese languages[3] compete with Chinese Mandarin (and, at least for children, even with English) in order to define the identity of the people of Shuiwei as well as the identity of the Taiwanese people. Especially in the central and southern regions of Taiwan, Taiwanese and Mandarin have taken the dichotomous characterization that wants them as representatives of different ethnic and political groups (Taiwanese vs. Chinese people, 本省人 *Běn shěng rén* vs 外省人 *Wài shěng rén*, DPP vs. KMT, please refer to Topos Sect. 3.3.3). Nevertheless, this rigid division between Chinese Mandarin and Taiwanese could lead to misunderstandings. In reality the situation is even more complex: different languages, such as Taiwanese and Chinese Mandarin, are not only used by different groups of people but also by the same group of people in different contexts.

The second way to apply the words of Gramsci to the situation of Shuiwei is from the point of view of the everyday activities. In fact, it is possible to recognize the links between language and what Gramsci described as common sense. It is concretely possible to see how the

---

[3] I will refer to Taiwanese (台語 *Táiyǔ*) to describe the Taiwanese Minnan language 臺灣閩南語 (*Táiwān mǐnnán yǔ*), also called Taiwanese Hokkien 臺灣福建話 (*Táiwān fújiàn huà*).

inconsistencies (in Gramsci's terms) which arise within the Circuit of Narration in the context of Lunbei Township, represent a vision of the dichotomy between the mainstream of the Taiwanese people who are generally involved in the practices of the Taiwanese Popular Religion and the Christian tradition shared by the majority of Shuiwei's inhabitants.

As the stories by which I started this chapter point out, Christians and non-Christians use different terms to refer to specific concepts or events linked to a particular system of beliefs. The use of specific words such as Amitofo or *Tiānzhǔ bǎoyòu* immediately situate the speaker within a precise social category. Certain words, then, have the power to identify who pronounces them. In other words, these terms should be considered as the "ambiguities and encrustations" described by Gramsci. They are, thus, the result of the "sedimentation and interweaving of conceptions of the world belonging to various social groups and to their ways of expressing and feel themselves" (Gramsci et al. 1971, Q 10, §44, p. 1330).

7.3.1 Logos, Politics, and Hegemony

As I mentioned above, from a social and political point of view there are many connections between the concrete situation of the languages used in Shuiwei and the political situation in Taiwan. The main language used among the villagers is Taiwanese. The Township government is trying to encourage the use of Zhaoan Hakka language among the children.

As a matter of fact, the question of language occupied a very important position in the political horizon of Taiwan. In 1953, the KMT-ruled government passed a law forbidding the use of Taiwanese or Japanese as a language of instruction. In 1964 the government of Chiang Kai-shek forbade the use of other languages except Chinese Mandarin in schools or official settings (Wachman 2016, pp. 107–108). Students who spoke Taiwanese at school were punished with beatings, fines, and other humiliations (Sandel 2003, p. 530). After the end of martial law, in 1987, the process of democratization started in Taiwan. In the 1990s, the demonstrations of many ethnic groups, such as the Hakka and the Taiwanese Aborigines, put an end to these language discrimination, and in 2001 Taiwanese and other local languages entered the elementary school curricula (Sandel 2003, p. 530). It is interesting to note that after 1953:

> Only the Presbyterian Church was permitted to use Taiwanese openly at this time. The Nationalists did not believe that allowing foreigners to continue

speaking and practicing the local languages would have a negative effect on the absorption of Mandarin by the locals. Because the church was dependent on the Church Romanization script for all its printed materials, there was no easy way for them to switch over to Mandarin. Church Romanization had been designed specifically for Taiwanese, and the spelling of the syllables and tonal diacriticals were particular to the Taiwanese topolect. Had the Presbyterian Church created a script based on Chinese characters, I doubt the Nationalists would have been so lenient in permitting them to use and print church materials in a script for a local language. (Beaser and Mair 2006, p. 5)

One of the most important consequences of this fact has been the strong identification of the Taiwanese Presbyterian Church with the Taiwanese speakers and with the political party that, as I already explained, takes the side of the "original" Taiwanese inhabitants (本省人 Běn shěng rén): the DPP (see Topos, Sect. 3.3.2). This identification is built in opposition to the KMT party, which leaders are considered as outsiders coming from the mainland. These people are considered as Mandarin-only speakers. It is not difficult to hear people, in and outside Shuiwei, referring to Chinese Mandarin as 北京話 Běijīng huà, the language of Beijing. Something far away from Taiwan in both geographical and political terms.

These historical facts are readable also in the social context of the Christian community of Shuiwei village. The importance of Taiwanese language for the Presbyterians of Shuiwei—which are openly sided in favor of the independence of Taiwan (and of the DPP party)—is highly remarkable. A few years ago, when the new Presbyterian Pastor in Lunbei decided to perform the Sunday services in Chinese Mandarin, a big portion of the Shuiwei community decided to boycott the Lunbei services. They started to go to 橋頭 Qiáotóu, a village not far from Shuiwei belonging to another township.

Also in the Catholic community the main language is Taiwanese. Many of the older members speak only Taiwanese and, although they understand, they don't speak Chinese Mandarin. This is also reflected in the political situation: the Catholic community of Shuiwei strongly supports the DPP (the totality of Catholic believers support the DPP).

At the beginning of my fieldwork the parish priest of Lunbei was Taiwanese. The Mass and all the Church activities were performed in Taiwanese. One year after our arrival, the priest was transferred to another parish. The new parish priest came from Mainland China, and although he had studied Taiwanese, he was not fluent in it. The Mass was celebrated in Taiwanese, but he made the homily in Chinese Mandarin. Because of him, almost all the Church activities were performed in Mandarin. Despite the change of language, I never heard any of the faithful complain or disagree because of this.

What we can read from this situation is that contrary to the Presbyterian community, the importance of being a family linked with all the Taiwanese and the Universal Church was considered by the faithful more important than the specific use of the language they consider as the mother-tongue and an ethnic and identity marker. The Shuiwei Catholic community openly supports the DPP and some of them are very well known among the local DPP party. Because of my involvement in village life, very often I was invited to lunches or dinners offered by DPP members of the Congress, or where some members of the Congress were invited. At the same time, DPP representatives came very often to Lunbei and also to Shuiwei to visit "some of their stronger supporters." Nevertheless, this political and ethnic involvement was not considered relevant in the matters related to their faith and their Church.

The last language introduced in Shuiwei by the Lunbei Township government is the local Hakka language. I already mentioned that the government of Lunbei Township considers Shuiwei as one of the 詔安 *Zhàoān* Hakka villages. Therefore, the children of the village should take non-compulsory courses in Hakka language.

7.3.2 Logos and Common Sense

As I previously stated, apart from the influence that different social groups' powers play on the logos of Shuiwei, there is another level where we can trace the importance of logos: on the daily activities of Shuiwei inhabitants. As I mentioned above, according to Gramsci the ambiguities and encrustations that are sedimented in the language are social and historical products. Among the particular context of Shuiwei village, these encrustations take the form of verbal expressions. These verbal expressions are related to the practical activities and the cosmologies which stand behind them.

These ambiguities present in the language are manifested especially within the dialogues that the Catholics from Shuiwei have between themselves and the non-Christians. Following the stories I reported, it is possible to find different levels of interactions between speakers and listeners. The

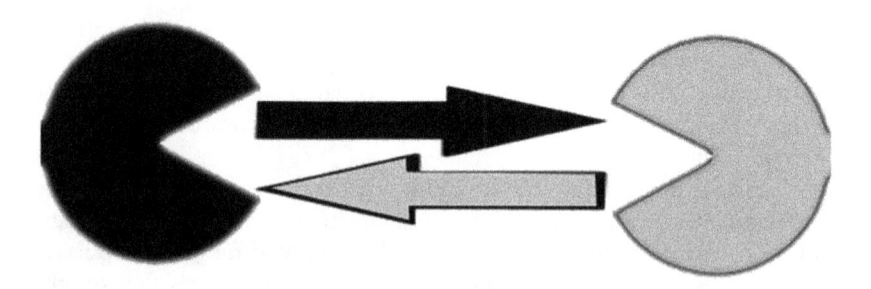

Fig. 7.2 Logos Schema 1

first layer can be easily recognized in the story told by Mrs. Li (Fig. 7.2). At this level the speakers use particular words belonging to different religious traditions—to different conceptions of the world belonging to various social groups. The way they use these particular words shows that both the speaker and the listener want to exhibit their faith. It is possible to observe that at this level there is not a real exigence of dialogue. These words are not used to begin a conversation. These expressions are an immediate way to show their own faith. There is a mutual exhibition/recognition of belonging to different communities.

We already stated that language—which for Gramsci is the manifestation of the thought and of the feelings of individuals and social groups—is the concrete form by which the socialization of people within the economic, productive, functional network that characterizes their life takes place. Following this line of reasoning, it is possible to recognize many social events as linked to this level of logos. These social events are related with the massive (if compared with other countryside villages in Taiwan) presence of Catholics in Shuiwei village and in the whole territory of Lunbei Township.

As I introduced earlier, besides Shuiwei village, Christianity is well represented in other villages of Lunbei Township. The Catholic and the Presbyterian churches are both situated in the village of 南陽 Nanyang, and on the main roads of Lunbei, it is very common to find stores with names unequivocally belonging to the Christian tradition (Agape, Sacred Heart, Charity). Pharmacies, dental clinics, private hospitals, and stores with agricultural products, in all these stores, people can find images of Holy Mary, sentences from the Holy Bible, crucifixes, and so on. The clinic 愛加倍 Agape (*Ài jiābèi*) is a private clinic of a young Taiwanese Catholic doctor.

Fig. 7.3 The Agape clinic

Apart from the name he chose for his clinic (Fig. 7.3), which for Taiwanese people (who clearly don't have any idea of the Christian meaning of this term) sounds like "extra love" or "add more love," inside the clinic sentences of the Gospel (Fig. 7.4) and Catholic images are present.[4]

In Fig. 7.4 it is possible to see the Agape's doctor between my wife and me. The sentence behind us comes from The First Letter to the Corinthians (13:7–8) "[Love] bears all things, believes all things, hopes all things, endures all things. Love never fails."

Apart from these images inside the clinic, even in the little plastic bag where the tablets are usually put, are written sentences such as God bless you (Fig. 7.5) and, again, The First Letter to the Corinthians (Fig. 7.6).

---

[4] The term "Agape" was used by Christ to describe the love among the persons of the Trinity; it is also the love he commanded his followers to have for one another (John 13:34–35). It is totally selfless love, which seeks not one's own advantage but only to benefit or share with another. As a proper noun, Agape is the so-called love feast celebrated in the early Church (I Corinthians 11:20–22, 33–34) (Leclercq 1907).

Fig. 7.4 In between myself (right) and my wife (left) is the text of The First Letter to the Corinthians

As for the verbal expressions I mentioned above, the main goal of these written words—which are part of a language and thus of logos—is not to establish a dialogue, but to show the belonging to a specific religion and community.

Continuing our analysis, it is possible to recognize another level of reading. Also this level is related to the coexistence of different cultural systems in the same place. It is characterized by reciprocal knowledge and, very often, by the overlapping of many daily activities: working together, sharing tea, playing card games, and so on (Fig. 7.7).

Figure 7.7 wants to illustrate the outcomes of the situation I described above. Within this level the story narrated by the storyteller is interpreted by the audience according to her/his own cultural parameters. In other

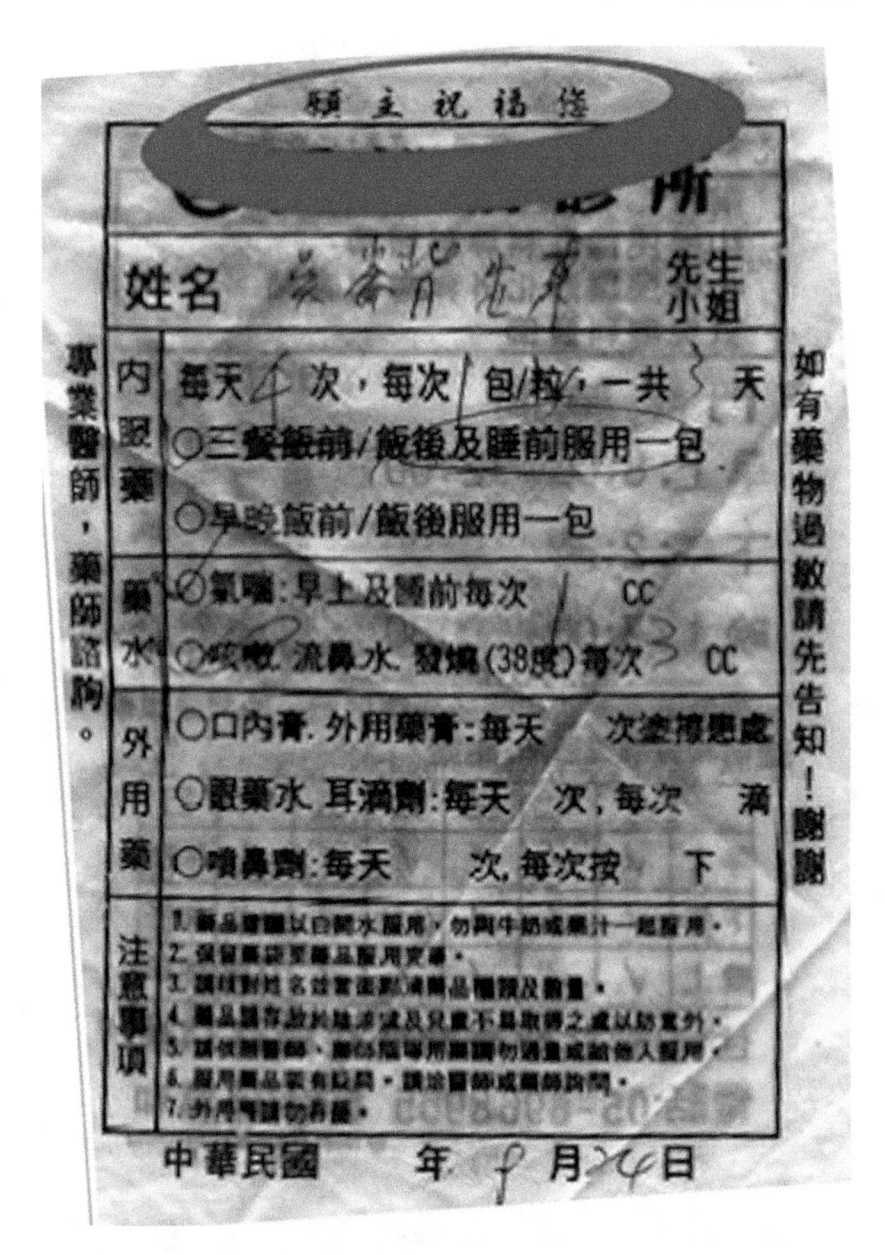

Fig. 7.5 May God bless you

Fig. 7.6 The First Letter to the Corinthians

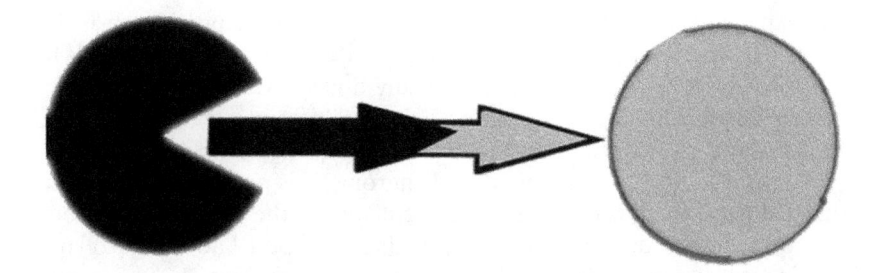

Fig. 7.7 Logos Schema 2

words, what comes out of the mouth (and brain) of those who tell and what enters the ears (and in the brain) of the listener is not exactly the same thing.

I would like to take a closer look at the stories I have been told by Mr. Liao and Fengrong. The verbal expressions used in these stories are linked to a precise cultural system. Terms such as 靈 *Líng* or 看一個日子 *Kàn yīgè rìzi* are undoubtedly linked to beliefs and practices belonging to the Chinese Popular Religion in Taiwan. From the Catholic's point of view, these terms don't belong to the Christian tradition but are used in order to let the other participants to the Circuit of Narration understand the meaning of the story. At the same time, non-Christians translate the meaning of the stories told by Catholic people, such as the one from Mr. Liao, by using these particular terms.

In the story narrated by Mr. Liao, all these concepts turn around the term 靈 *Líng*. As I mentioned above, this term is linked with the cultural environment of the Taiwanese Popular Religion. The god or gods worshiped by people are always believed to have *Líng* for the individual worshiper (Jordan 1972, p. 103). The success of big temples in Taiwan is attributed to the proven *Líng* of their gods and goddesses. That means that the god is able, throughout his/her power to solve the requests of the worshipers. The reputation of a god to be *Líng* can influence people's choice of a god or of a temple: if this god satisfies my exigencies or helps me solve my problems, I will continue to go to him; otherwise, I will change the god and the temple. This concept is very far away from the traditional Catholic doctrine. According to it, even with a high degree of localization, God—as well as Mary or other saints—is always the same. Above all this concept is not completely getting the point of Mr. Liao. Of course, there are many levels of understanding which are clearly overlapped, such as the belief that there was a miracle, probably related to the Virgin Mary. On the other hand, as Mr. Liao told me many times, "Mother Mary is *Líng*, not the Mary in our garden 不是我們院子裏的聖母很靈，聖母媽媽很靈 *Bùshì wǒmen yuànzi lǐ de shèngmǔ hěn líng, shèngmǔ māmā hěn líng*."

Also in the first story narrated by Fengrong, it is possible to recognize this dialogical level, not only for the peculiarity of the terms involved but also because the dialogue is based on the reciprocal knowledge of the interlocutor different faith. The architect was aware that Fengrong was a Catholic, and Fengrong was familiar with the practices of the Chinese Popular Religion in Taiwan. I asked Fengrong if the architect, at the end of the day, really "looked" for a propitious day. This had been his answer: "Probably, I don't know, and actually I don't care. When we started the work, we did not stop. That was enough for me. 有可能，我不知道。其實我不管。他開始工作就沒停掉，就好了！ *Yǒu kěnéng, wǒ bù zhīdào. Qíshí wǒ bùguǎn. Tā kāishǐ gōngzuò jiù méi tíngdiào, jiù hǎole!*."

Among the stories that I have selected for this chapter, a special place must be given to the last two. The special feature of these stories is that the Circuit of Narration within which these stories are born is only composed of Catholic believers (Fig. 7.8).

Within this level, the individual uses religious terms and anecdotes in order to define herself/himself or a certain situation. In this level the context of Lunbei which made the Christian terms appear as "encrustation of irrational thought" completely changes. In the context of Shuiwei village, the sentences and the anecdotes linked with the Catholic faith

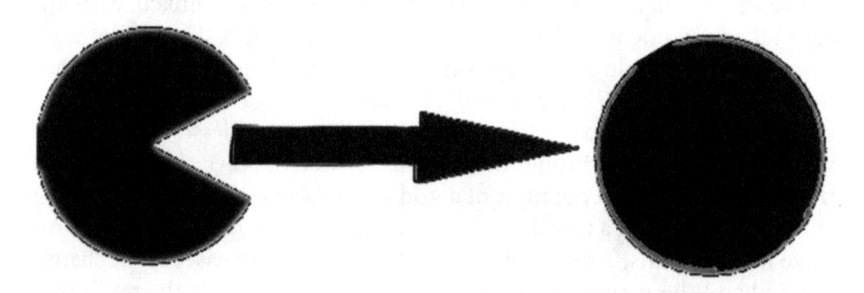

Fig. 7.8 Logos Schema 3

are part of the villagers' common sense. They are, in Gramsci's words, expressing a sort of hegemonic system.

This happens because the Circuit of Narration is entirely composed of people who share the same religion. Within this context, the "common sense," the way people interpret the surrounding reality, is clearly oriented to one religion, not only because the people of Shuiwei share the same faith but also because the many activities they share are linked with their faith.

It is possible to say that within this level, what are considered as "incrustations" or "anomalies" within the Taiwanese Popular Religion context become shared common knowledge and a (sometimes) privileged way of expression within the context of Shuiwei village.

The story of Fengrong could be understood only by a Catholic audience. The decision to follow the words of the Gospel as an operating instruction and to put four big stones in the basement of the house could sound very odd for Taiwanese people. Especially if we consider that the number four, which in Mandarin Chinese is pronounced 四 *Sì*, has the same sound of the word death 死 *Sǐ*, it is quite common that buildings, and consequentially elevators, don't have a fourth floor. The sequence of numbers skips the "dangerous" number letting people go directly from third to the fifth floor, or—as an alternative—to the F floor, the initial of the English word four (Lazzarotti 2014, p. 109).

The "lost sheep" episode is also situated on this level. To quote a passage of the Gospel was probably the quickest way for the "lost sheep" to introduce himself and his situation within his family. The pronunciation of these words identifies who speaks and who listens as belonging to the same community.

7.3.3 *Logos and the Ever-Changing Context*

In this chapter I considered logos not only as a way of communication but also—as the story of the Tower of Babel told us—as a way to construct identities and social groups. This happens because language is certainly one of the fundamental tools of cultural transmission. For this reason, language has always been seen as a characterizing element of individual identity (together with ethnicity, religion, etc.), especially because it identifies a speaker as belonging to a certain group. At the same time, language contributes to the creation of the collective identity of a group of people and also acts as an element of differentiation of a specific group of people from other groups (Zappettini 2016).

In the context of Shuiwei, it is possible to read both these tendencies. On the one hand, we can recognize the position of the Presbyterian Church and, partially, of the DPP. This approach seems to underline that the close relationship between language and identity is seen in existentialist, static, and deterministic terms. Language represents a "natural" expression of the collective character of the ethnos that can determine or influence the way of thinking of the individual. In other words, the way you talk defines you; therefore when the Pastor of Lunbei tried to change the ritual language (and thus partially the community language), most of the Presbyterian from Shuiwei decided to leave that community.

On the other hand, in the example offered by the Catholic community, the choice of a specific language—and thus of a specific logos—seems the result of a process of social construction subject to historical, political, and religious factors, and therefore something fluid and continuous changing. With the arrival of a Mainlander priest, the Catholics of Shuiwei switched their ritual language (and also partially their community language) from Taiwanese to Mandarin, without any particular complication.

Of course these situations are not absolute and "static," but they are very dynamic and adapted to the various contexts that a person or a group of persons could meet in their everyday life. For example, the Catholics from Shuiwei (which I already introduced as strong supporters of DPP) shared—and I think this situation did not change today—the idea that Taiwanese is the language of Taiwan and they use Taiwanese to talk each other. At the same time, I had friendly and fruitful conversations in Mandarin with many Presbyterian believers. They knew that my Taiwanese level was not enough to have a deep conversation about politics or religion and decided to talk in Mandarin. In this case the proverbial politeness that identify the Taiwanese people played an important role in the choice of the language they used with me.

The construction of logos as ethnos builder not only influences the choice of the language that a community should use but also changes the relations between the social groups and among them. For example, the choice to implement the study of Hakka language in the Lunbei's elementary schools leads to an interesting phenomenon. Zhaoan Hakka are a small minority of the whole Hakka community in Taiwan. As I already mentioned, in the early 1990s, the Hakka people have begun to claim the right to speak their language as an opposition to the KMT's decision to ban all languages except Mandarin (Logos, Sect. 7.3.1). The main opponent of Hakka, as language and as ethnic group, was Mandarin and the Mandarin speakers—in other words the KMT government.

With the end of the dictatorship and the implementation of the new DPP policy of discovering (or rediscovering) the local roots, scholars started to study and research local languages such as the different Hakka's dialects and the aboriginal people's languages. At the same time, the government decision to insert local languages in the school curricula started the production of textbooks, language certification's tests, TV programs, Hakka languages competitions, and so on. In other words, what began with this was the commercialization of the local traditions and, among them, local languages. Within this market, the first competitors are not more the Mandarin speakers, but the other Hakka speaker communities. Other Hakka communities are, in fact, the opponents in Hakka Language Contests organized by the Hakka TV, and very often the Zhaoan Hakka textbooks are edited by experts from other Hakka groups (one of the reasons for this is that there are no Zhaoan Hakka representatives in the National Hakka Council), and Lunbei people often complain about the influence of other Hakka dialects on their own textbooks. It is common to hear the local teachers complain about the choice or the pronunciation of certain words as presented in the textbooks.

Among this macro (political, social, historical) context, logos, just like the other four elements, is an always changing element. What seems to be the non-changing—or at least a less-changing—part of logos is the micro (personal, religious) context made by the Circuit of Narration.

The different levels I introduced in this chapter show that the elements which characterize the Circuit of Narration (the terms 阿彌陀佛 Amitofo or 天主保佑 Tiānzhǔ bǎoyòu, the term 看一個日子 Kàn yīgè rìzi, or the Gospel sentences) are not necessary linked with a certain or specific language, but are linked deeper with symbols and cosmological values. These values could be considered as the ones who concretely give a meaning to the life of the people, and the symbols (and among them the words) which represent them, are the ones that help people to orient themselves in their everyday life.

References

Altan, C.T. 1995. *Ethnos e Civiltà. Identità Etniche e Valori Democratici*. Milano: Feltrinelli.
Beaser, D., and V.H. Mair. 2006. The Outlook for Taiwanese Language Preservation. *Sino-Platonic Papers* 172: 1–18.
Forgacs, D., and G. Nowell-Smith. 1985. *Selections from Cultural Writings*. Cambridge: Harvard University Press.
Gensini, S. 2012. Appunti su 'Linguaggio','Senso Comune'e 'Traduzione'in Gramsci. *Il cannocchiale. Rivista di studi filosofici* 3: 163–193.
Gramsci, A., Q. Hoare, et al. 1971. *Selections from the Prison Notebooks*. Lawrence and Wishart London.
Jordan, D.K. 1972. *Gods, Ghosts, & Ancestors: Folk Religion in a Taiwan Village*. Berkeley: University of California Press.
Lazzarotti, M. 2014. Modern Life and Traditional Death. Tradition and Modernization of Funeral Rites in Taiwan. *Fu Jen International Religious Studies* 8 (1): 108–126.
Leclercq, H. 1907. Agape. *The Catholic Encyclopedia* 1: 775–848.
Sandel, T.L. 2003. Linguistic Capital in Taiwan: The KMT's Mandarin Language Policy and its Perceived Impact on Language Practices of Bilingual Mandarin and Tai-gi Speakers. *Language in Society* 32 (4): 523–551.
Tanaka, K.K. 1990. *The Dawn of Chinese Pure Land Buddhist Doctrine: Ching-ying Hui-yuan's Commentary on the Visualization Sutra*. Albany: SUNY Press.
Wachman, A.M. 2016. *Taiwan: National Identity and Democratization*. New York: Routledge.
Zappettini, F. 2016. Lingua e Identità Sociale. *Geografia Interculturale: Spazi, luoghi e non luoghi* 1: 1–21.

CHAPTER 8

Conclusions

8.1 Other Stories, Other Worlds

When we moved to Lunbei, my wife and I were living in Lunquan, but almost every night we went to visit Fengrong and A-Ying, a Catholic couple who lived in Shuiwei. One evening we went with A-Ying to visit some of her neighbors. At that time, we had just arrived in Lunbei and were laughing and commenting on the joke that greeted us when we arrived. "When a 演戲 Yǎnxì traditional performance will take place in Shuiwei, I will give you back your money" (Introduction, Sect. 1.1).

A-Ying, who became Catholic only after her wedding, told us a story related to this joke. "Actually, there is another story related to this joke. I heard it from someone who lives in 下街 xià jiē. They said that a family who was living in 下街 xià jiē, was able to have a child after a long wait. They were so happy and grateful that they decided to organize a 演戲 yǎnxì. After a short time, unfortunately, it happened that their newborn baby died. The fact was interpreted as a sign that the people buried in the village had been disturbed by the noise of the 演戲 yǎnxì. From that moment no one has ever dared to organize a 演戲 yǎnxì in the village."

I tried several time to find someone who could confirm the story A-Ying told us, but apart from someone who told me she he already heard it, nobody was able to indicate which family was the one described in the story. Most of the people collocated this story in an ancient time, remote in time and memory. The collocation in the past gives an explanation of why nobody was able to identify which family was affected by this event. Even if it is impossible to reach the concrete source of the story (the affected family), through the passing of time, and especially through the process of narration from one person to another, everybody assumes that this story is true. This story (with all the cultural elements linked with it) leads us to a very important consideration. What the process of storytelling helps us to build, it is not a true image of the world, but a verisimilar one—a plausible image of a credible world.[1]

The different interpretations of the same event, made by two groups of people (the Christians and the non-Christians) with (sometimes and somehow) contrasting identities, built up different stories and consequentially different worlds. For the Christians, the main reason why in Shuiwei no Yǎnxì are performed is because the majority of the inhabitants are Christian and because there is no main temple in their village. For the non-Christian inhabitants of Shuiwei, the explanation of this fact (and the subsequent story related with it) is linked to the Taiwanese Popular Religion's way to deal with extraordinary and unexpected events: to consider them as influenced by supernatural and (very often) malignant forces. This makes even more sense if we consider that the only people who are buried within the boundaries of the village are the ones considered the ancestors of the Catholic community (Epos, Sect. 4.3).

This story thus assumes an interesting and particular meaning. A meaning strongly linked with the sense of *alterity* and with the immanent sense of difference through which the other's actions and moral values are judged and interpreted.

At the same time, this story reveals another important thing: the (cumbersome) presence of the fact. The fact that no *Yǎnxì* is performed in Shuiwei village is something immovable and difficult to hide for both the Christian and the non-Christian communities. It is when these unavoidable facts or events pass through the sieve of the five elements that stories, and thus the worlds, are created.

---

[1] From the Latin verisimilis. Having the appearance of truth. Probable (Merriam-Webster.com 2017).

8.2 The Discovery of the Other

As many of the stories are linked to the Christian community of Shuiwei, the one narrated by A-Ying is full of meanings. For A-Ying, as well for all the Christian inhabitants of Shuiwei, 下街 *xià jiē* represents the "non-Christian" part of the village. 下街 *xià jiē*, developed along the National Road N.154, is the most recent part of the village. Many new structures, such as the village's elementary school and activities center, are all located in 下街 *xià jiē*. The Christians, and especially the Catholics, refer to 下街 *xià jiē* as somewhere distant from the original Shuiwei, which is the part of the village that I described in genos (Sect. 4.3.1, see Fig. 3.9) as the "proper Catholic area."

In 下街 *xià jiē*, just at the boundaries of the village of Shuiwei, stands an agricultural produce store. The owner of the shop is a non-Christian whose family name is Zhong. He married a Catholic woman whose surname is also Zhong.[2] Her brother and also her sister-in-law from time to time work in the store, taking care of different tasks. Christian and non-Christian farmers sit together under the large porch of this shop. Every day they spend a considerable amount of time chatting together, drinking tea, and, especially in summer nights, playing cards. Christians and non-Christians, if observed during the moments they pass in this store, are difficult to distinguish. Apart from these moments, both Christian and non-Christian farmers share the same education system and watch the same television programs. Being in contact every day for a considerable amount of time, they share many of their daily experiences.

Nevertheless, Shuiwei is still described by the non-Christian people of Lunbei as a different place. As I tried to demonstrate, Shuiwei is different because the people who inhabit it live according to different taboos and different traditions. They have other kinds of rituals and have different ways to solve their problems. In other words, they live in a different topos and share a different epos. Very often they act according to a different ethos and use a different logos. In addition, they belong to different genos. Because of this, although they share almost the same everyday experiences, Shuiwei is still considered a "different place."

When processed through an immanent—because it is historically constructed—frame of interpretation, the differences of behavior construct

---

[2] I already introduced this family in Genos, Sect. 4.4.

different narrations and, thus, different worlds. Taking as an example the story narrated by A-Ying, Christians and non-Christians, through their narrations, build different locus: a locus free from superstitions and taboos for the Christian inhabitants and a locus animated by other ancestors and thus by other ghosts for the non-Christian villagers.

The five elements, which provide the conceptual frames that interpret the various events, acted in this case as lenses that help the different parts to focus on their different construction of the world. This happens because the behavioral contrasts are interpreted, bringing them back into the sieve formed by the five elements. Since the five elements stress the different identity constructions, the differences of behavior are sieved by them following a "schema of contrast." This schema of contrast is based on the fact that the differences are immanent to any interpretation. From this contrast comes the story and thus the construction of a locus. This happens because, as I previously mentioned, "each story comes from conflict, without conflict there are no events, and therefore no story" (Pinardi and De Angelis 2008).

In other words, the frame of meanings that are used in order to interpret an event (such as an extraordinary behavior) are built on the idea of the immanent difference of the other. As suggested by (Altan 1995, p. 24), I consider this immanence as particularly linked with the elements of epos (the historical construction of a common past) and ethos (the ethical, the moral aspects of a society).

The importance of the historical background and, above all, of the reconstruction of the historical meeting between Christianity and the Taiwanese cultural background played an important part in the identification of Shuiwei village as a place ontologically different from the surrounding areas. In fact, the historical meeting between Christianity and local culture involves different levels of understanding and interpretation.

It is exactly within these levels of interpretation that ethos—with the interdictions and the ritual disputes linked with it—played a fundamental role in the construction of the alterity of Shuiwei as a locus.

The sieve formed by the five elements attaches different values to the actions and to the way of behaving of the other. These values are always changing because they are defined by the context—the locus—where different conceptions of the world meet each other. In the space created by these encounters, alterity is discovered and narrated according to the patterns formed by the five elements. Alterity thus is both a result and a parameter that the storyteller, as well as the audience, uses in order to build the world where the story should take place.

Inside the space formed by these encounters, there are certainly many levels of contact which in turn are linked with different levels of understanding and interpretation. The differences of understanding and interpretation are linked to an immanent scale of values which ultimately direct the symbolic construction of the world where the stories take place and consequentially the construction of the world where we live in.

8.3 Locus, Narration, and the Other Us

Let's try now to go back (metaphorically) to 下街 *xià jiē* and the agricultural product store. This place and the cohabitation of Christians and non-Christians show us an interesting element. If it is certainly true that the differences are immanent, it is also true that they are not constantly intrusive. In many aspects of daily life, these differences are simply covered by the common behavior shared both by Christians and non-Christians.

The patterns of interpretation—based on the differences and on the contrast between the behavior considered standard and the one of the other (in our specific case the unexpected behavior of the Christian inhabitants of Shuiwei)—are applied only when the event is related to one or more of the five elements. When these points are not particularly stressed, the differences do not appear or are not considered important in order to define the other. In this case, the differences don't generate narration and consequentially don't contribute to the construction of the Locus.

When the focus is pointed on other aspects, or when the five elements are constructed on different concepts (e.g. the Taiwanese sense of identity, local political issues), the diversities between Christians versus non-Christians and Lunbei versus Shuiwei are not considered as relevant. In other words, within different frames of meanings, the differences based on people's faith are not able to stimulate a narration based on differences and contrasts between Christians and non-Christians.

From another point of view, there is another element we should take into consideration. Through the daily contact and the everyday sharing of experiences, it sometimes happens that the alterity of Shuiwei becomes familiar and one of the constituents of the non-Christian system of meaning. The long historical coexistence of people in some way belonging to different systems of meaning reduced the immanent diversity into a familiar sphere.

Through the process of narration, the sense of alterity that comes from the events linked with Shuiwei as locus and with its inhabitants is inserted into the local common knowledge and becomes the local common feeling.

If we take the story told to me by Fengrong in the second chapter (Locus, Sect. 2.1) as an example, it is evident that what Fengrong did was openly in contrast with all the taboos and the restrictions linked to the many rules which managed the access to the temple in that specific moment.

Fengrong entered in the wrong place (because he was a Catholic believer) in the wrong moment (because he belonged to a forbidden zodiacal sign) and did the wrong thing (a Catholic cannot take part in the ritual changing of the incense sticks inside the temple). Nevertheless, this singular event happened precisely because Fengrong was considered as someone completely "other" by the people in charge of managing the temple. If Fengrong had not been a well-known Catholic faithful (therefore belonging to something ontologically different from the environment of the Taiwanese Popular Religion), it is very likely that his request to enter the temple and change the incense sticks would not have been taken into account. It is because everybody in that moment shared the common knowledge of Fengrong alterity that things worked out in that particular way.

But the story of Fengrong brings us toward another very important point: Fengrong was, at least in that specific moment, a visible sign of alterity. But what happened just after this moment? It happened that this particular event—and the alterity expressed by it—became narration, and thus it has been added to the many other narrations about Shuiwei village and its inhabitants.

I already mentioned during this work that narration contributes to bringing the unexpected, the different, within a fabric of common references. It is thus through narrative, or storytelling, that individual actors are able to mediate transactions between the ordinary, the unexpected, and the possible (Mattingly et al. 2008, p. 14).

The extraordinary event which had Fengrong as the main character became a story that could be narrated according to existent and shared patterns of meanings. But above all the creation of a story based on this particular kind of event created different parameters of understanding and thus different narrations and different worlds.

The process of storytelling lets the unexpected become familiar and consequentially inserted in the *verisimilar* version of the world, which reassures and comforts us. Or that gives us the sense of being alive.

8.4 Alterity, Narration, and Our Life

During the process of my fieldwork and also during the writing of this thesis, I came to realize the central point that alterity occupied in the construction of Shuiwei village as locus. Alterity was probably the starting point of my interest toward this topic. The discovery of alterity, its construction, the way people manage it during their everyday life and especially within their narrations. All these topics attracted my attention during my fieldwork.

The construction of alterity is intimately connected with narration. I would say that these two aspects are different faces of the same coin. In the specific case of Shuiwei, this village represents a place ontologically different from the surrounding environment. This is certainly related to the cultural context shared by the most of the Han people. Within the complex cosmology shared by the majority of the Taiwanese people, each place is linked to natural (e.g. *fēngshui*) and supernatural (e.g. gods, ghosts, and ancestors) ties. The cultural universe that gives life to these natural and supernatural entities provides the interpretation of Shuiwei as an other place. A place where many of the known rules and social behaviors are not running in the standard way. Because of this particular context, the narration about Shuiwei creates a locus with a particular and charismatic reputation. This locus, symbolically constructed by these narrations, influences the people who live inside and outside it. In other words, thanks to its intrinsic alterity—born from the narration of it—locus becomes an existent in and of itself.

Throughout this thesis I have tried to demonstrate that the ties that connect place and alterity are strongly interwoven with the process of narration. The way we live our life is linked with the way we narrate it and we narrate ourselves. At the same time, the way we live our life is linked also to the way we narrate—we construct—the other, as well as the way others narrate—construct—us. I think this is something that we have all experienced. Maybe when we were kids or teenagers or when we were strangers in another country. The way others describe us influence our choices, direct our actions, and open or close us to the world around us. In a certain sense, we can say that we define our identity only in the relationship with those who are different from us, who are *other* to us.

In this work I have tried to demonstrate how a place, its identity, its *Genius Loci*, is built not only by its inhabitants or their narratives but—especially—by those who are external to it. Their narratives are an active constituent of the place. Very often their description of our place gives new light through which we can increase—or at least modify—our sense of place and influence the way we perceive the places we inhabit.

I hope that this approach will help the branch of Anthropology called Anthropology of Space and Place to consider alterity as a fundamental and constituent element of place and of narration. Considering alterity as the core of the narrative process and as the center of the symbolic construction of a place, it will help to better define the subject of study and to let anthropological analysis to become more and more refined in order to face the challenges of this interconnected and glocalized world.

References

Altan, C.T. 1995. *Ethnos e Civiltà. Identità Etniche e Valori Democratici*. Milano: Feltrinelli.

Mattingly, C., N.C. Lutkehaus, and C.J. Throop. 2008. Bruner's Search for Meaning: A Conversation between Psychology and Anthropology. *Ethos* 36 (1): 1–28.

Merriam-Webster.com, T. 2017. Verisimilar. http://www.merriam-webster.com/dictionary/verisimilar. Accessed June 12, 2016.

Pinardi, D., and P. De Angelis. 2008. *Il Mondo Narrativo: Come Costruire e come Presentare L'Ambiente e i Personaggi di una Storia*. Torino: Lindau.

Index

A
Agency, 22, 23, 28–30, 33, 51
  narration, 3
  of place, 4, 96
Altan, Carlo Tullio, 10–13, 37–40, 45, 51, 76, 77, 103, 124, 141, 165, 166, 186
Alterity, 4, 11, 12, 14, 28, 34, 36, 39, 40, 51, 158, 184, 186–190
  concept of, 34, 37, 40
  ontology, 158, 188, 189
Ancestors, 8, 13, 54, 55, 68, 69, 106, 125, 144, 145, 152, 153, 186, 189
  apical, 13, 107, 136
  Catholic, 152
  concept of, 12, 55
  cult of, 13, 54, 64, 69, 96–98, 105–109, 118, 123, 126, 130, 131, 134, 135, 145; prohibition, 109, 110, 116, 125, 135
  Hakka, 2
  Jesus, 110, 116, 125, 126, 132, 135; prohibition, 126, 128
  rites for the, 2, 13, 96, 97, 107, 108, 127, 151
  Shuiwei, 131, 135, 184; Jesus, 136; prohibition, 136
  worship, 6, 103–107, 125, 153

C
Circuit of Narration, 3–5, 10, 14, 20–24, 27, 28, 38, 169, 177–179, 181
Coherence, 24, 38
  external, 24
  internal, 24
Context of contrast, 27, 146, 169, 171, 178, 179

E
Epos, 10, 12–14, 38, 76–78, 94, 96, 97, 110–112, 115, 141, 152, 166, 185, 186
  of Shuiwei, 13, 78, 82
Ethnos, 37–40, 141, 165, 166, 180

Ethos, 10, 12–14, 38, 78, 107, 115, 135, 142, 143, 145–151, 154, 157, 158, 185, 186
   context of contrast, 148, 149, 158, 159
   contingencies, 154
   Geertz, 142
   of Shuiwei, 13
   social fact, 145
Evangelization, 85, 95, 128
   of China, 141, 152
   experience of, 56
   method of, 28, 84, 96, 97
   process of, 34, 86, 154
   project of, 86, 95, 110, 132
   of Taiwan, 78, 82, 85, 89, 91, 111, 132

G

Genealogy, 45, 48, 71, 79, 106, 107, 155
   Lunbei's families, 111
   Zhong family, 115, 117, 118, 120, 136
Genos, 10, 12–14, 38, 44, 48, 69, 96, 99, 103, 123–125, 136, 185

H

Hakka, 61–64, 67, 68, 70–72, 102, 115, 116, 169, 180
   identity, 62, 63
   language, 62, 63, 67, 168, 169, 171, 180, 181

I

Identity, 4, 7, 14, 15, 30, 32, 33, 36, 46, 76, 78, 95, 108, 141, 148, 190
   alterity, 190
   construction, 170; language, 179

   construction of, 39, 108, 109, 126, 186; Chinese culture, 122; context of contrast, 148; conversion, 109; Hakka, 115
   ethnic, 141
   language, 168, 171, 180
   local, 62
   of locus, 14, 39, 56
   of Lunbei, 61
   maintaining, 39
   narration of, 69
   national, 38
   of place, 54, 56
   sense of, 4, 13, 30
   Taiwan, 62, 68, 187
   of Yunlin, 61
Immanence, 22, 28, 51, 69, 95, 97, 185–187
   sense of, 27, 28, 96, 184

L

Locus, 4–6, 11, 14, 15, 29, 34, 36–39, 51, 56, 68, 72, 79, 96, 158, 186, 187, 189
Logos, 10, 12, 14, 38, 82, 165–169, 171, 172, 174, 179–181, 185
   of Shuiwei, 171

N

Narration, 68, 166, 187
   agency, 3
   agency of place, 4
   alterity, 14, 159, 186, 188–190
   concept of, 27
   context, 27, 96
   context of, 20
   context of contrast, 28, 95, 157, 158, 187
   difference, 29, 68, 188
   five elements, 10, 187
   history, 77, 78, 90, 97

identity, 76, 77
Locus, 4–6, 37, 69, 72, 186, 187, 189
myth, 79
place, 28, 51; locus, 40
process of, 25, 51, 184, 188, 189
Shuiwei, 113
time of, 24
Narrative, 190
  context, 56
  context of contrast, 51, 54, 69
  difference, 72
Narrative world, 3, 20–22, 26–28, 37–39, 166

O
Otherness, 4, 11, 29, 51, 95, 109, 123, 146–148, 150, 158, 183, 185–190

P
patriliny, 13, 46, 103–105, 108, 116

S
Sense

of alterity, 11, 14, 28, 34, 188
of belonging, 4, 13, 32, 33, 77, 81, 127, 136
of brotherhood, 13, 80
common, 14, 15, 25, 26, 142, 147, 148, 158, 159, 166–168, 171, 179
of continuity, 56
of difference, 27, 28, 46, 48, 51, 69
of disclosing, 11
of diversity, 3, 14, 28
of filial piety, 153
of Genos, 136
of identity, 4, 13, 77, 84, 187
of otherness, 11, 184
of place, 31–33, 46, 56, 190
of positioning, 30
and stability, 38
of unity, 79, 80

T
Topos, 10, 12, 14, 38, 45, 46, 51, 69, 72, 81, 87, 113, 115, 121, 125, 126, 168, 170, 185

CPSIA information can be obtained
at www.ICGtesting.com
Printed in the USA
BVHW010158220720
584295BV00001B/2

9 783030 434601